# Sharing the
# *Burden*

# *Sharing the Burden*

STRATEGIES FOR PUBLIC AND PRIVATE
LONG-TERM CARE INSURANCE

Joshua M. Wiener
Laurel Hixon Illston
Raymond J. Hanley

The Brookings Institution
*Washington, D.C.*

Copyright © 1994
THE BROOKINGS INSTITUTION
1775 Massachusetts Avenue, N.W., Washington, D.C. 20036

*Library of Congress Cataloging-in-Publication data:*

Wiener, Joshua M.
    Sharing the burden : strategies for public and private long-term
    care insurance / Joshua M. Wiener, Laurel Hixon Illston, Ray-
    mond J. Hanley.
        p.   cm
    Includes bibliographical references (p. 245) and index.
    ISBN 0-8157-9378-2 (cloth)—ISBN 0-8157-9377-4 (pbk.)
    1. Insurance, Long-term care—United States. I. Illston, Laurel
    Hixon. II. Hanley, Raymond J. III. Title.
    HD7102.U4W48 1994
    368.3′8′00973—dc20                                              94-1616
                                                                        CIP


9      8      7      6      5      4      3      2      1

*Composition by Harlowe Typography Inc.,*
*Cottage City, Maryland*
*Printed by R.R. Donnelley and Sons, Co.*
*Harrisonburg, Virginia*

# ⓑ THE BROOKINGS INSTITUTION

The Brookings Institution is an independent organization devoted to nonpartisan research, education, and publication in economics, government, foreign policy, and the social sciences generally. Its principal purposes are to aid in the development of sound public policies and to promote public understanding of issues of national importance.

The Institution was founded on December 8, 1927, to merge the activities of the Institute for Government Research, founded in 1916, the Institute of Economics, founded in 1922, and the Robert Brookings Graduate School of Economics and Government, founded in 1924.

The Board of Trustees is responsible for the general administration of the Institution, while the immediate direction of the policies, program, and staff is vested in the President, assisted by an advisory committee of the officers and staff. The by-laws of the Institution state: "It is the function of the Trustees to make possible the conduct of scientific research, and publication, under the most favorable conditions, and to safeguard the independence of the research staff in the pursuit of their studies and in the publication of the results of such studies. It is not a part of their function to determine, control, or influence the conduct of particular investigations or the conclusions reached."

The President bears final responsibility for the decision to publish a manuscript as a Brookings book. In reaching his judgment on the competence, accuracy, and objectivity of each study, the President is advised by the director of the appropriate research program and weighs the views of a panel of expert outside readers who report to him in confidence on the quality of the work. Publication of a work signifies that it is deemed a competent treatment worthy of public consideration but does not imply endorsement of conclusions or recommendations.

The Institution maintains its position of neutrality on issues of public policy in order to safeguard the intellectual freedom of the staff. Hence interpretations or conclusions in Brookings publications should be understood to be solely those of the authors and should not be attributed to the Institution, to its trustees, officers, or other staff members, or to the organizations that support its research.

---

# Foreword

A key issue in the debate about reforming the U.S. health care system is how to finance long-term care for the elderly. The current delivery system is heavily tilted toward institutional care, even though the elderly express a desire for care at home. The cost of care for the chronically disabled far exceeds the resources of the average family and is not normally covered by either private insurance or medicare. Elderly people must rely on their own or their family's income and assets to pay for care or, when these are depleted, turn to welfare.

This study analyzes the major options for reforming the way long-term care for the elderly is financed. It explores private long-term care insurance, changes to the medicaid program, the federal-state health care program for the poor, and social insurance. The authors recommend a reform strategy that combines all three approaches.

Joshua M. Wiener is a senior fellow in the Brookings Economic Studies program; Laurel Hixon Illston is a senior research analyst in that program; Raymond J. Hanley is a former Brookings senior research analyst and is now a senior analyst at the Office of Financial Management of the State of Washington. David L. Kennell and Lisa Marie B. Alecxih of Lewin-VHI, Inc., were equal partners with the authors in developing and revising the Brookings-ICF Long-Term Care Financing Model and provided invaluable help in formulating the simulated options. Peter Robertshaw of Lewin-VHI, Inc., supplied computer programming assistance. The authors wish to thank Soma Datta, Katherine M. Harris, and Nancy A. Loube, who provided research assistance; Martha Gottron and Caroline Lalire, who edited the manuscript; David Bearce and Laura Kelly, who verified it; Susan L. Woollen, who prepared the manuscript for typesetting; Norman G. Turpin, who managed the production process; and Carolyn J. Hill, E. Carole Hingleton, Diane C. Maranis, and Colette M. Solpietro, who provided staff assistance. Florence Robinson prepared the index.

Special thanks are extended to the Brookings Advisory Panel on Long-Term Care (listed on the next page) for their expert guidance and for their comments on early drafts. Comments by many people greatly improved the final manuscript. In particular, the authors wish to thank Henry J. Aaron, Susan A. Coronel, Robert B. Friedland, Katherine M. Harris, Peter Kemper, F. Peter Libassi, Brenda C. Spillman, Joseph White, and Linda Wray.

Funding for this study was provided by the Henry J. Kaiser Family Foundation, Merrill Lynch, Inc., Merck & Company, Inc., and the Teachers Insurance and Annuity Association–College Retirement Equities Fund. Dennis F. Beatrice, William Henkel, and Bruce L. Boyd of these organizations gave help and encouragement to the authors. Brookings is grateful for this support.

The views expressed here are those of the authors and should not be attributed to the persons or organizations whose assistance is acknowledged, or to the trustees, officers, or other staff members of the Brookings Institution.

BRUCE K. MAC LAURY
*President*

*April 1994*
*Washington, D.C.*

# The Brookings Advisory Panel
# on Long-Term Care

# Contents

APPENDIXES

TABLES

Contents xv

FIGURES

# Introduction and Summary

The United States is now engaged in a historic debate over how, not if, our health care system should be overhauled. President Clinton's call for reform has focused national attention on the problems and possible cures for uncontrolled costs and lack of adequate health insurance. Although this debate is focused primarily on acute care, it is also about long-term care. Americans suffer not only acute illnesses requiring care in hospitals and by physicians, but also chronic conditions that require long-term care either at home or in nursing homes. To begin to address these problems, the Clinton administration is proposing major new initiatives for long-term care.

Alzheimer's disease, osteoporosis, heart disease, multiple sclerosis, muscular dystrophy, and stroke are just a few of the many diseases that cause chronic disability. Long-term care is the help needed to cope, and sometimes to survive, when physical or mental disabilities impair the capacity to perform the basic tasks of everyday life, such as eating, bathing, dressing, and housekeeping.

Most long-term care services are provided by family members and friends of the disabled person, often at considerable personal sacrifice. Paid services are offered by nursing homes, home health workers, home-makers and personal care workers, adult day care centers, and respite programs for family caregivers. Costs are high. A year in a nursing home cost more than $37,000 in 1993.[1]

Long-term care reform is not central to the inner logic of providing basic insurance to the uninsured and controlling acute care expenditures, but there are at least four reasons why it should be part of health care reform. First, the current long-term care system is broken and needs to be fixed. The United States does not have, either in the private or

1

public sector, satisfactory mechanisms for helping people anticipate and pay for long-term care. Long-term care is one of the two leading causes of catastrophic out-of-pocket health care costs for the elderly; the other is prescription drugs.[2] The disabled elderly and nonelderly find, often to their surprise, that neither medicare nor private insurance covers the costs of nursing home and home care. Instead, the disabled must rely on their own resources or, when these have been exhausted, turn to welfare in the form of medicaid, the federal-state health care program for the poor. Finally, despite the strong preference of the disabled for home- and community-based services, the available financing is highly skewed toward institutional care.

Second, President Clinton's proposed acute care benefit package for people under age 65 is substantially more generous than existing medicare benefits, creating equity problems. The political difficulty is that, with the exception of prescription drugs, most elderly already have most of this additional coverage through their supplemental private insurance. For them, expanded acute care coverage would not provide new benefits, but it would entail substantial new government expenditures. Expanded long-term care services would be a new benefit for both the elderly and the nonelderly.

Third, pressure to control acute care costs will create strong incentives either to substitute nursing home and home care for hospital services or, less benignly, to reclassify acute care services as long-term care. In either case, the need for long-term care services will escalate sharply, even though the financing mechanism to pay for them will be lacking.

Finally, inclusion of long-term care garners substantial additional popular support for general health care reform. Although public opinion polls, especially those sponsored by interest groups, must be viewed cautiously, surveys sponsored by Consumers Union and by the American Association of Retired Persons find much greater enthusiasm for health reform if long-term care benefits are included.[3] In one survey, for example, 57 percent of respondents said that their support for the Clinton health plan would increase if home and community care were included.[4]

Although the debate over long-term care reform has many facets, it is primarily an argument over the relative merits of private versus public sector approaches. Differences over how much emphasis to put on each sector depend partly on values that cannot be directly proved or disproved. Some believe that the primary responsibility for care of the elderly and disabled belongs with individuals and their families and that government should act only as a payer of last resort for those unable to provide for themselves. The opposite view is that the government should take the lead in ensuring care for all disabled older people, regardless of financial need, by providing comprehensive, compulsory social insurance. In this view, the private sector plays little or no role. Between these polar positions, many combinations of public and private responsibility are possible, and most people would probably opt for some middle ground.

The choice of emphasis between public and private programs depends not just on political ideology, but also on whether private and public initiatives are affordable, whom they would benefit, and whether they can reduce catastrophic costs and realign the delivery system. For example, if it were demonstrably possible to market private long-term care insurance that would protect a large majority of the population from financial hardship and reduce dependence on medicaid, then many people would see less need for new government programs. Conversely, if private insurance were to prove widely unaffordable or otherwise encounter barriers that prevent people from voluntarily purchasing policies, then the case for an expanded public role would be stronger.

It is in the areas of the affordability of public and private initiatives, their distributional consequences, and their impact on long-term care financing where empirical analysis is helpful and where we hope to make our contribution with this research. As such, this study is a continuation and extension of the research begun at the Brookings Institution with *Caring for the Disabled Elderly: Who Will Pay?* by Alice M. Rivlin and Joshua M. Wiener, with Raymond J. Hanley and Denise A. Spence, published in 1988.

That earlier book examined an extremely wide range of public and private financing options; this study focuses on private and public insurance and on changes to the medicaid program. We made this choice because our earlier analysis strongly indicated that reform strategies based on risk pooling (such as insurance) rather than on asset accumulation and use (such as individual retirement accounts for long-term care and home equity conversions) were more likely to have an impact on the long-term care system. The problem with individual savings and asset utilization strategies is that everyone must save quite a lot each year to accumulate enough to pay for potential catastrophic long-term care expenses, but only a minority will actually incur those expenses. On an average day, only 4.2 percent of the elderly and a negligible proportion of the nonelderly are in nursing homes.[5] Because relatively few people face a need for services that involve a large outlay of funds, long-term care lends itself to insurance and risk pooling, whereby many people contribute to a fund to cover the extraordinary expenses of the few.

This new study goes well beyond the earlier book in three ways. First, for both public and private sector options, this research includes an extensive analysis of the impact of different strategies on catastrophic out-of-pocket costs. Second, it extends the analysis of private insurance by conducting sensitivity analyses and by exploring in depth employer-sponsored policies and strategies to promote purchase. Finally, this research analyzes several prototype public insurance options that were not in the policy debate when the simulations for the earlier book were done.

Although we use a wide variety of data to assess different financing options, our quantitative analysis is based on results from the Brookings-ICF Long-Term Care Financing Model, version 2, which we developed jointly with the consulting firm of Lewin-VHI, Inc. This microsimulation model, which incorporates a great deal more recent data, is a major revision of the model used in *Caring for the Disabled Elderly: Who Will Pay?*

Although this study aims at the broad issues of reform, a caveat is in order. People can and do require long-term care at any age; this study, however, is limited to the physically and cognitively impaired elderly population. It does not include the mentally ill, developmentally disabled, or nonelderly physically disabled—all important populations with pressing needs but beyond the scope of this study. This research contributes to our understanding of long-term care, but it does not claim to address the needs of the entire disabled population.

Our analysis of options for reforming long-term care leads us to recommend a mixed public-private system. First, public, non-means-tested programs should be expanded to cover more of the costs of home care and nursing home care. Second, the financial eligibility requirements of medicaid should be liberalized so that people forced to rely on the program are not as severely impoverished as they are currently. And, finally, private long-term care insurance should be encouraged to play a larger role in the financing of care. A key to doing so will be reaching people well before they become elderly. Private insurance should not be expected to play the leading role in reforming or financing long-term care, however. Our recommendations are consistent with, but more comprehensive than, President Clinton's proposals.

## Long-Term Care in the 1990s

Most older people are physically active, able to care for themselves, and not in need of long-term care.[6] Of the 29.3 million Americans aged 65 and older in 1987, less than a quarter (6.3 million) were disabled on the average day.[7] Of this group, 3.1 million had severe disabilities and were either in a nursing home or were living in the community.[a]

The prevalence of disability rises steeply with advancing age. Only about 12 percent of people aged 65 to 74 were disabled in 1987, but that proportion rises to 69 percent for people aged 85 and older.[8] Today the fastest growing age group in the population is the very elderly, the group most likely to need long-term care.[9] Largely because women live longer than men, the disabled elderly are disproportionately very old widows. Three-quarters of all nursing home residents are, in fact, unmarried.[10]

Not all disabled people are old. More than 40 percent of all community-based adults who need assistance with personal care are under age 65.[11] In addition, the nonelderly disabled population makes up about 10 percent of the nursing home population.[12] Although disability is much more prevalent among those over age 65, many more people are under age 65 than over. So even a low disability rate among those under age 65 produces a significant number of nonelderly disabled people.

Despite their numbers, we know relatively little about the characteristics and service needs of disabled people under age 65. We do know that they tend to make less use of paid services, such as home care and nursing homes, than do the elderly. But we do not know why.

### WHO PROVIDES LONG-TERM CARE?

Although many people think long-term care is synonymous with nursing homes, the predominant provider of long-term care in the United States is the family. Only about 22 percent of the disabled elderly were in nursing homes in 1987.[13] Those with more severe disabilities were more likely to be in institutions, but even among the severely disabled, considerably less than half were in nursing homes.

The elderly express strong preferences for remaining in their own homes as long as possible and for being cared for by relatives.[14] Nearly

a. "Severely disabled" is defined here as having difficulty with at least two of the five activities of daily living—eating, bathing, dressing, toileting, and getting in and out of bed.

84 percent of the disabled old people who were not in nursing homes received assistance from relatives and friends, sometimes supplemented by paid services.[15] The majority of unpaid caregivers are female relatives of the disabled, usually wives, daughters, or daughters-in-law.[16]

Families devote enormous time and energy to the care of elderly relatives. One study estimated that more than 27 million unpaid days of informal care are provided each week.[17] Other studies suggest caring for elderly relatives imposes large emotional and physical strains on families.[18]

The strong role of the family in long-term care runs counter to the myth that American families, who supposedly took care of their aging relatives at home "in the good old days," are now "dumping" them in nursing homes. In fact, in the past, few families cared for an elderly parent because relatively few people lived long enough to experience a prolonged period of disability.[19] Because of increased longevity, the odds of being called upon to provide parent care are much higher now than they were in the past.

Although nursing homes serve less than a quarter of the disabled elderly, they dominate long-term care financing. In 1986 there were 16,033 nursing homes with 1.6 million beds, more beds than in acute care hospitals.[20] Many nursing home patients reside there for a long time, but more than half stay for fewer than six months. About half of these short-stay patients are discharged alive and return to the community. Expenditures for nursing home and home care for the elderly in 1993 were estimated at $54.7 billion and $20.7 billion, respectively.[21]

### HOW ARE THE BILLS PAID?

The striking fact about long-term care financing is that only a trivial portion of the bill is paid by any form of insurance. Most private health insurance policies do not cover long-term care; only about 1 percent of total long-term care expenditures are paid by private insurance. Medicare covers short stays in skilled nursing facilities, but medicare spending amounted to less than 5 percent of nursing home expenditures in 1991.[22]

The disabled elderly who use long-term care pay for it out of their own or their family's income and assets—or they turn to welfare. Out-of-pocket spending accounts for a little more than half, and medicaid and medicare for a little less than half, of all spending for nursing home care. Medicaid is the dominant source of public funding for long-term care, accounting for 62 percent of government spending for nursing home and home care for the elderly in 1993.[23]

Because the cost of an extended stay in a nursing home exceeds the financial resources of most elderly, it is not surprising that 61 percent of all nursing home residents in 1987 depended on welfare to help pay for their care.[24] Many nursing home patients are not poor when they enter the nursing home, but some become poor by depleting their income and assets paying for care, a process known as "spending down."[25] Medicaid patients have less access to services than do private-pay patients, mostly because medicaid payment rates are lower.

Because medicaid is intended for the needy, eligibility is limited to those who meet a strict means test. In 1993 unmarried individuals were not eligible for medicaid if they had more than $2,000 in assets, generally not counting the value of the home. Nursing home residents who meet the asset test and whose medical expenses exceed their ability to pay must contribute all of their income, except for a small personal needs allowance (usually $30 a month), to help pay for their care. Only then will medicaid help pay the bills.

## Methods: The Brookings-ICF Long-Term Care Financing Model

The Brookings-ICF Long-Term Care Financing Model is a large, integrated, microsimulation model that projects the size, financial position, disability status, and nursing home and home care use and expenditures of the elderly through the year 2020. In addition, expenditures are extrapolated to 2050. (See chapter 2 and appendix A for more complete descriptions of the model.) It is designed to evaluate public and private sector options for long-term care financing reform.

Like all computer models, the Brookings-ICF Long-Term Care Financing Model embodies a large number of assumptions. Our mortality and economic assumptions generally follow those of the Social Security Administration actuaries' middle path. Thus, the model assumes that elderly mortality rates will continue to decline and that the economy, inflation, and wages will continue to grow at modest levels. In particular, real wages and fringe benefits are assumed to grow at 1.5 percent a year; general inflation is assumed to be 4.0 percent a year. Because of the large labor component involved, nursing home and home care prices are assumed to grow 1.5 percent a year faster than general inflation. Disability rates are assumed to remain constant, as are nursing home and home care use rates.

## Base Case: Increasing Strains on the System

As the population of disabled elderly increases, additional pressures on the long-term care financing system are inevitable. The "base case" simulates what may happen if no changes are made in the way long-term care services are organized, used, and reimbursed between 1993 and 2018. The results of this simulation are summarized in tables 1-1 and 1-2. Alternative financing options are compared with this benchmark scenario.

During the next twenty-five years, the number of elderly will grow rapidly, as will the use of and expenditures for nursing home and home care. The overall number of elderly will grow from about 33 million in 1993 to 49 million in 2018, with the population aged 75 and older increasing from 14 million to 20 million. The total number of elderly using nursing homes is projected to increase from 2.2 million in 1993 to 3.6 million in 2018. Similarly, the number of home care users is projected to increase from 5.2 million to 7.4 million over the same period.[b]

The financial status of the elderly is likely to improve substantially over the next twenty-five years. Including the institutionalized population and people without income or assets, overall real median income is projected to increase from $15,523 in 1993 to $24,832 in 2018, and median housing and financial assets are projected to increase from $104,039 to $163,306 over that same period. Although the elderly aged 75 and older will continue to have lower income and assets than the younger elderly, all age groups are projected to have more income and assets in the future.

Not surprisingly, nursing home and home care expenditures for the elderly are projected to increase rapidly, from $75.4 billion in 1993 to $166.2 billion in constant 1993 dollars in 2018. Indeed, expenditures rise a good deal faster than use, primarily because prices of nursing home and home care are likely to increase faster than general consumer prices. Despite projected improvements in the financial status of the elderly, medicaid spending increases nearly as fast as total long-term care expenditures.

A major goal of long-term care reform is to reduce out-of-pocket

b. These figures represent the total number of users during the course of a year, not just the number of users on a given day. The figures for home care include those who used medicare home health care services after suffering an acute illness as well as those who are chronically disabled and use unskilled home care.

TABLE 1-1. *Thirty-Year Projection: Number of Elderly, Finances, and Use of Long-Term Care, Selected Periods*[a]

| Item | All elderly | 65–74 | 75–84 | 85 and older |
|---|---|---|---|---|
| | | | *Age* | |
| | | *1993* | | |
| Number of elderly (millions)[b] | | | | |
| In the population | 32.7 | 18.6 | 10.5 | 3.6 |
| Age distribution (percent) | (100) | (57) | (32) | (11) |
| In a nursing home[c] | 2.2 | 0.3 | 0.8 | 1.1 |
| Age distribution (percent) | (100) | (13) | (36) | (51) |
| Receiving home care services[d] | 5.2 | 2.0 | 2.0 | 1.2 |
| Age distribution (percent) | (100) | (38) | (38) | (23) |
| Median family income (1993 dollars)[e] | 15,523 | 18,882 | 12,927 | 9,536 |
| Median family assets (1993 dollars)[f] | 104,039 | 119,131 | 95,413 | 54,244 |
| Housing | 74,112 | 86,887 | 68,430 | 36,050 |
| Financial | 19,362 | 27,238 | 15,840 | 3,721 |
| | | *2018* | | |
| Number of elderly (millions)[b] | | | | |
| In the population | 49.2 | 29.1 | 13.9 | 6.2 |
| Age distribution (percent) | (100) | (59) | (28) | (13) |
| In a nursing home[c] | 3.6 | 0.5 | 1.1 | 2.0 |
| Age distribution (percent) | (100) | (14) | (31) | (56) |
| Receiving home care services[d] | 7.4 | 3.0 | 2.5 | 1.9 |
| Age distribution (percent) | (100) | (41) | (34) | (26) |
| Median family income (1993 dollars)[e] | 24,832 | 30,214 | 20,873 | 14,106 |
| Median family assets (1993 dollars)[f] | 163,306 | 174,530 | 157,753 | 133,927 |
| Housing | 122,177 | 131,841 | 116,428 | 81,876 |
| Financial | 43,141 | 51,755 | 35,981 | 14,981 |

SOURCE: Brookings-ICF Long-Term Care Financing Model.

a. In this and other tables in this chapter, 1993 represents the five-year average for the period 1991–95; and 2018 represents the five-year average for the period 2016–20.

b. Elderly aged 65 and older.

c. Number in a nursing home at any time during the year.

d. Number using paid home care services at any time during the year, including the nonchronically disabled elderly.

e. Family income is joint income for married people and individual income for unmarried people. Income sources are social security, pensions, supplemental security income, individual retirement accounts, wages, and asset earnings. Families and individuals without income are included.

f. Includes families without assets.

catastrophic costs, but these financial burdens can be measured many different ways. Because medicaid requires that nursing home patients spend down virtually all of their assets and contribute virtually all of their income to the cost of care, one measure of the extent of catastrophic costs is the number of medicaid nursing home patients. The average annual number of elderly medicaid nursing home patients is likely to increase from 1.4 million in 1993 to 2.0 million in 2018.

TABLE 1-2. *Thirty-Year Projection: Long-Term Care Spending, Selected Periods*[a]
*Billions of 1993 dollars*

| Payment source | 1993 | 2018 | Percent increase |
|---|---|---|---|
| | | *Nursing home services* | |
| Medicaid | 22.4 | 49.0 | 119 |
| Medicare | 4.3 | 10.0 | 133 |
| Patient out-of-pocket | 28.0 | 67.2 | 140 |
| TOTAL | 54.7 | 126.2 | 131 |
| | | *Home care services* | |
| Medicaid | 3.6 | 5.2 | 44 |
| Medicare | 9.4 | 19.0 | 102 |
| Other payers[b] | 2.2 | 4.3 | 95 |
| Patient out-of-pocket | 5.5 | 11.5 | 109 |
| TOTAL | 20.7 | 40.0 | 93 |

SOURCE: Brookings-ICF Long-Term Care Financing Model. Figures are rounded.
a. Nursing home and home care inflation is assumed to be 5.5 percent a year. General inflation is assumed to be 4 percent; long-term care inflation in excess of general inflation is assumed to be 1.5 percent a year.
b. Other payers include state and local expenditures, social services block grants, Older Americans Act and Department of Veterans' Affairs home care funds, charity, and out-of-pocket expenditures by people other than the service recipient.

An alternate measure of catastrophic costs is to calculate the proportion of a patient's income and assets that are spent on nursing home care. The model projects that the proportion of nursing home admissions who will spend more than 40 percent of their income and financial assets on care will be fairly stable at about 40 percent of nursing home admissions during the simulation period.

## Problems of Current System and Goals of Reform

The current system of financing and organizing long-term care satisfies almost no one. Pooling the risks of long-term care is not widespread in either the public or private sector. Families and governments are simply coping with the rising costs of long-term care as best they can. Long-term care reform should embody at least five different and sometimes competing goals.

### A NORMAL LIFE RISK

The most important goal of reform should be to treat long-term care as a normal risk of living and of growing old. Mechanisms should be established so that people will know how they will pay for services should they need them. The costs of long-term care should not come as an unpleasant surprise that causes severe financial distress to individuals and their families. Right now the pain and anxiety inherent in becoming disabled or in caring for a disabled relative are compounded by worries about paying for care. One of the great fears of the elderly is that they will be a burden on their children.

## PROTECTING AGAINST CATASTROPHIC COSTS

With very little public or private insurance coverage available against the high costs of long-term care, it is not surprising that users of long-term care services incur very high out-of-pocket costs. Less than one-tenth of elderly nursing home users can afford to pay for a year of nursing home care solely out of income.[26] Even when nursing home and home care patients do not end up on medicaid, long-term care still imposes a costly burden that can be financially crippling.

Protecting the elderly against the financial burdens of long-term care means, in part, preventing the elderly from impoverishing themselves simply because they need nursing home or extensive home care. Currently, many of the middle-class elderly spend all of their income for long-term care and then resort to their life savings when income alone does not cover the costs. Some of these people will deplete their savings and assets and be forced to rely on medicaid. Other middle-class elderly, particularly those with higher incomes, may not actually spend down to medicaid but may exhaust most of their assets.

The principles of the current long-term care financing system contrast radically with those of the medicare program, the government program that finances acute care for the elderly. Virtually no one argues that the sick or even terminally ill should use all of their income and deplete their assets to pay for their hospital or physician care, yet doing so is routine in long-term care.[27]

## PREVENTING DEPENDENCE ON WELFARE

A separate but related concern is to save elderly people who have been financially independent all their lives from depending on welfare—medicaid—with its stigma, inferior access, and perhaps lesser quality of care. Although more than half of current nursing home residents are eligible for medicaid, an unknown but probably substantial portion of residents were not eligible for the program when they were living in the community or became eligible shortly before admission. This group probably had low levels of assets but too much income to qualify for medicaid in the community. The high costs of nursing home care, however, make them eligible for medicaid as soon as they enter the nursing home. Although few data are available on this issue, Burwell and others found that only 27 percent of Michigan medicaid patients spent down after entering the nursing home, but that another 35 percent enrolled in medicaid when they were admitted to the nursing home.[28] In other words, more than 60 percent of the medicaid nursing home patients were not eligible for medicaid before admission to the nursing home.[29] In our view, this group has not received enough attention in reform proposals.

**TILTING TOWARD HOME CARE**

Reform of the financing system should also aim at creating a more balanced delivery system by expanding paid home care services, such as home health care, personal care, homemaker help, meals on wheels, and adult day care. The overwhelming majority of disabled elderly are at home and want to stay there. Only a minority of the chronically disabled elderly, however, receive any formal care at home but rely instead on informal care provided by family and friends. On the average day in 1989 only 29 percent of the disabled elderly living at home were using any paid in-home care.[30]

Public expenditures for long-term care for the elderly are overwhelmingly for nursing home rather than home care. In 1993 only about 36 percent of government long-term care expenditures for the elderly were for home care services.[31] Nearly 62 percent of that was for the medicare home health benefit, much of which is geared toward post-acute rather than long-term care. Although private insurance coverage of long-term home care has improved greatly over the last few years, few people have policies with broad coverage.

At the same time, interest in home care is strong. For example, the long-term care component of President Clinton's reform proposal focuses on expanding home care. In a 1992–93 public opinion survey conducted by LH Research for HealthRight, more than 80 percent of respondents favored a new federal home care program.[32]

**DESIGNING AN AFFORDABLE SYSTEM**

Political reality and common sense dictate that any new reform system be affordable, both to the user and the government. Although few agree on what constitutes society's willingness to pay for long-term care services, raising taxes to pay for public programs is always difficult, even for popular programs. Greater attention, however, needs to be given to how much long-term care costs society overall and less to the level of government expenditures. Just because expenses are in the private sector does not mean that society does not incur them. Nonetheless, the more ambitious proposals for long-term care reform cost more and, at some point, are not politically viable.

## Private Long-Term Care Insurance

Private sector approaches are appealing because they reflect the American tradition of individuals' taking responsibility for their own lives.[c] Private insurance, in particular, offers the possibility of prefunding the inevitable societal burden that will occur when the baby boom generation needs long-term care. The classic virtue of the competitive market is its flexibility to adapt to individual needs and wants and to local conditions.[d] Moreover, the large federal budget deficit and general concern about the competency of government have made large-scale expansions in almost all public programs difficult to enact. In the case of long-term care, some have voiced the hope that private sector initiatives could hold down public spending on medicaid. The marked improvement in the financial position of the elderly in the past twenty years has also made it more plausible to argue that private sector financing—especially private insurance—might be widely affordable in the future.

Although 97 percent of the elderly have medicare coverage and almost two-thirds have private supplemental health insurance, insurance against the potentially devastating costs of long-term care is relatively rare and very recent.[33] The Health Insurance Association of America reports that the number of policies ever sold increased from 815,000 in 1987 to 2.9 million in 1992;[34] the number of policies actually in force, however, is considerably lower. Thus, perhaps 4 to 5 percent of the elderly and a negligible percentage of the nonelderly have some kind of private long-term care insurance.

c. Government, of course, has assisted individuals in any number of situations. It has been used to promote transportation, help the development of industry, protect the family farm, and provide a wide variety of arrangements for personal financial security.
d. There is a potential conflict between prefunding and flexibility, however, in that individuals may be locked into insurance contracts that embody current delivery system concepts and that will be outdated by the time they actually use the services.

## INDIVIDUAL PRIVATE INSURANCE PRODUCTS

Private long-term care insurance is overwhelmingly sold on an individual basis to the elderly population, with the insured paying the entire premium. This is in contrast to acute care insurance, which is provided primarily by employers, who shoulder most of the cost.

Partly because of the high administrative costs and the relatively short period available for reserves to build, private long-term care insurance sold to the elderly is quite expensive. As a result, numerous studies conclude that only between 10 and 20 percent of the current elderly can afford high-quality private long-term care insurance.[35]

During the last few years, the substantial number of American households that carry life insurance policies has stimulated interest in using this mechanism—especially cash-value policies that accumulate reserves—to finance long-term care. Because most nursing home patients end their stay because of death, insurers use "accelerated death benefits" to pay benefits a bit earlier than they would otherwise. The principal drawbacks of this approach are that many Americans do not have cash-value life insurance, and most of those that do have policies with only a small cash value. In 1991 the average face value of cash-value life insurance policies was only about $26,000.[36] As a result, these policies cannot absorb much of the cost of long-term care.

## STRATEGIES TO IMPROVE AFFORDABILITY

Various options have been proposed to improve the affordability of private long-term care insurance. These include encouraging people to buy insurance when they are still young and in the work force, providing tax deductions or tax credits for the purchase of insurance, and providing easier access to medicaid for people who buy an approved long-term care policy.

### Employer-Sponsored Policies

If people bought long-term care insurance when they were younger, especially through employer groups, then premiums could be significantly lower and therefore more affordable. Reserves and interest earnings have more time to build when they are bought by people at age 45 rather than at age 65, and group policies have lower administrative costs than policies sold individually. Although employer-sponsored long-term care insurance is the fastest growing of all private insurance markets, only 350,000 policies had been sold as of 1992.[37]

Selling private long-term care insurance to an employer-based, younger population is conceptually sound, but it will be difficult. First, marketing will be extremely hard. In general, 45-year-old workers have other, more immediate financial concerns, such as child care, mortgage payments, and college education for their children. Experience to date is that few employees who are offered private long-term care insurance actually purchase it.[38]

Second, selling to the nonelderly population raises several difficult pricing and product design considerations. An actuary pricing a private long-term care insurance product for a 45-year-old must predict what is going to happen forty years into the future, when the insured is 85 years old and likely to need services. Small changes in assumptions compounded over long periods of time can drastically change a product's profitability. Closely related to the issue of pricing is the issue of product design. Although employer-sponsored plans are sometimes better than the individually marketed products available, most policies do not deal well with the inevitable inflation in nursing home and home care.

Third, employers may be willing to offer private long-term care insurance, but they are unlikely to help pay for it as they do acute care insurance. The uncertain tax status of employer contributions for private long-term care insurance undoubtedly complicates matters, and employers are not looking to contribute to another fringe benefit for retirees. It is no secret that acute care insurance premiums have skyrocketed, and companies are looking for ways to cut back on their expenses. In addition, large employers typically face huge unfunded liabilities for the acute care insurance for retirees.

*Tax Incentives to Purchase Insurance*

Another set of options would improve the affordability of private long-term care insurance by offering purchasers of such insurance a deduction or credit on federal income taxes. The effect of either a deduction or a credit is to reduce the net price of insurance policies, making them more affordable. Some insurance advocates also argue that a tax incentive would signal potential purchasers that the government considers long-term care insurance to be a worthwhile product.

Tax incentives are potentially inefficient because benefits are likely to go primarily to people who would have bought the policies anyway. Thus the government's cost per additional policy sold will be high.

In addition a tax incentive is, by definition, a revenue loss that will increase the federal deficit unless offset by other revenue increases or spending cuts. Some advocates of tax incentives argue that reductions in medicaid expenditures will offset the tax loss. For the level of incentives commonly suggested, our simulations suggest that this is not the case. At least through 2018 the tax loss will be at least four times the savings from public programs.

*Easier Access to Medicaid: A Public-Private Partnership*

A third option to promote private insurance is to provide easier access to medicaid for purchasers of a state-approved private long-term care insurance policy. In these public-private partnerships, which are being tried in California, Connecticut, Indiana, Iowa, and New York, policyholders are allowed to keep more of their financial assets than usual and still receive nursing home benefits under medicaid. This strategy allows the insured to obtain lifetime asset protection without having to buy an insurance policy that pays lifetime benefits. Moreover, supporters argue that the scheme will be roughly budget neutral, with medicaid savings offsetting the new benefits.

This approach raises several issues. First, is it appropriate to use medicaid, a means-tested welfare program designed for the poorest of the poor, to protect the assets of primarily upper-middle- and upper-income elderly?

Second, how important is "asset protection" as a motivator in the purchase of private long-term care insurance? In a 1990 survey of new long-term care insurance purchasers, LifePlans, Inc., found that asset protection was one of many reasons people purchased insurance but that only 14 percent listed it as the "most important" reason.[39]

The third concern is whether easier access to medicaid will actually induce substantial numbers of people to purchase long-term care insurance who would not otherwise have bought it. Indeed, one of the major reasons people buy long-term care insurance is to avoid the need to apply for welfare.

## PRIVATE INSURANCE SIMULATION RESULTS

Simulations using the Brookings-ICF Long-Term Care Financing Model show that private insurance for long-term care can grow substantially. Figure 1-1 summarizes the assumptions used for our simulations of the principal private insurance options, and table 1-3 summarizes the results. These assumptions are relatively generous to the potential role of private long-term care insurance and are meant to

FIGURE 1-1. **Private Long-Term Care Insurance: Assumptions for Key Simulations**

---

- *Policies:* Insurance policies cover two or four years of nursing home and home care and pay an initial indemnity value of $60 a day for nursing home care and $30 a visit for home care in 1986. Indemnity values increase by 5.5 percent a year, compounded annually. Premiums for nonelderly increase by 5.5 percent a year until age 65 and then are level. All nondisabled persons who meet affordability criteria buy as much insurance as they can afford.

- *SPEND5PCT:* All elderly with $10,000 or more in nonhousing assets purchase insurance if it costs no more than 5 percent of their income.

- *TAXFAVINS:* Elderly who purchase insurance receive an income-related tax credit of up to 20 percent of the premium cost. All elderly with $10,000 or more in nonhousing assets purchase insurance if the policy costs no more than 5 percent of their income.

- *CTINS:* Elderly who purchase private long-term care insurance may receive medicaid nursing home benefits while retaining liquid assets beyond what is normally allowed. The additional assets equal the amount that the private insurance policy pays out in benefits. All elderly with $10,000 or more in nonhousing assets purchase insurance if the policy costs no more than 7 percent of their income.

- *GROUPINS:* Individuals as young as age 40 purchase group or individual long-term care insurance policies. Nonelderly purchase policies if premiums are between 2 percent and 4 percent of income (depending on age). Elderly with $10,000 or more in nonhousing assets purchase insurance if it costs no more than 5 percent of their income.

- *ADBENEFITS:* Individuals with cash-value life insurance use it to finance their nursing home stay. The amount they use is 2.5 percent a month of the face amount of the life insurance, following a six-month deductible.

---

establish a rough upper bound of the impact. They are not a prediction of what will happen.

The simulation results suggest that the private long-term care insurance industry is at a crossroad. So long as private insurance is aimed principally at the elderly population, its market penetration and ability to finance long-term care will remain restricted, even twenty-five years into the future. Because of the limited market penetration, private insurance will not substantially reduce catastrophic out-of-pocket costs among the elderly. Moreover, private insurance expenditures will be made mostly on behalf of the upper-income elderly and thus will have almost no effect on medicaid expenditures.

The story would change substantially if employers could be convinced to offer private long-term care insurance to their active employees and if workers could be convinced to buy the policies. The simulation results

TABLE 1-3. *Private Insurance Strategies: Key Simulation Results for Major Options, 2018*

| Option | Percent of elderly with private insurance[a] | Percent of total long-term care spending paid by private insurance[b] | Percent of private insurance spending on nursing home patients with incomes >$40,000[c] | Percent reductions in medicaid nursing home spending[d] | Percent reductions in catastrophic out-of-pocket spending for nursing home patients[e] |
|---|---|---|---|---|---|
| SPEND5PCT | 20 | 9 | 70 | −2 | −6 |
| TAXFAVINS | 28 | 12 | 64 | −3 | −8 |
| CTINS | 32 | 14 | 61 | −4 | −11 |
| GROUPINS | 76 | 29 | 29 | −28 | −26 |
| ADBENEFITS | 85 | 1 | 31 | −1 | 0 |

SOURCE: Brookings-ICF Long-Term Care Financing Model. Figures are rounded.

a. Because age at initial participation varies by option, the denominators (elderly population) are different for each option. Participation for SPEND5PCT, TAXFAVINS2, and CTINS is expressed as the percent of elderly age 67 and older. Participation in GROUPINS is the percent of elderly age 65 and older.

b. Total long-term care expenditures vary by option.

c. Income is presented in 1993 dollars.

d. Medicaid nursing home expenditures for the base case are $49 billion.

e. Defined as 40 percent or more of income and nonhousing assets.

clearly suggest that the affordability problem would largely be solved by selling properly structured policies to the nonelderly. Indeed, private insurance could eventually play a significant role in financing long-term care and could meaningfully reduce catastrophic out-of-pocket costs and medicaid expenditures. The real market penetration, however, is certain to be much less than the simulation because of other barriers to purchase, such as the lack of interest by the nonelderly.

## Why Public Strategies Should Take the Lead

Private insurance is not a panacea. Although the market can and should grow, private insurance is likely to play only a modest role in financing nursing home and home care. The limits of the private sector mean that greater attention should be given to reforming our public programs.

There are two broad approaches to publicly financing long-term care. The means-tested welfare program—medicaid—can continue as the principal government program to finance care, but be liberalized so that it does not require total impoverishment, or more long-term care can be provided on a non-means-tested basis through social insurance. These two approaches need not be mutually exclusive. Indeed, many reform proposals combine the two strategies and include a role for private insurance as well.

## A MEANS-TESTED MEDICAID STRATEGY

Proposals for medicaid reform generally include using more lenient financial eligibility standards—raising the level of protected assets and increasing the amount of income nursing home patients can retain for personal needs—and expanding home care coverage. By liberalizing medicaid eligibility criteria, the safety net can be cast more widely so that fewer people face complete impoverishment before receiving benefits.

The most compelling argument for means-testing is that it targets public expenditures to those people with the greatest financial need. In the context of long-term care, those who advocate continued reliance on medicaid believe that the proper role of government is to finance only that part of care that is beyond the resources of the elderly. They believe that people with high levels of income should either purchase private insurance or pay for their care out of pocket. Because it does not provide universal coverage, a medicaid liberalization strategy is also the least expensive of all public reform options.

The other major advantage is that medicaid reform is an incremental approach, building on an existing program with administrative systems already in place. Adjusting the existing system may be more politically feasible than creating a largely new program.

A welfare strategy has several drawbacks, however. Because medicaid helps to fund care only after the disabled have depleted their income and assets, it does not prevent the elderly from incurring catastrophic costs. Moreover, because benefits are available only to the impoverished, a perverse incentive exists to transfer, underreport, or shelter wealth of any appreciable size. Perhaps the most disconcerting aspect of using a means-tested program to finance most public long-term care is that a significant number of people who have been financially independent all their lives end up on welfare. An underlying assumption of welfare programs is that only a relatively small proportion of the population should depend on them. Yet, with long-term care, it is the many, not the few, who rely on welfare.

Despite the large number of middle-class beneficiaries currently on the program, medicaid still retains some of the stigma of a welfare program. Fragmentary evidence from other programs for the elderly indicates that less welfare stigma may be associated with medicaid and long-term care than is often assumed.

More important than the question of stigma is whether means-tested programs such as medicaid can garner enough public and political support to sustain them. Ironically, although "enactability" is supposed to be the strong suit of incremental changes, public opinion polls suggest only meager support for means-tested approaches, especially when compared with programs that provide universal coverage.[40]

## NON-MEANS-TESTED APPROACHES

A social insurance approach to financing long-term care offers coverage regardless of financial status. This approach explicitly recognizes long-term care as a normal risk of growing old. Advocates of social insurance see no cogent reason why long-term care should be financed primarily through a welfare program, while acute health care and income support for the elderly are financed through the non-means-tested programs of medicare and social security.

Social insurance is the only approach that guarantees universal or near-universal coverage. That is, social insurance covers the able-bodied and the currently disabled, the young and the old, and people of all levels of income and wealth. In this way, social insurance avoids the risk of adverse selection that affects private insurance and the administrative costs of screening out high risks.

Because social insurance programs provide benefits without regard to income, they have the political advantage of including middle- and upper-class beneficiaries as part of their constituency. These beneficiaries generally wield more political power than the impoverished, and programs benefiting them, such as social security and medicare, tend to be more politically stable than programs for the poor. Given the immense popularity of medicare and social security, it should not come as a great surprise that Americans generally favor a social insurance approach to long-term care.[41]

Social insurance can also deliberately create a more balanced delivery system by providing broad coverage of home care. Reflecting this concern, all of the major proposals for public long-term care insurance offer such coverage.

The primary disadvantage of a social insurance approach is its cost. The combination of an intractable budget deficit and resistance to new taxes makes this a formidable barrier. An uncertain national economic future, the costs associated with a rapidly aging population, and the added financial burden of extending acute care health insurance to the uninsured all compound the political difficulties of enacting an expensive new social insurance program.

Nonetheless, most of the costs of the program will be incurred by society, with or without such a program. This is also true for medicaid liberalization, although the level of expenditures would be lower. Much of what a public program would do is to shift individual nursing home and home care expenditures from the private sector to the public sector, rather than create new spending. To the extent that the presence of public insurance would increase overall costs to society by increasing use of nursing home and home care, the same is also true for the widescale purchase of private insurance, since both types of insurance have similar cost-increasing features.[e]

Because social insurance provides benefits regardless of the recipient's income, critics argue that it will be a windfall to upper-income elderly who could otherwise afford to pay for long-term care themselves. The income and asset profile of nursing home patients, however, shows that this is a much overstated argument.[42] Our simulation results suggest that the overwhelming majority of new expenditures are likely to go to people with quite modest financial status.

Detractors also contend that it would be unfair to create yet another program—in addition to social security and medicare—that benefits mostly the elderly but is financed mostly by the nonelderly. As such, a major new program for long-term care would be "generationally inequitable."

There are at least three responses to such concerns. First, many disabled persons are not elderly, and virtually all proposals would benefit the nonelderly as well as the elderly. Second, because family care is the backbone of community-based long-term care, middle-aged caregivers will benefit from an expanded federal home care program. Third, generational-equity concerns are based on a narrow, cross-sectional perspective of benefits and tax payments at one moment in time rather than over a lifetime. Like public education for children, social insurance for long-term care responds to a need that exists across the course of life and thus benefits all groups. Indeed, the current nonelderly population is likely to live much longer—and need more long-term care—than the current generation of elderly.

**EXAMINATION OF FOUR SOCIAL INSURANCE PROTOTYPES**

Several specific social insurance proposals to cover long-term care have been introduced in Congress. All of these plans provide fairly compre-

e. The main feature that would increase use, and therefore costs, is the lowering of the net price of services to consumers.

hensive home care and are generally differentiated by the type and duration of nursing home coverage they provide. "Home care coverage only" proposals offer no new nursing home coverage, "front-end" plans offer first-dollar nursing home coverage of limited duration, "back-end" nursing home coverage entails lengthy deductible periods, and "comprehensive" models have little or no deductible periods and cover nursing home care no matter how long the stay. All of these proposals are easily combined with liberalization of the medicaid program and, except for the comprehensive prototype, with the expansion of private insurance.

### Home-Care-Only Strategies

Home-care-only strategies, such as those proposed by President Clinton and the late Representative Claude Pepper, would boldly shift financing away from the nursing home as the predominant setting for long-term care. Under this design, no major changes would be made to nursing home coverage, but coverage for a wide variety of in-home services would be offered.

There are several reasons to concentrate on home care. Foremost, the disabled elderly prefer home care because it allows them to maintain a sense of independence, helps reduce unmet care needs, lessens their feelings of being a burden on relatives, and increases their confidence that they will receive the care they need. Approximately 70 percent of disabled elderly living in the community in 1982 were receiving help solely from their family and friends, often at great personal sacrifice of time, effort, emotional strain, and sometimes financial expense.[43] Home care programs can help caregivers by offering respite from their daily responsibilities.

Improving access to services in the home and thus creating a more balanced delivery system has great appeal. Nursing home care, however, not home care, is the major cause of catastrophic costs related to long-term care and welfare dependency among the elderly.[44] A home-care-only strategy would do little to address these problems.

### Home Care and Front-End Nursing Home Coverage

A second strategy would similarly cover comprehensive home care but also provide public insurance for the first part or "front-end" of a nursing home stay (for example, the first six months). Legislation introduced by the Senate and House Democratic leadership based on recommendations from the U.S. Bipartisan Commission on Comprehensive

Health Care (the so-called Pepper Commission) embodies this approach. The rationale for front-end coverage is that incremental public expenditures should be concentrated on people who are living in the community or who have the greatest probability of returning home after a nursing home stay. Most people who return to the community have relatively short lengths of stay in the nursing home.[45] It is also the least expensive of the options that provide some coverage for nursing home care. Finally, front-end nursing home coverage is a logical expansion of the existing skilled nursing facility benefit offered under medicare.

One of the disadvantages of this strategy is that many people can already afford to finance short nursing home stays. This approach does little to assist people with long lengths of stay and very large nursing home bills. For that reason this proposal is often combined with liberalization of medicaid financial eligibility rules.

*Home Care and Back-End Nursing Home Coverage*

A third strategy would offer comprehensive home care, but provide nursing home coverage only after a very long deductible period (the so-called "back-end" of a nursing home stay). For example, the public insurance plan proposed by Senator George Mitchell would cover home care with a modest deductible and coinsurance, but provide public nursing home insurance only for those patients who stay longer than two years.[46] This approach explicitly assumes that insurers will offer and large majorities of elderly will purchase private insurance to fill in the costly deductible period. Here, in theory at least, private and public insurance are neatly combined into a package where public insurance offers a "backstop" to private coverage.

The strongest argument for back-end coverage is that the government would pay for the unquestionably catastrophic costs of long nursing home stays, a role that many feel is most appropriate. Relying on a vast expansion of private sector insurance makes back-end coverage a highly risky strategy, however, because so few elderly currently have any kind of private coverage. If the assumptions about the supply or demand for insurance are wrong, nursing home residents would face upwards of $74,000 (the approximate cost of two years in a long-term care facility) in out-of-pocket costs before receiving any public insurance benefits.

Another disadvantage to back-end coverage is that few of the long-stay patients targeted by such an approach are discharged alive.[47] Thus, it provides asset protection for heirs—arguably a less appropriate role for government.

*Comprehensive Coverage for Home and Nursing Home Care*

A fourth strategy, comprehensive coverage, has been introduced in two different forms by Representative Henry Waxman and by Representative Fortney "Pete" Stark.[48] Both bills cover comprehensive nursing home and home care after a relatively short deductible period and with moderate coinsurance levels. This strategy seeks to solve directly the problems of long-term care within the structure of a government program, without relying on private insurance to fill the gaps. This approach has the advantage of establishing a single payer, thus enabling the government to control payment rates and service delivery. Of all the options, a comprehensive strategy would be best at financing needed care, reducing catastrophic costs, and equalizing access to nursing home care and home care.

The costs of a comprehensive program, however, would be by far the highest of all four options, and other spending priorities would be squeezed. Also, certain disadvantages pertain to any program that is totally dependent on government financing. For example, the system could become rigid and bureaucratic, unable to respond to the individual needs of the disabled. Arguably, quality may suffer when all patients are publicly sponsored because nursing homes will no longer have to compete to attract higher-paying private pay patients.

## RAISING THE MONEY

Any responsible new public program for long-term care (or any other program for that matter) will need to avoid adding to the federal budget deficit. From a long-term care policy perspective, any number of financing sources would be acceptable so long as they raised enough money to pay for the program. Potential sources include payroll, income, value-added, estate, cigarette, and alcohol taxes, insurance premiums, and savings in medicare, medicaid, and other public programs. Politically, of course, the difficulty of raising significant new taxes has blocked public expansion of long-term care and, more generally, of health care for the uninsured.

Three general principles, however, should guide the financing structure for the new program. First, although the elderly are not likely to be able to finance all, or even a majority of the expenditures, they should, out of fairness, pay a significant share of the cost of the program. This probably means some kind of insurance premium and, perhaps, an

FIGURE 1-2. **Medicaid Liberalization and Social Insurance Options: Simulation Assumptions**

- *Medicaid Liberalization:* Medicaid financial eligibility standards increased to allow single individuals and married couples to keep $30,000 and $60,000, respectively, in nonhousing assets. Personal needs allowance increased to $100 a month. Home care for severely disabled (persons with problems with two or more activities of daily living or substantial cognitive impairment) expanded and available to people with incomes below 150 percent of federal poverty level. Private insurance available for nursing home and home care.

- *Home Care Only:* Broad, non-means-tested home care coverage of unlimited duration provided to severely disabled elderly. Twenty percent coinsurance rate; medicaid pays coinsurance for population with incomes below 150 percent of poverty level. Medicaid liberalization changes listed above included. Private insurance available for nursing home care.

- *Front-End:* Combines home care only program with coverage of first six months of nursing home stay. Twenty percent coinsurance for nursing home care. Private insurance available for uncovered period of nursing home stays.

- *Back-End:* Combines home care only program with unlimited nursing home coverage after a two-year deductible period. Twenty percent coinsurance for nursing home care. Private insurance available to cover deductible period.

- *Comprehensive:* Combines home care only program with unlimited nursing home coverage with no deductible. Twenty percent coinsurance for nursing home care. No private insurance available to cover coinsurance.

---

increase in the estate tax. Second, states should contribute to the cost of the program. States are likely to have a major administrative and policy role in any new program, and it is therefore essential that they have a financial stake in the program. Third, for all but the medicaid liberalization option, the level of expenditures needed will likely necessitate fairly broad-based sources of financing—payroll, income, or value-added taxes—or large cuts in other programs. It is unlikely that enough small taxes can be stitched together to raise reliably the money needed.

### PUBLIC PROGRAM SIMULATION RESULTS

To evaluate the various types of public long-term care options, medicaid liberalization and the four social insurance prototypes were simulated. Figure 1-2 summarizes the simulation assumptions, and tables 1-4 and 1-5 summarize the results. All of the social insurance prototypes include changes to the medicaid program.

Incremental public spending—that is, public expenditures above current levels of spending—for these options in 1993 for fully implemented

TABLE 1-4. *Medicaid Liberalization and Social Insurance Strategies: Key Simulation Results, Selected Periods*[a]

| Option | Incremental public cost (billions of 1993 dollars)[b] | Percent of incremental public spending on nursing home patients with incomes >$40,000[c] | Percent reduction in catastrophic out-of-pocket spending for nursing home patients[d] |
|---|---|---|---|
| | | *1993* | |
| Medicaid liberalization | 6.0 | 1 | −33 |
| Expanded home care only | 20.8 | 0[e] | −33 |
| Front-end | 23.2 | 14 | −34 |
| Back-end | 32.5 | 11 | −41 |
| Comprehensive | 49.1 | 11 | −61 |
| | | *2018* | |
| Medicaid liberalization | 4.3 | 10 | −21 |
| Expanded home care only | 35.2 | 0[e] | −23 |
| Front-end | 44.5 | 19 | −31 |
| Back-end | 66.6 | 28 | −33 |
| Comprehensive | 109.4 | 26 | −54 |

SOURCE: Brookings-ICF Long-Term Care Financing Model.
a. All social insurance strategies include liberalized medicaid benefits.
b. In billions of 1993 dollars.
c. Income in 1993 dollars.
d. Defined as 40 percent or more of income and nonhousing assets.
e. Incremental public expenditures for the elderly with incomes of $40,000 or more actually went down under this option because of the purchase of private insurance among this group.

programs varies from $6.0 billion for medicaid liberalization alone to $49.1 billion for a comprehensive long-term care program. In 2018 these incremental expenditures are projected to vary from $4.3 billion to $109.4 billion for these same options. These expenditures are only for the elderly; including the nonelderly disabled would increase the level of expenditures. Contrary to the claims of critics, the overwhelming majority of incremental expenditures under these programs would be for elderly with relatively modest incomes. Finally, compared with the private insurance options, public options do a better job of reducing catastrophic out-of-pocket costs.

Table 1-5 offers an illustration of what level of taxation would be required to pay for the various reform options with a payroll tax. Assuming that every dollar of earnings is subject to the payroll tax, a 1.28 percent payroll tax would be required in 1993 (employer and employee portions combined) and 3.43 percent tax in 2048 to finance existing public programs. For the various options, the total public costs would require between a 1.48 and 2.80 percent payroll tax in 1993. Projected to the year 2048, these rates range from 3.83 percent to 7.75 percent.

TABLE 1-5. *Total Expenditures for Public Long-Term Care as a Percentage of Payroll for the Base Case and Public Insurance Options, Selected Periods*

| Option | Payroll tax[a] | | |
| --- | --- | --- | --- |
| | 1993 | 2018 | 2048[b] |
| Base case | | | |
| Total costs | 2.37 | 3.61 | 6.85 |
| Public costs | 1.28 | 1.80 | 3.43 |
| Medicaid liberalization only | 1.48 | 1.93 | 3.83 |
| Expanded home care only | 1.89 | 2.42 | 4.58 |
| Front-end nursing home | 1.99 | 2.59 | 4.91 |
| Back-end nursing home | 2.28 | 3.15 | 6.08 |
| Comprehensive nursing home | 2.80 | 3.98 | 7.75 |

SOURCE: Brookings-ICF Long-Term Care Financing Model.
a. Combined employee and employer contributions. No ceiling on taxable salaries.
b. 2048 represents the five-year average for the period 2045–50.

Because this payroll tax would be additional to social security, medicare, and any new acute health care taxes, it is not trivial, but neither is it enormous. And, again, to a significant degree, it represents an expense that society as a whole will incur with or without a new program.

## Recommendations

The principal options for reforming the financing of long-term care are private insurance, medicaid liberalization, and social insurance. Even with public strategies to promote it, only a minority of the elderly are likely to have private long-term care insurance in the foreseeable future.

Because private insurance is not likely to change the way in which nursing home and home care is financed, greater attention should be given to reforming public programs. Medicaid liberalization costs less and concentrates expenditures on the lower-income population, but public support for means-tested programs is minimal, and those who do rely on medicaid often face inferior access to care of uncertain quality. Social insurance offers better protection against impoverishment and can spread the risk of incurring expenses for long-term care across everyone. But all social insurance strategies are expensive.

In the end, a mixed system of private insurance, medicaid liberalization, and expansion of social insurance is desirable. Our recommendations are in line with, but are more far-reaching than, the proposals put forth by President Clinton. In general, we favor the strategy set forth by the Pepper Commission—including home care and front-end nursing home coverage under social insurance, liberalizing medicaid financial eligibility, and leaving a substantial role for the private sector to provide asset protection to the upper-middle-income and wealthy elderly.[49] According to our simulations, this approach would reduce the proportion of nursing home admissions who incur catastrophic out-of-pocket costs by 31 percent in 2018, about the same as the back-end strategy but considerably less than the comprehensive approach. Although limited to the severely disabled, the public programs would be available to all persons regardless of age. Under this proposal, private insurance would be subject to strict federal regulations. In addition, the tax status of private long-term care insurance would be clarified, mostly in a direction favorable to private insurance. This overall approach has a price tag for the elderly of $23 billion in 1993 and $45 billion in 2018, which, while not cheap, is in the realm of the possible.

The social insurance program that we envision is very different from the traditional concept of social insurance as embodied in social security or medicare. States rather than the federal government would be primarily responsible for designing and administering the program, albeit largely with federal funds. In addition, the program would be budgeted, rather than open ended. Finally, to maximize service flexibility and ensure that states could stay within their budgets, individuals would not have a "legal entitlement" to a defined set of services. Instead, individuals would be entitled to an assessment, a plan of care, and services on a funds-available basis. Expenditure levels would be indexed annually to account for nursing home and home care inflation and the number of disabled elderly and nonelderly.

Funding for the medicaid liberalization and new social insurance program should come from a combination of payroll taxes, premiums paid by the elderly, medicare savings, and continued federal and state contributions for what would have been spent in the existing medicare and medicaid programs.

Our proposal has five advantages. First, by providing additional long-term care on a universal basis, it furthers risk pooling as a way to finance long-term care. Second, by focusing on people who are either at home or have the greatest chance of returning home after a nursing home stay, it concentrates new spending on people who have the greatest need for financial protection. In our view, protecting the assets of those who will die in a nursing home deserves a lower priority. Third, aggressively expanding home care brings more balance to the delivery system and provides the services that older people want. Fourth, increasing the level of income and assets that medicaid nursing home patients can keep would provide a significant increase in the level of financial protection against catastrophic costs, while still requiring individuals to contribute a substantial amount of their income and assets before obtaining help from the government. Fifth, these public sector initiatives allow private insurance to expand, while guaranteeing that consumers will be protected against inadequate policies.

## Chapter Two

# The Model and Base Case

To help evaluate various public and private strategies for financing long-term care, we worked with Lewin-VHI, Inc., to revise extensively and update the Brookings-ICF Long-Term Care Financing Model, a micro-simulation model that we used in *Caring for the Disabled Elderly: Who Will Pay?*[1] This model projects the size and status of the elderly population, the elderly's expected use of nursing home and home care, and their financial resources to pay for these services. This model can project the cost of financing long-term care both under current policy and under proposed public and private financing mechanisms. The model can also estimate how new mechanisms would affect different groups in the elderly population and spending from existing private sources and public programs, such as medicaid. Thus, for example, the model can estimate medicaid savings that would result from expanding private insurance; it can also estimate how coverage under various public insurance programs would affect out-of-pocket costs.

We have three goals in using this model. First, we hope to put some quantitative boundaries around the claims of advocates for various reforms, and to do so in a manner that is consistent across interventions, thereby facilitating comparisons. Second, although the projections are almost certain to be inaccurate to some extent, they provide an order of magnitude estimate on a variety of important issues. Projecting into the future is critical both to take advantage of the improved financial status of the elderly, which may make private insurance more affordable, and to assess more fully the changing financial burden of providing long-term care as the population ages. Finally, we hope to illustrate the consequences of a set of assumptions, encouraging debate about what behavior must change in order to arrive at different results.

Although much uncertainty exists, the model projects simultaneously many characteristics of the older population that will affect the need for and use of long-term care, together with the financial resources likely to be available to pay for it. Comparisons of the costs and effects of different schemes can provide insight into the relative advantages and disadvantages of various financing approaches, even if some economic or behavioral assumptions prove invalid.

This chapter describes the Brookings-ICF Long-Term Care Financing Model. We explain the methodology in general terms (a detailed description can be found in appendix A), highlight key assumptions, and point out some of the limitations of the model. In the second part of the chapter, we discuss the base case, or what is likely to happen if current policies are continued without change. We also show how the findings of the model are sensitive to different economic and demographic assumptions. The last section explains how we used the model to develop premiums for the prototype private long-term care insurance policies that are used in the simulations of private insurance in chapters 3 and 4.

## The Model

The Brookings-ICF Long-Term Care Financing Model is a microsimulation model, meaning that it starts with a sample of actual people and simulates what happens to each of them individually. The model begins with a nationally representative sample of the adult population, with a record for each person's age, gender, income, assets, and other characteristics. It simulates changes in the population from 1986 through 2020, indicating for each person both general changes, such as age and economic status, and changes specific to long-term care, such as onset and recovery from disability, use of care, and method of paying for care. More aggregate projections are made through 2050.

In general, this version of the Brookings-ICF Long-Term Care Financing Model differs from the earlier version in two ways. First, it uses much more recent data than the first model does. The late 1980s saw an explosion of data on long-term care and the elderly. Second, this version of the model is much more sophisticated and provides more "fine-grained" sets of probabilities. In the first model, for example, people were characterized as either disabled or nondisabled; the revised model characterizes people as nondisabled, disabled with problems with only instrumental activities of daily living, disabled with problems with one activity of daily living, and disabled with problems with two or more activities of daily living.[a]

In the base case, these changes are simulated on the assumption that current public programs and private funding mechanisms remain unchanged. The changes can also be simulated assuming additional private financing, such as increased purchase of private long-term care insurance, or new public financing programs. In all cases, these simulations are greatly affected by the choice of assumptions about the overall economy and human behavior, such as rates of nursing home and home care use.

## STRUCTURE OF THE MODEL

The Brookings-ICF Long-Term Care Financing Model has six major components.

*Representative population data base.* The model starts with a population data base. Using the 1979 Current Population Survey (CPS), the first part of the model contains information on a representative sample of 28,000 adults of all ages. The 1979 CPS provides information about income, assets, family structure, and earning histories. It also contains social security earnings histories for each person in the sample.

*Income simulator.* The second part of the model simulates labor force activity, income, and marital status for each person, using a modified version of Lewin-VHI's Pension and Retirement Income Simulation Model (PRISM). Using data from the 1985 National Nursing Home Survey and the 1984 Survey of Income and Program Participation, the model also simulates housing and financial assets for the elderly.

*Disability of the elderly.* Disability rates for the elderly are projected using probability estimates derived primarily from the 1982–1984 National Long-Term Care Survey and the 1982 New Beneficiary Survey. The model assigns one of four disability levels to each person as he or she turns age 65 and then simulates a disability level for each year thereafter. Annual changes vary by age, marital status, and prior level of disability.

*Use of long-term care services.* For each year of the simulation, the model determines which people enter a nursing home, their length of stay, and

a. The term "activities of daily living," or ADLs, refers to the basic tasks of everyday life, such as eating, bathing, dressing, toileting, and getting in and out of bed. As useful as they are, ADLs do not measure the full range of activities necessary for independent living in the community. To begin to fill this gap in disability classification, the "instrumental activities of daily living," or IADLs, were developed. The IADLs encompass a range of activities that are more complex than those needed for the ADLs, including handling personal finances, preparing meals, shopping, traveling, doing housework, using the telephone, and taking medications.

whether they are discharged alive or dead. The model uses nursing home admission probabilities estimated from longitudinal data from the 1982 and 1984 National Long-Term Care Surveys adjusted by data from the 1985 National Nursing Home Discharge Survey. It also simulates the use of paid home care services for disabled people not in nursing homes, using data from the 1982 and 1984 National Long-Term Care Surveys.

*Sources and levels of payments.* The fifth part of the model simulates the sources of payment and the level of expenditures for every person receiving nursing home or home care services. It is based on data from the 1985 National Nursing Home Survey and the 1984 National Long-Term Care Survey; data on medicare and medicaid are from the Health Care Financing Administration. Incorporated into the model are eligibility requirements for medicare, medicaid, and other public programs.

*Aggregate expenditures and service use.* Finally, the model accumulates expenditures for medicare, medicaid, private insurance, and other payers; out-of-pocket expenditures; and service use for the simulated persons each year.

### MODEL ASSUMPTIONS

Because all projections depend on assumptions about future trends, the choice of parameters regarding, for example, death and disability, the economic environment, and eligibility for public programs greatly affects the simulation results.

*Assumptions about death and disability.* The projections are based on the Social Security Administration's mid-range mortality assumptions (alternative II-B), which assume substantial improvements in longevity over time.[2] Disability rates are assumed to remain constant but to vary by age, gender, and marital status. Controlling for these variables, we assume that the population becomes neither sicker nor healthier.

*Economic assumptions.* Our economic assumptions also follow the alternative II-B assumptions from the Social Security Administration. Over the long run, general inflation is assumed to be about 4 percent a year. The model follows labor force participation forecasts of the Bureau of Labor Statistics through the year 2000, which project substantial growth of women in the work force. Real wage growth reflects actual rates until 1986 and then follows Social Security Administration projections, which vary between 1.0 percent and 2.4 percent annually.

*Use of long-term care.* Nursing home admission rates are kept constant throughout the projection period, implying that the supply of nursing home beds will increase as necessary to accommodate more admissions from an increasingly larger elderly population. Thus, the model assumes that demand for nursing home care in the future will be no more or less constrained by the bed supply than it is now.

Because use of long-term care, especially home care, is likely to be affected by the availability of new financing, however, the impact of higher rates of use has been included in the evaluation of financing options. Finally, we assume that there is no substitution between home care services and nursing home care.[3]

*Reimbursement rates.* Payment rates for nursing home and home care vary by source of payment—medicare, medicaid, private pay, and other payers—but all are assumed to increase by 5.5 percent a year.[4] This projected rate of growth is based on the long-run assumption, made in 1989 by the Social Security Administration Office of the Actuary, that the consumer price index will increase at 4.0 percent a year, real wages at 1.3 percent a year, and fringe benefits at 0.2 percent a year. This assumption presumes nursing home and home care prices will increase to keep pace with projected growth in wages and fringe benefits in the rest of the economy.

*Public program eligibility requirements.* Unless changes in public programs are explicitly being simulated, program benefits and financial eligibility rules are assumed to increase only by the rate of inflation. For medicaid beneficiaries, the spousal impoverishment provisions of the Medicare Catastrophic Coverage Act of 1988 are modeled.

### EXTRAPOLATION TO 2050

To more fully evaluate the financing necessary to fund government program options, we extrapolated public expenditures from 2021 to 2050, the period when the "baby boom" generation will need long-term care. We did this by calculating age-specific, per capita, long-term care expenditures for the elderly in the period 2016–20 and then inflating them by 5.5 percent (a 1.5 percent real increase) a year. Expenditures for each subsequent year were achieved by multiplying the age-specific, per capita costs by the projected number of elderly in each age group in each year, as estimated by the Social Security Administration actuaries.[5] Estimates of the projected payroll are also taken from Social Security Administration assumptions.

### A GUIDE TO INTERPRETING THE SIMULATIONS

In interpreting the results from the simulations, several features of the model must be kept in mind. First, all tables and figures present information only on the elderly population. Nursing home and home care expenditures and use for the nonelderly population are not included, nor are expenditures and use by residents of intermediate care facilities for the mentally retarded. Second, all expenditures are in constant 1993 dollars to eliminate the effect of general inflation but not the extra increase in costs of nursing home and home care. Nominal amounts would be dramatically higher.

Third, most tables are presented for the years 1993, 2008, and 2018. These figures are actually the five-year average of the experience for the periods 1991–95, 2006–10, and 2016–20, respectively. The period 2016–20, which is the latest period the full model projects, presents the options at a relatively mature stage and takes advantage of the expected increase in income of the elderly between 1986 and 2020. This projection is particularly important for an evaluation of private insurance options, because of their current low rates of penetration.

Two types of tables are presented. The first gives average long-term care expenditures by source of financing and number of beneficiaries during a five-year period (for example, 2016, 2017, 2018, 2019, and 2020) and is presented as the number for the midpoint for that period (in this case, 2018).

The second type of table disaggregates expenditures by social and economic characteristics and presents the data on an "admission cohort" basis for the entire length of stay in a nursing home or use of home care. In other words, it identifies all people who started using long-term care services during a specific five-year period (for example, 2016–20) and follows them until they leave the nursing home or stop using home care services, even when the service extends beyond the time period being examined. The expenditures are totaled for each day that nursing home or home care is used. If the length of stay in a nursing home is three years, for example, this second type of table aggregates the expenditures for all three years, not just for one year. Thus, expenditures for long-stay patients are more dominant in the second set of tables than they are in the first.

A major focus of our evaluation of the different options is how they affect catastrophic out-of-pocket costs for the elderly. Three different measures present data on a single episode of nursing home use rather than on lifetime experience. First, the number of nursing home patients receiving medicaid can be considered a rough proxy for the number of people in nursing homes who incur catastrophic out-of-pocket costs. This is because people receive medicaid assistance only after they have used up almost all of their assets and only if they contribute virtually all of their income toward the cost of care.

The second approach to catastrophic costs measures the absolute level of out-of-pocket costs—that is, the average level of out-of-pocket expenditure and proportion of nursing home admissions spending more than a certain level (in this case, $20,000). The third strategy recognizes that financial status, especially for the elderly, is a function of assets as well as income. This last measure therefore estimates the proportion of nursing home admissions who spend more than 40 percent of their income and assets to pay for care.[6] Likewise, in an attempt to measure how efficiently the various options target those most in need, we estimate the proportion of new expenditures that would be spent on those who otherwise would have spent more than 40 percent of their income and assets for care.

In acute care, it is commonly argued that catastrophic costs are reached when people spend $3,000 or 10 percent or more of their income for health care. Because some of the costs of nursing home care involve ordinary living expenses, higher levels of expenditures are not necessarily excessive. The $20,000 level and 40 percent of income and assets threshold that we have chosen are, admittedly, arbitrary cutoffs, but represent very substantial out-of-pocket payments.

## Base Case: Projecting the Current System Forward

The base case projects what will happen if no changes are made in the way long-term care services are organized, used, and reimbursed. Alternative financing options discussed in subsequent chapters are compared with this scenario.

### DEMOGRAPHIC CHARACTERISTICS OF THE ELDERLY

The demographic imperative of long-term care is evident in the first set of tables. First, there will be many more elderly people. The number aged 65 years and older is projected to grow from 32.7 million in 1993 to 49.2 million in 2018, an increase of 50 percent in just one-quarter of a century (figure 2-1). The number of elderly aged 85 and older, who account for much of the need for long-term care among the older population, is projected to grow from 3.6 million in 1993 to 6.2 million in 2018, an increase of 72 percent. This sharp increase results primarily from the expected large decreases in mortality rates for this age group.

FIGURE 2-1. **Number of Elderly, by Age, Selected Periods**[a]

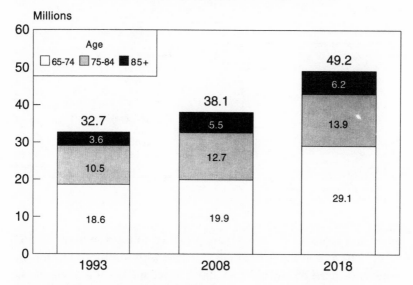

SOURCE: Brookings-ICF Long-Term Care Financing Model.
a. In this and other figures and tables in this chapter, 1993 represents the five-year average for the period 1991–95; 2008, the five-year average for the period 2006–10; and 2018, the five-year average for the period 2016–20.

## FINANCIAL CHARACTERISTICS OF THE ELDERLY

The financial status of the elderly will improve. The median real income for all elderly (including the institutionalized population and those with no income), which was $15,523 in 1993, will increase to $24,832 (in constant 1993 dollars) in 2018 (table 2-1). Median income of the 85 and older population is much lower, however, and will increase from only $9,536 in 1993 to $14,106 in 2018.

Similarly, the assets of the elderly are also projected to grow. Median nonhousing assets for all elderly (including the institutionalized popu-

TABLE 2-1. *Median Annual Family Income, by Age, Selected Periods*[a]
*1993 dollars*

| Age group | 1993 | 2008 | 2018 |
|---|---|---|---|
| 65–74 | 18,882 | 26,810 | 30,214 |
| 75–84 | 12,927 | 16,906 | 20,873 |
| 85 and older | 9,536 | 11,804 | 14,106 |
| TOTAL | 15,523 | 20,323 | 24,832 |

SOURCE: Brookings-ICF Long-Term Care Financing Model.
a. Family income is joint income for married people and individual income for unmarried people. Income sources are social security, pensions, supplemental security income, individual retirement accounts, wages, and asset earnings.

T A B L E 2-2. *Median Family Assets, by Age and Asset Type, Selected Periods*[a]
*1993 dollars*

| Age group | 1993 | 2008 | 2018 |
|---|---|---|---|
| | *Housing assets* | | |
| 65–74 | 86,887 | 115,024 | 131,841 |
| 75–84 | 68,430 | 103,379 | 116,428 |
| 85 and older | 36,050 | 70,822 | 81,876 |
| TOTAL | 74,112 | 103,705 | 122,177 |
| | *Financial assets* | | |
| 65–74 | 27,238 | 45,387 | 51,755 |
| 75–84 | 15,840 | 26,803 | 35,981 |
| 85 and older | 3,721 | 10,143 | 14,981 |
| TOTAL | 19,362 | 32,379 | 43,141 |

S O U R C E: Brookings-ICF Long-Term Care Financing Model.
a. Includes individuals or couples with no housing or financial assets.

lation and those with no assets) are projected to increase from $19,362 in 1993 to $43,141 in 2018 (table 2-2). As with income, assets for the population aged 85 and older are much lower and will reach only about $15,000 in 2018.

## USE OF LONG-TERM CARE

The increase in the numbers of elderly is expected to cause a concomitant increase in nursing home and home care use. Indeed the increase in long-term care use is projected to grow even faster than the increase in the overall number of elderly. Figure 2-2 shows that the number of elderly in nursing homes during the year is projected to increase 64 percent, from 2.2 million in 1993 to 3.6 million in 2018. Similarly, the number of home care users is projected to increase more than 42 percent, rising from 5.2 million in 1993 to 7.4 million in 2018 (figure 2-3). Nursing home care increases faster than home care because nursing home use is more sensitive to changes in the number of very old elderly.

## EXPENDITURES FOR LONG-TERM CARE

Consistent with the expected increases in use, total long-term care expenditures will also rise substantially. If the current configuration of long-term care is continued, total expenditures for nursing home and home care will more than double in real terms, increasing from $75 billion in 1993 to more than $168 billion in 2018 (table 2-3). Total expenditures for long-term care are projected to reach $509 billion in 2048. Expenditures increase faster than the number of nursing home

FIGURE 2-2. **Nursing Home Population, by Age, Selected Periods**[a]

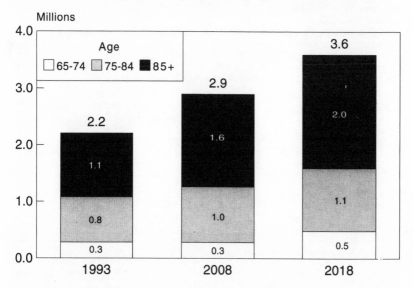

SOURCE: Brookings-ICF Long-Term Care Financing Model.
a. All nursing home users during the course of a year.

FIGURE 2-3. **Home Care Users, by Age, Selected Periods**[a]

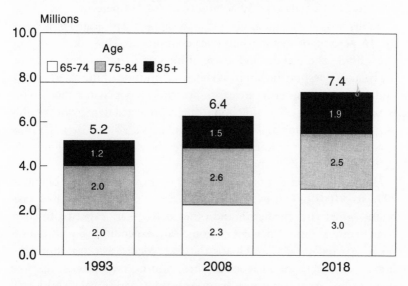

SOURCE: Brookings-ICF Long-Term Care Financing Model.
a. All home care users during the course of the year.

TABLE 2-3. *Total Expenditures for Nursing Home and Home Care, by Source of Payment, Selected Periods*
Billions of 1993 dollars

| Payment source | 1993 | 2008 | 2018 | Percent increase, 1993 to 2018 |
|---|---|---|---|---|
| Total | 75.4 | 119.9 | 168.2 | 123 |
| Nursing homes | | | | |
| Medicaid | 22.4 | 35.4 | 49.0 | 119 |
| Medicare | 4.3 | 7.6 | 10.0 | 133 |
| Patients' cash income | 17.0 | 28.3 | 42.6 | 151 |
| Patients' assets | 11.0 | 17.2 | 26.6 | 142 |
| TOTAL | 54.7 | 88.5 | 128.2 | 134 |
| Home care | | | | |
| Medicaid | 3.6 | 4.4 | 5.2 | 44 |
| Medicare | 9.4 | 15.1 | 19.0 | 102 |
| Other payers[a] | 2.2 | 3.1 | 4.3 | 95 |
| Out-of-pocket payment | 5.5 | 8.8 | 11.5 | 109 |
| TOTAL | 20.7 | 31.4 | 40.0 | 93 |

SOURCE: Brookings-ICF Long-Term Care Financing Model.
a. Other payers include state and local expenditures, social service block grants, Older Americans Act and Department of Veterans' Affairs home care funds, charity, and out-of-pocket expenditures by people other than the service recipient.

and home care users because price increases, like the rest of medical care, are likely to exceed general inflation.

Nursing home care will absorb more than 72 percent of this spending. Institutional expenditures are expected to grow from $54.7 billion in 1993 to $128.2 billion in 2018, an increase of 134 percent.

Public programs—medicare and medicaid—are projected to account for 46 percent of nursing home expenditures in 2018, down slightly from 1993. The income and assets of nursing home patients make up the balance. Despite the improved financial position of the elderly, medicaid's share of long-term care expenditures does not change much. That is because the cost of nursing home care is projected to increase roughly as quickly as income and assets for people aged 75 and over. Thus, in relation to the cost of nursing home care, the elderly are likely to be no better off in the future than they are now.

Home care expenditures are expected to grow from $20.7 billion in 1993 to $40.0 billion in 2018, an increase of 92 percent. Public programs—medicare, medicaid, and other payers—are expected to cover consistently about 72 percent of home care expenditures, with out-of-pocket payments accounting for the rest. Medicare expenditures for home health care are included in these figures, even though many of these skilled, post-acute care services are not traditionally considered long-term care. A major uncertainty in these projections is whether the

TABLE 2-4. *Total and Public Expenditures for Long-Term Care as a Percentage of Gross Domestic Product and Total Payroll, Selected Periods*[a]

| Year[b] | Total expenditures as percent of | | Public expenditures as percent of | |
|---|---|---|---|---|
| | GDP | Total payroll | GDP | Total payroll |
| 1993 | 1.21 | 2.37 | 0.65 | 1.28 |
| 2008 | 1.36 | 2.86 | 0.72 | 1.51 |
| 2018 | 1.55 | 3.61 | 0.77 | 1.80 |
| 2028 | 1.71 | 4.29 | 0.85 | 2.14 |
| 2038 | 2.04 | 5.75 | 1.02 | 2.88 |
| 2048 | 2.14 | 6.85 | 1.07 | 3.43 |

SOURCE: Brookings-ICF Long-Term Care Financing Model.
a. Public expenditures are medicaid and medicare and, for home care, other payers.
b. Here and in table 2-9, 2028 represents the five-year average for the period 2025–2030; 2038, the five-year average for the period 2035–2040; and 2048, the five-year average for the period 2045–2050.

dramatic increase in medicare expenditures that has occurred since 1989 will be sustained.[7]

Although spending will be growing, the burden will not be as large as commonly assumed because the economy will be expanding as well (table 2-4). Assuming that the economy grows at a real rate of 2.5 percent a year, long-term care will less than double as a percentage of gross domestic product (GDP) and will not quite triple as a percentage of payroll between 1993 and 2048. For example, total long-term care expenditures for the elderly as a share of GDP will increase from about 1.21 percent in 1993 to 2.14 percent in 2048. Similarly, total expenditures will increase from about 2.37 percent of payroll in 1993 to 6.85 percent in 2048.

## CATASTROPHIC OUT-OF-POCKET COSTS

The heavy reliance on out-of-pocket payments to finance long-term care means that substantial numbers of disabled elderly will incur catastrophic costs. Table 2-5 shows that the number of people who rely on medicaid to help finance their nursing home payment will increase by 43 percent from 1.4 million in 1993 to 2 million in 2018. Average out-of-pocket spending for a nursing home stay will approach $44,000 in 2018, up from $28,100 in 1993. Furthermore, the proportion of nursing home admissions who spend more than $20,000 (in constant 1993 dollars) out of pocket is projected to increase from 27 percent to more than 33 percent. Finally, approximately 36 percent of all nursing home patients spent more than 40 percent of their income and financial assets to pay for care in 1993, a proportion that is estimated to increase only slightly during the next twenty-five years.

TABLE 2-5. *Measures of Catastrophic Costs of Nursing Home Care, Selected Periods*

| Measure | 1993 | 2008 | 2018 |
|---|---|---|---|
| Number of medicaid patients (in millions)[a] | 1.4 | 1.7 | 2.0 |
| Absolute out-of-pocket expenditure[b] | | | |
| Average out-of-pocket spending (thousands of 1993 dollars) | 28.1 | 34.7 | 43.9 |
| Percentage of admissions spending more than $20,000 out-of-pocket | 26.5 | 28.0 | 33.1 |
| Relative out-of-pocket expenditure[c] | | | |
| Percentage of admissions spending more than 40 percent of income and assets on care | 36.0 | 35.8 | 39.2 |

SOURCE: Brookings-ICF Long-Term Care Financing Model.
a. Patients who are financed by medicaid at any time during the year.
b. These data are based on total out-of-pocket payments for an admission cohort over the entire length of the nursing home stay.
c. The numerator is equal to the out-of-pocket contribution to nursing home care for the entire length of stay; the denominator is equal to income during the stay plus nonhousing assets.

## Sensitivity Analyses

By using alternative assumptions, the model can show how sensitive the results are to the assumptions chosen. Three key assumptions regarding long-term care financing concern the inflation rate for nursing home and home care, the proportion of the elderly with disabilities, and the overall growth in the economy.

### NURSING HOME AND HOME CARE INFLATION

Nursing home and home care expenditures are very sensitive to the projected long-term care inflation rate. Using a 4.5 percent or a 6.5 percent annual inflation rate produces expenditure levels for nursing home care that are substantially different from those produced with a 5.5 percent inflation rate (table 2-6). Under a 6.5 percent annual inflation rate, total expenditures are 40 percent larger in 2018 than they are under the benchmark 5.5 percent assumption; under a 4.5 percent assumption, they are 21 percent less. During that same time period, medicaid expenditures for nursing home care are expected to be two-thirds higher than the benchmark for the high inflation assumption and 37 percent lower for the low inflation assumption. In 2018 medicaid expenditures under the high-inflation assumption would be almost three times as large as those under the low-inflation assumption.

Lowering nursing home and home care inflation will not be easy. Long-term care is extremely labor intensive, and much of it involves

TABLE 2-6. *Expenditures for Nursing Home Care, by Source of Payment, under High, Medium, and Low Inflation Assumptions, Selected Periods*
Billions of 1993 dollars

| Payment source | 1993 | 2008 | 2018 | Percent increase, 1993 to 2018 |
|---|---|---|---|---|
| | | *6.5 percent inflation assumption* | | |
| Medicaid | 25.8 | 50.2 | 81.4 | 216 |
| Medicare | 4.8 | 10.1 | 14.2 | 196 |
| Patients' cash income | 18.5 | 30.5 | 43.0 | 132 |
| Patients' assets | 12.9 | 24.1 | 40.9 | 217 |
| TOTAL | 62.0 | 114.9 | 179.5 | 190 |
| | | *5.5 percent inflation assumption* | | |
| Medicaid | 22.4 | 35.4 | 49.0 | 119 |
| Medicare | 4.3 | 7.6 | 10.0 | 133 |
| Patients' cash income | 17.0 | 28.3 | 42.6 | 151 |
| Patients' assets | 11.0 | 17.2 | 26.6 | 142 |
| TOTAL | 54.7 | 88.5 | 128.2 | 134 |
| | | *4.5 percent inflation assumption* | | |
| Medicaid | 21.6 | 26.8 | 30.9 | 43 |
| Medicare | 4.3 | 6.5 | 7.8 | 81 |
| Patients' cash income | 17.8 | 29.8 | 45.3 | 154 |
| Patients' assets | 10.8 | 13.4 | 17.6 | 63 |
| TOTAL | 54.5 | 76.5 | 101.6 | 86 |

SOURCE: Brookings-ICF Long-Term Care Financing Model. Figures are rounded.

hands-on, personal services, where opportunities for substantial gains in productivity are few. Thus, reducing nursing home inflation to a rate that approximates the consumer price index would mean substantially reducing wages of nursing home and home care workers relative to the rest of the work force. It is doubtful that people could be recruited to work for relatively lower wages, and quality of care could be adversely affected. Indeed, advocates for improving quality of care argue that nursing home and home care employees need to be better trained and more highly paid than they are now.[8] Moreover, some evidence suggests that nursing home patients have become more disabled, a factor that is likely to increase staffing levels and their associated costs.[9]

## DISABILITY RATES

A key variable in determining the future demand for and cost of long-term care services is the health of the elderly. Researchers continue to speculate about whether future generations will live longer but more disabled lives or increasingly healthy lives.[10]

To assess the effects of varying disability rates on long-term care expenditures and use, three different scenarios were simulated (table 2-7). Under the high disability scenario, elderly disability rates gradually

TABLE 2-7. *Total Expenditures for Long-Term Care under Different Disability Assumptions, by Source of Payment, 2018*[a]
Billions of 1993 dollars

| Payment source | High disability | Constant disability | Low disability |
|---|---|---|---|
| Total long-term care | 215.0 | 168.3 | 134.3 |
| Medicaid | 72.8 | 54.2 | 44.2 |
| Medicare | 31.9 | 28.9 | 26.4 |
| Other payers[b] | 5.5 | 4.3 | 4.4 |
| Out-of-pocket | 104.8 | 80.9 | 59.3 |
| Nursing homes | 172.6 | 128.2 | 95.8 |
| Medicaid | 65.4 | 49.0 | 39.0 |
| Medicare | 14.5 | 10.0 | 7.5 |
| Patients' cash income | 56.0 | 42.6 | 30.3 |
| Patients' assets | 36.7 | 26.6 | 19.0 |
| Home care | 42.3 | 40.1 | 38.6 |
| Medicaid | 7.3 | 5.2 | 5.3 |
| Medicare | 17.4 | 19.0 | 18.9 |
| Other payers[b] | 5.5 | 4.3 | 4.4 |
| Out-of-pocket | 12.1 | 11.6 | 10.0 |

SOURCE: Brookings-ICF Long-Term Care Financing Model.
a. Under high disability, rates increase so that in 2020, 70-year-olds have the same disability rate as 75-year-olds did in 1986. Under low disability, rates decrease so that in 2020, 70-year-olds have the same disability rate as 65-year-olds did in 1986.
b. See note a, table 2-3.

increase so that the disability rate in 2020 is the same as the disability rate for people five years older in 1986. For example, a person aged 70 in 2020 would have the same chance of being disabled as a 75-year-old in 1986. In this scenario people live longer but more disabled lives. Under the no-change scenario (base case), disability rates remain constant, controlling for age and marital status. In this scenario, people live longer but face no higher risk of disability at a given age and marital status. Under a low-disability scenario, elderly disability rates decline so that the rate of impairment in 2020 is the same as the disability rate for people five years younger in 1986. For example, a person aged 70 in 2020 would have the same chance of being disabled as a 65-year-old in 1986. In this scenario, people live longer and less disabled lives.

The effects of varying the disability rates are significant, but expenditures and use increase substantially even under the more optimistic assumptions. Total long-term care expenditures under the low-disability assumptions are 57 percent lower than those under the high-disability scenario. But even with the low-disability assumptions, real long-term care expenditures by 2018 are projected to be 77 percent higher than in 1993 (not shown). In the low-disability scenario the total number of people who use nursing homes and home care in 2018 is 23 percent

TABLE 2-8. *Number of Elderly Using Long-Term Care Services under Different Disability Assumptions, 2018*[a]
*Millions*

| Assumption | Total long-term care | Nursing home care | Home care |
|---|---|---|---|
| High disability rates | 12.8 | 4.9 | 7.9 |
| Constant disability rates | 11.0 | 3.6 | 7.4 |
| Low disability rates | 9.9 | 2.7 | 7.2 |
| | *Percent change from constant disability rates* | | |
| High disability rates | 16.4 | 36.1 | 6.8 |
| Low disability rates | −10.0 | −25.0 | −2.7 |

SOURCE: Brookings-ICF Long-Term Care Financing Model.
a. Under high disability, rates increase so that in 2020, 70-year-olds have the same disability rate as 75-year-olds did in 1986. Under low disability, rates decrease so that in 2020, 70-year-olds have the same disability rate as 65-year-olds did in 1986.

lower than in the high-disability scenario but substantially greater than in 1993 (table 2-8). Home care use and expenditures are less strongly affected by different disability assumptions because some home care use covered by medicare is for people who are not chronically disabled but who need only post-acute services.

## GROWTH IN THE ECONOMY

Although the number of disabled elderly likely to use long-term care will grow dramatically by 2048, the economy will also grow. Consequently, the financial burden of long-term care will largely depend on how fast the economy grows (table 2-9). Under a low-growth assumption (1.5 percent real growth a year), total long-term care expenditures for the elderly increase from 1.21 percent of GDP in 1993 to 3.67

TABLE 2-9. *Total and Public Expenditures for Long-Term Care as a Percentage of Gross Domestic Product, by Different Growth Rates, Selected Periods*[a]
*Percent of GDP*

| Year | Total expenditures | | | Public expenditures[b] | | |
|---|---|---|---|---|---|---|
| | Low growth | Medium growth | High growth | Low growth | Medium growth | High growth |
| 1993 | 1.21 | 1.21 | 1.21 | 0.65 | 0.65 | 0.65 |
| 2008 | 1.60 | 1.36 | 1.16 | 0.84 | 0.72 | 0.61 |
| 2018 | 2.00 | 1.55 | 1.20 | 1.00 | 0.77 | 0.60 |
| 2028 | 2.42 | 1.71 | 1.21 | 1.21 | 0.85 | 0.60 |
| 2038 | 3.18 | 2.04 | 1.31 | 1.59 | 1.02 | 0.66 |
| 2048 | 3.67 | 2.14 | 1.26 | 1.84 | 1.07 | 0.63 |

SOURCE: Brookings-ICF Long-Term Care Financing Model.
a. Low growth is 1.5 percent real growth in GDP a year, medium growth is 2.5 percent real growth in GDP a year, and high growth is 3.5 percent real growth in GDP a year.
b. Public expenditures include medicaid, medicare, and, for home care, other payers.

percent in 2048, almost a threefold increase. In contrast, under a high-growth assumption (3.5 percent real growth a year), total expenditures grow from 1.21 of GDP in 1993 to only 1.26 percent in 2048, barely a 4 percent increase. High economic growth rates would minimize the burden of increased expenditures for long-term care.

## Pricing Prototype Private Insurance Policies

In our simulations of private long-term care insurance, we use policies and premiums generated with the Brookings-ICF Long-Term Care Financing Model rather than actual policies available in the marketplace.[11] Actuaries from the Actuarial Research Corporation reviewed our premium pricing methodology.

Prototype policies have several important advantages over actual products that real companies are offering. First, they can be designed to have far better coverage than most existing policies. Many existing policies have significant benefit limitations; we know from earlier work that these restrictions have a major effect on the simulation results. Moreover, because products are rapidly changing and improving, we believe it is more important to model what policies will look like in the future.

Second, with prototype policies, we have far greater flexibility in designing benefits. For example, we believe that premiums for policies sold to the younger population should be indexed until retirement to take wage growth into account. Because few existing policies currently index premiums, we would have had to estimate an adjustment to make existing policies fully usable.

Third, because the prototype premiums were developed using the output from the model, there is an internal consistency between the premiums and the simulation results. Moreover, since we specify the pricing assumptions, we do not have to guess about the methodology used for pricing policies available in the marketplace.

### PREMIUM PRICING METHODOLOGY

Insurance premiums have a benefit portion (known to economists as the "actuarially fair premium" and to actuaries as the "net premium") and an administrative and profit portion. Using output from the Brookings-ICF Long-Term Care Financing Model, the basic pricing strategy is to make the present value of the benefit stream equal to the present value of the premium payment stream and then to apply a factor to account for administrative and profit costs. Appendix B discusses the premium pricing methodology in detail.

In brief, the methodology has four main steps: First, to calculate the present value of the benefit stream, it is assumed that each individual belonging to a specific age cohort (for example, 65–69, 70–74) purchases an insurance policy with a defined set of benefits. The stream of benefit payments is simulated in the model for each year between 1986 and 2020. The stream is discounted to find the present value of the total benefit payment in 1986. The benefit stream implicitly discounts for mortality.

Second, to calculate the present value of premiums, we arbitrarily assign all policyholders an annual premium. The aggregate stream of premium payments for each year between 1986 and 2020 is simulated in the model, and the premium stream is then discounted back to 1986. Like the benefit stream, the premium stream implicitly discounts for mortality.

Third, to establish the actual cost of the benefit portion of the premium, the ratio of the present value of aggregate benefit payments to the present value of aggregate premium payments is calculated. Multiplying this loss ratio by the arbitrary premium yields the actuarially fair premium for each year.

Finally, the actuarially fair premium is divided by the loss ratio to calculate the final premiums. A loss ratio of 70 percent is used for individual policies and 80 percent for group products.

## POLICIES AND PREMIUMS

As shown in figure 2-4, the core policies that are used in the simulations cover two or four years of nursing home and home care after a deductible period. Home care is available only to persons who have two or more problems with the activities of daily living or who have cognitive impairments. The policies paid $60 a day for nursing home care and $30 a visit for home care in 1986. The benefit is indexed for inflation at 5.5 percent a year (1.5 percent more than the projected growth in the consumer price index).

Premiums for the prototype policies are shown in table 2-10. Comparisons with roughly comparable policies on the market and other prototype policies developed by the Actuarial Research Corporation, William M. Mercer, Inc., and the National Association of Insurance Commissioners Actuarial Task Force on Long-Term Care suggest that our premiums are reasonable and within the ballpark of currently marketed policies.[12] For example, according to a survey of large sellers of

## 48   The Model and Base Case

FIGURE 2-4.  **Characteristics of Prototype Private Long-Term Care Insurance Policies**

---

- Policies cover two or four years of nursing home care after a sixty-day deductible and two or four years of home care after a thirty-visit deductible. Home care is available only to persons who have two or more problems with the activities of daily living or have cognitive impairments.[a]

- In 1986, the policies paid $60 a day in the nursing home and $30 a visit for home care. The benefit is indexed for inflation at 5.5 percent a year (1.5 percent more than the projected growth in the consumer price index).

- Policies are purchased only by persons who have no problems with the activities of daily living or the instrumental activities of daily living.[b]

- Lapses of policies by policyholders are assumed to be 5.0 percent a year for two years, 3.0 percent a year for years three through eight, then no lapses after that.

- Individual policies have a loss ratio of 70 percent, and group policies have a loss ratio of 80 percent.[c]

- Use of nursing home care by the insured population is assumed to increase gradually by 20 percent over a ten-year period; home care use is assumed to increase by 80 percent immediately.

- Premiums increase by 5.5 percent a year from ages 40 through 64 and then are level from age 65 on.

- The premium assumes a discount rate of 7.5 percent, 3.5 percent above projected general inflation.

---

a. For our purposes, the activities of daily living are eating, bathing, dressing, getting in and out of bed, and toileting.
b. The instrumental activities of daily living comprise a range of activities, including handling personal finances, meal preparation, shopping, traveling, doing housework, using the telephone, and taking medications.
c. That is, 70 or 80 percent of the premium is benefit payments; the rest is for administration, marketing, profits, taxes, and so on.

private long-term care insurance, the average premium for a policy roughly comparable to ours, purchased at age 65, was $1,894, compared with our estimate of $1,923.[13]

## Conclusion

Future long-term care use and expenditures for the elderly will be influenced by the aging of the population, changing mortality rates, public and private financing sources, disability rates, use patterns, income and asset levels, health services inflation, and many other variables. The interaction of these forces will determine the costs of long-term care over the next twenty-five years and beyond. The Brookings-ICF

TABLE 2-10. *Initial Individual and Group Premiums for Two-Year and Four-Year Private Long-Term Care Insurance Policies*[a]

| | Individual | | Group | |
|---|---|---|---|---|
| Age | Two-year | Four-year | Two-year | Four-year |
| 40 | 239 | 343 | 209 | 301 |
| 42 | 267 | 383 | 233 | 336 |
| 44 | 298 | 428 | 260 | 375 |
| 46 | 333 | 478 | 291 | 419 |
| 48 | 372 | 534 | 325 | 469 |
| 50 | 416 | 597 | 363 | 524 |
| 52 | 465 | 667 | 406 | 585 |
| 54 | 541 | 778 | 474 | 680 |
| 56 | 631 | 907 | 552 | 793 |
| 58 | 736 | 1,058 | 644 | 925 |
| 60 | 859 | 1,235 | 751 | 1,079 |
| 62 | 996 | 1,437 | 871 | 1,257 |
| 64 | 1,210 | 1,745 | 1,058 | 1,527 |
| 66 | 1,469 | 2,119 | 1,285 | 1,854 |
| 68 | 1,704 | 2,468 | 1,491 | 2,160 |
| 70 | 1,893 | 2,752 | 1,657 | 2,408 |
| 72 | 2,100 | 3,074 | 1,837 | 2,690 |
| 74 | 2,245 | 3,293 | 1,964 | 2,876 |
| 76 | 2,400 | 3,527 | 2,100 | 3,075 |
| 78 | 2,549 | 3,771 | 2,246 | 3,296 |
| 80 | 2,689 | 4,039 | 2,401 | 3,524 |
| 82 | 2,836 | 4,375 | 2,481 | 3,828 |
| 84 | 2,991 | 4,687 | 2,617 | 4,038 |

SOURCE: Brookings-ICF Long-Term Care Financing Model.
a. Premiums are indexed by 5.5 percent a year until the insured is age 65 and are level thereafter.

Long-Term Care Financing Model simulates those interactions to permit assessment of a variety of financing options.

The base case and the sensitivity analyses indicate that long-term care expenses will impose an increasing burden on society despite continued economic growth. Nursing home and home care use is likely to continue to increase substantially between 1993 and 2018. Because long-term care prices are likely to increase faster than general inflation, expenditures will rise substantially faster than use. The base case is discouraging for those who had hoped that rising future incomes would make it easier for the elderly to afford long-term care. To a large extent, the increasing price of nursing home and home care will offset increases in the financial position of the elderly.

Also presented in this chapter are the methodology and premiums for prototype private long-term care insurance policies. These premiums will be used extensively in the simulations in the next two chapters.

## Chapter Three

# Private Long-Term Care Insurance

American society uses private insurance to protect against loss from catastrophic events such as hospitalization, automobile accidents, home fires, theft, and early death. Insurance against the potentially devastating costs of long-term care, however, is relatively rare. Although private long-term care insurance as such did not exist before the mid-1980s, the market is growing and rapidly changing. Surveys conducted by the Health Insurance Association of America (HIAA) found that the number of companies selling long-term care insurance increased from 75 in 1987 to 135 in 1992. The number of policies ever sold increased from 815,000 in December 1987 to more than 2.9 million in December 1992.[1,a]

The long-term care insurance market has three components—the individual market, the employer-sponsored market, and the life insurance rider market. The individual market overwhelmingly dominates private long-term care insurance. Although much smaller, sales through the employer-sponsored and life insurance market are increasing, and some think they represent the greatest potential sources of future growth. This chapter considers the potential of the current private long-term care insurance system, while the next chapter analyzes various public subsidies to promote private insurance.

The simulations for private long-term care insurance unsubsidized by the public sector provide sharply different results between policies geared toward initial purchase by the elderly and those geared toward initial purchase by the nonelderly. So long as private insurance is aimed

a. Because of lapses and deaths, the number of policies in force is substantially less than the total number sold, probably on the order of 2 million.

principally at the elderly population, its market penetration and ability to finance long-term care likely will remain limited, even twenty-five years into the future. Similarly, because of their typically low face value, long-term care riders to life insurance policies are unlikely to play a significant role in financing long-term care.

If employers could be convinced to offer private long-term care insurance to their active employees, and if workers were willing to buy the products, then a substantial majority of people could afford good quality long-term care insurance. Selling policies to the nonelderly in large numbers will be difficult, however, and will not substantially affect how nursing home and home care is financed for a long period of time.

## Barriers to Private Long-Term Care Insurance

Although the market is evolving rapidly, relatively few policies are in force because of barriers on both the demand and supply sides. On the demand side, there are at least three major obstacles—affordability, lack of knowledge about the risks of long-term care, and misinformation about current coverage.

Historically, the elderly have been disproportionately poor and unable to afford significant premium payments. This is less true now as improvements in public and private pensions have increased the income of the elderly substantially during the last twenty years. Most current evidence suggests that the elderly as a whole are roughly as well off financially as the nonelderly population.[2] The population aged 85 and older, people with disabilities, women, and minorities have not fared as well financially and still have poverty rates well above those in the nonelderly population.[3]

Despite improvements in their financial status, most elderly still find it difficult to afford good quality long-term care insurance. The average annual premium for individual policies with inflation protection and some nonforfeiture benefits offered by the fifteen leading sellers in 1991 was $2,525 at age 65 and climbed rapidly to $7,675 at age 79.[4] Not surprisingly, then, purchasers of these policies have substantially higher income and many more liquid assets than has the general population.[5] Most affordability studies[b] find that only a relatively small minority of

b. The results of any study of affordability depend on assumptions about how much of their income (and perhaps assets) people are willing to spend on insurance, as well as on assumptions about the kind of coverage offered. It follows then that the more liberal these assumptions are, the more affordable insurance will be.

the current elderly population—generally 10 to 20 percent—can afford private long-term care insurance.[6] Projections suggest that these percentages will increase, but that the bulk of the elderly will still not be able to afford policies in the future.[7]

Other research has found the percentage of the elderly who can afford private insurance to be higher, but these studies have done so by assuming purchase of policies with limited coverage, by assuming that the elderly would use their assets as well as income to pay premiums, or by excluding a large proportion of the elderly from the pool of people considered interested in purchasing insurance.[8]

Virtually all of the affordability studies cited above, including our own, used some admittedly arbitrary criteria in determining who could and could not purchase policies.[9] For example, in most of the simulations of private insurance in *Caring for the Disabled Elderly,* individuals purchased insurance if it cost no more than 5 percent of their income and if they had $10,000 in nonhousing assets.[10] The rationale for the 5 percent of income figure was that it represented a 50 percent increase in out-of-pocket health care expenses for the noninstitutionalized elderly. It was also believed that elderly purchasers had to have at least a modest amount of assets before they would be willing to buy a relatively costly insurance policy. Thus, the assumptions seemed a generous maximum for assessing the possible impact of private insurance. A 1990 survey of private long-term care insurance purchasers found that a substantial majority spent less than 5 percent of their income on insurance, but it is possible that, with more information about the risks of needing long-term care and about the limitations of existing coverage, more people would be willing to spend a higher proportion of their income for insurance.[11]

Critics argue that all affordability studies are flawed because they do not measure consumers' actual willingness to pay. These critics suggest that actual purchasers of insurance be surveyed to establish the willingness to pay for private insurance. Because so few people have actually purchased or even seriously considered buying private long-term care insurance, however, it is not clear that the survey results could be applied to the general population. Despite the controversy over what proportion of the elderly can afford long-term care insurance, there is little doubt that the number who can afford it far exceeds the number of people who are insured.[12]

Other factors contributing to the low number of long-term care policies sold are lack of knowledge about the risk of needing long-term care and confusion over the coverage currently available through existing public programs and private carriers. Most people either are unaware of or deny the risk of ever needing long-term care. Yet research suggests that people who live to age 65 face more than a four-in-ten chance of spending some time in a nursing home and a one-in-four chance of spending more than a year.[13] People seem willing to accept the possibility that they will someday need acute care services, but few are willing to admit that they face a significant lifetime risk of becoming disabled and needing nursing home or home care.

Although the situation has improved substantially, there is still a great deal of misinformation about what is and is not covered by the insurance policies that people have. Many people think that medicare and their medicare supplemental health insurance policies cover extensive nursing home and home care services, when they do not.[14] Obviously, people feel no need to buy additional coverage for long-term care if they think they already have it.

Although substantial barriers remain on the demand side, considerable progress has been made on the supply side over the last few years. Indeed, the capacity to supply private long-term care insurance is now much greater than the demand for it. Nonetheless, because they lack large-scale claims experience, insurance actuaries remain uneasy about whether long-term care (especially home care) is an "insurable" event and whether these products will be profitable.

The question of insurability has three main components. One is the extent to which the event being insured against is under the control of the insured. More precisely, to what extent will there be "moral hazard," or increased use induced by insurance coverage?[15] Several factors lead insurers to worry about moral hazard in long-term care. First, insurance lowers the out-of-pocket price of services. Because people usually buy more of a good or service when the price is lower, a likely consequence of more widespread insurance will be increased admissions to nursing homes and use of home care. How much of an increase is hard to estimate, however, and that uncertainty makes premiums difficult to price. Second, social, not strictly medical, considerations are the key determinants of long-term care use,[16] as is evidenced by the many disabled elderly who might medically qualify for long-term care services but do not currently receive any.[17] In 1986 nursing home utilization varied across states by a factor of two.[18]

The reluctance of the elderly to enter nursing homes, however, reduces the likelihood of a large increase in nursing home use. But the inherent desirability of some home care services, especially the less medically oriented services such as housekeeping, meal preparation, and shopping, means that their use is likely to increase substantially if covered by insurance.

The second component of insurability is whether people can easily forecast their individual need for the insured benefits. In this instance, if people can predict whether they will use long-term care services, those most in need of services may disproportionately buy insurance because it will usually be less expensive than paying for services out of pocket. This "adverse selection" could drive use beyond expected levels and force insurance companies to raise premiums to avoid losing money. That, in turn, would cause low-risk purchasers to drop their policies, pushing both average use and premiums even higher. To protect against adverse selection, insurers usually screen out people with health problems and refuse coverage for preexisting conditions.

The third component is whether the total costs associated with the insured event are predictable for the population as a whole, a precondition necessary to calculate insurance premiums. In this regard, long-term care insurance is probably the riskiest product insurers can sell. Not only is there little claims experience with an insured population, but the vast majority of claims will be made far into the future. Long-term care is needed principally by the very elderly, especially those aged 85 and older. Thus, a very long time is likely to elapse between initial purchase of the insurance policy and its eventual use. For example, a policy bought at age 65 probably will not be used for twenty years; a policy bought at age 45 probably will not be used for forty years. For the insurers, unforeseen changes in disability or mortality rates, utilization patterns, or the rate of return on financial reserves can dramatically change a profitable policy into a highly unprofitable one. The uncertainty of the future also affects consumers.

## The Individual Market

Private long-term care insurance is overwhelmingly sold on an individual, one-on-one basis to the elderly population, with the insured paying the entire cost of the premiums. As of 1992 the individual and group association market accounted for 82 percent of all sales. The average age of purchasers in this market is 68 years old.[19] This pattern contrasts sharply with the acute care insurance market, in which insurance is provided to the nonelderly as well as the elderly, primarily through employment-based groups where employers shoulder most of the cost. The high administrative costs of selling policies one at a time (high commissions to agents in the first year that the policy is in force are customary) and the comparatively limited time for reserves and interest earnings to build help make private long-term care insurance sold on an individual basis to the elderly quite expensive.

## MODEL ASSUMPTIONS AND RESULTS

To assess the financing potential of individual long-term care policies sold to the elderly, we modeled the purchase of insurance using a wide range of affordability criteria. This approach allows an assessment of the sensitivity of the results to different assumptions, which are detailed in figure 3-1.

The simulations vary by the amount of income and assets that elderly people use to purchase the insurance. In simulations SPEND3PCT, SPEND5PCT, and SPEND7PCT, individuals are assumed to purchase private long-term care insurance if it costs no more than 3, 5, or 7 percent of their income, respectively. They must also have a minimum of $10,000 in nonhousing assets. In simulation SPENDASSETS, individuals spend 7 percent of their income and up to 1 percent of their financial assets. In all simulations, all persons who meet the affordability criteria at age 67 are assumed to purchase insurance, thereby making affordability the only barrier to the purchase of insurance in the model. Age 67 was chosen because most elderly have left the work force by then and are living on their retirement income.[20] Individuals with problems with the activities or instrumental activities of daily living are not allowed to purchase policies.

In evaluating other private insurance strategies (later in this chapter and in chapter 4), SPEND5PCT is used as a benchmark, along with the base case, against which other options are compared. SPEND5PCT was chosen because it requires a relatively large increase in out-of-pocket costs for the elderly and, in our view, represents a realistic maximum of the potential role for individual private insurance whose sale is oriented toward the elderly.

In the simulations in this section, nondisabled elderly individuals may purchase private long-term care insurance that covers either two years each or four years each of nursing home and home care, depending on what they can afford. Payment rates begin at $60 a day for nursing home care and $30 a visit for home care; both rates are indexed for inflation by 5.5 percent annually. Premiums for these policies were estimated

FIGURE 3-1. **Assumptions for Simulations of Individual Private Long-Term Care Insurance Sold to the Elderly**

- People buy one of two policies: the first covers four years of nursing home care after a sixty-day deductible and four years of home care after a thirty-visit deductible; the second covers two years of nursing home care after a sixty-day deductible and two years of home care after a thirty-visit deductible. Home care benefits are limited to persons with two or more problems with the activities of daily living or cognitive impairment.[a]

- The payment rate in 1986 is $60 a day for nursing home care and $30 a visit for home care. Benefits are increased annually by 5.5 percent.

- Initial annual premiums for the four-year policy vary from $2,337 at age 67 to $4,687 at age 84; for the two-year policies, from $1,617 at age 67 to $2,991 at age 84. Although premiums are level, initial premiums are increased by 5.5 percent a year for new purchasers to reflect nursing home and home care inflation.

- All individuals and couples buy insurance if they have $10,000 or more in nonhousing assets and if the premium costs no more than 3 percent (SPEND3PCT), 5 percent (SPEND5PCT), or 7 percent (SPEND7PCT) of their income. In SPENDASSETS, individuals spend 7 percent of their income and 1 percent of their nonhousing assets. Married couples purchase only one policy if they can afford one but not two policies for the prescribed percentage of income.

- Individuals who have problems with the instrumental activities of daily living or the activities of daily living may not purchase policies.[b]

- In 1986, people aged 67–84 are eligible to purchase the policies. After 1986 people purchase the policy when they turn age 67.

- Individuals let the policies lapse if the premium exceeds 20 percent of their income.

- Demand from holders of four-year policies is assumed to increase nursing home use by 20 percent and covered home care use by 80 percent. For insureds with the two-year policy, nursing home use is assumed to increase by 15 percent and covered home care use by 80 percent.

---

a. The activities of daily living are eating, bathing, dressing, getting in and out of bed, and toileting.
b. The instrumental activities of daily living comprise a range of activities, including handling personal finances, meal preparation, shopping, traveling, doing housework, using the telephone, and taking medications.

using the Brookings-ICF Long-Term Care Financing Model, according to the methodology described in chapter 2 and appendix B. Annual premiums for the two-year policies vary from $1,617 at age 67 to $2,991 at age 84. Similarly, annual premiums for the four-year policy vary from $2,337 at age 67 to $4,687 at age 84.

The proportion of elderly projected to have long-term care insurance in 2018 ranges from 6 percent for SPEND3PCT to 37 percent for SPENDASSETS; 20 percent of the elderly might have insurance under the SPEND5PCT option (figure 3-2). Thus, although the number of

FIGURE 3-2. **Elderly Participation in Private Long-Term Care Insurance Options Sold to the Elderly, Selected Periods**[a]

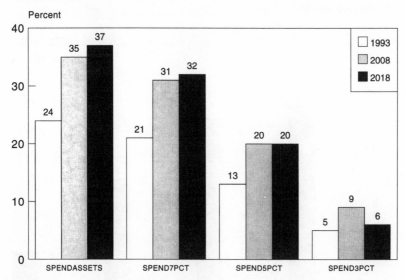

Percent

SOURCE: Brookings-ICF Long-Term Care Financing Model.

a. Aged 67 and older. Population aged 67 and older in 1993 is 28.6 million, in 2008 is 33.2 million, and in 2018 is 42.1 million. In this and other figures and tables in this chapter, 1993 represents the five-year average for the period 1991–95; 2008 represents the five-year average for the period 2006–10; and 2018 represents the five-year average for the period 2016–20.

elderly with private long-term care insurance increases substantially over the simulation period, only a minority of the elderly would have policies under any one of the options.

If private insurance grows along these lines, its importance in financing nursing home and home care services will increase somewhat (figure 3-3). It is noteworthy that the proportion of nursing home and home care expenditures paid by private insurance is substantially less than the proportion of elderly with insurance. This is because medical underwriting excludes the disabled from purchasing policies, younger elderly who use less long-term care are more likely to have insurance than are older elderly, and simulated policies do not cover all expenses. By 2018 private insurance geared to purchase by the elderly is estimated to pay only 3 to 16 percent of total nursing home expenditures and between 2 and 12 percent of total home care expenditures (table 3-1). Under the middle option, SPEND5PCT, private insurance would finance 10 percent of nursing home expenditures and 6 percent of home care expenditures. Overall, this would be a large increase over the 1 or 2 percent of these expenditures private insurance currently pays, but it is not likely

FIGURE 3-3. **Insurance Expenditures as a Proportion of Long-Term Care Spending under Private Insurance Options Sold to the Elderly, Selected Periods**

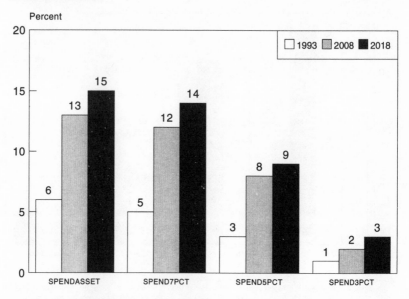

SOURCE: Brookings-ICF Long-Term Care Financing Model.

to have a significant impact on the way nursing home and home care is reimbursed.

Because good quality long-term care insurance is expensive, insurance premiums are most affordable to upper-middle- and upper-income elderly. Figure 3-4 shows that in 2018, the proportion of private insurance expenditures for nursing home care that are made on behalf of persons with incomes above $40,000 a year varies from 81 percent for SPEND3PCT to 57 percent for SPENDASSETS; for SPEND5PCT, it is 70 percent.

Some advocates of private long-term care insurance have argued that purchase of policies by middle-income elderly could reduce medicaid nursing home expenditures by preventing these policyholders from depleting their income and assets.[21] Table 3-2 suggests that these hopes are not likely to be realized with individual policies marketed to the elderly. All options have a negligible impact on medicaid nursing home expenditures in 2018, compared with the base case.

How well will private insurance geared to the elderly reduce catastrophic out-of-pocket costs? Table 3-2 also shows the projected reduc-

TABLE 3-1. *Total Expenditures for Nursing Home and Home Care, by Source of Payment, Base Case and Private Insurance Options Sold to the Elderly, 2018*
Billions of 1993 dollars

| Payment source | Base case | SPENDASSETS | SPEND7PCT | SPEND5PCT | SPEND3PCT |
|---|---|---|---|---|---|
| Total long-term care expenditures | 168.2 | 177.3 | 175.9 | 173.2 | 170.2 |
| Nursing home | | | | | |
| Medicaid | 49.0 | 45.8 | 46.5 | 48.0 | 48.8 |
| Medicare | 10.0 | 10.4 | 10.4 | 10.3 | 10.1 |
| Private insurance | 0.0 | 21.8 | 19.4 | 12.5 | 4.4 |
| Family cash | 42.6 | 34.8 | 35.3 | 37.3 | 40.5 |
| Family assets | 26.6 | 21.0 | 21.4 | 23.2 | 25.8 |
| TOTAL | 128.2 | 133.8 | 132.9 | 131.3 | 129.6 |
| Home care | | | | | |
| Medicaid | 5.2 | 5.2 | 5.2 | 5.2 | 5.2 |
| Medicare | 19.0 | 19.5 | 19.4 | 19.2 | 19.1 |
| Other payers[a] | 4.3 | 3.6 | 3.6 | 3.9 | 4.2 |
| Private insurance | 0.0 | 5.1 | 4.4 | 2.6 | 0.7 |
| Out-of-pocket | 11.5 | 10.1 | 10.3 | 11.0 | 11.5 |
| TOTAL | 40.0 | 43.5 | 43.0 | 41.9 | 40.6 |

SOURCE: Brookings-ICF Long-Term Care Financing Model.

a. Other payers include state and local expenditures, social service block grants, Older Americans Act and Department of Veterans' Affairs home care funds, charity, and out-of-pocket expenditures by people other than the service recipient.

TABLE 3-2. *Effect on Medicaid of Private Insurance Options Sold to the Elderly, Selected Periods*

| Option | Percentage reduction from base case | | |
|---|---|---|---|
| | 1993 | 2008 | 2018 |
| | *In medicaid nursing home expenditures* | | |
| SPENDASSETS | 1.3 | 6.5 | 6.5 |
| SPEND7PCT | 0.9 | 4.5 | 5.1 |
| SPEND5PCT | 0.0 | 3.1 | 2.0 |
| SPEND3PCT | 0.0 | 1.1 | 0.4 |
| | *In number of medicaid nursing home patients* | | |
| SPENDASSETS | 0.3 | 4.2 | 4.5 |
| SPEND7PCT | 0.9 | 3.5 | 4.3 |
| SPEND5PCT | 0.5 | 2.2 | 1.9 |
| SPEND3PCT | 0.1 | 0.5 | 0.1 |

SOURCE: Brookings-ICF Long-Term Care Financing Model.

FIGURE 3-4. **Insurance Expenditures for Nursing Home Care under Private Insurance Options Sold to the Elderly, by Income of Patients, 2018**[a]

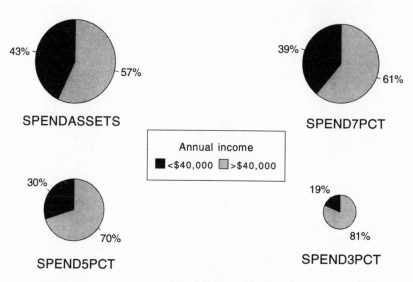

SPENDASSETS

43%    57%

SPEND7PCT

39%    61%

Annual income
■ <$40,000   ▢ >$40,000

SPEND5PCT

30%    70%

SPEND3PCT

19%    81%

SOURCE:: Brookings-ICF Long-Term Care Financing Model.
a. These data are based on the total payments for an admission cohort over the entire length of their stays in nursing homes. For a person who is admitted to a nursing home in 2018 for a two-year stay, for example, we totaled two years' worth of nursing home expenditures and then calculated the proportion of those expenditures paid by private long-term care insurance.
Total insurance expenditures are $23.7 billion under SPENDASSETS, $21.1 billion under SPEND7PCT, $13.3 billion under SPEND5PCT, and $4.0 billion under SPEND3PCT.

tion in the number of medicaid nursing home patients from the base case in 2018, which indicates the effects will probably be small. People who are able to afford private long-term care insurance and people who are likely to use medicaid appear to be separate populations.

Absolute levels of out-of-pocket nursing home costs decline considerably under private insurance, but average expenditures remain at fairly high levels (see table 3-3). In 2018 the options geared to the elderly reduce average out-of-pocket expenses for a nursing home stay from about $44,000 in the base case to a low of $35,000 for SPENDASSETS and SPEND7PCT; the out-of-pocket cost for SPEND5PCT is $38,000. The proportion of nursing home admissions who incur out-of-pocket expenses of $20,000 or more falls from 33 percent in the base case to a low of 27 percent for SPENDASSETS.

Nor do these private insurance options appear to have much of an effect on the proportion of income and financial assets paid out of pocket. For options focusing on the elderly, the percentage of nursing home admissions who spend more than 40 percent of their income and

TABLE 3-3. *Effect of Private Insurance Options Sold to the Elderly on Catastrophic Out-of-Pocket Expenditures for Nursing Home Care, 2018*

| Measure | Base case | SPENDASSETS | SPEND7PCT | SPEND5PCT | SPEND3PCT |
|---|---|---|---|---|---|
| Absolute expenditure[a] | | | | | |
| Average out-of-pocket spending (thousands of 1993 dollars) | 44 | 35 | 35 | 38 | 42 |
| Percentage of admissions spending more than $20,000 out of pocket | 33 | 27 | 27 | 29 | 32 |
| Relative expenditure[b] | | | | | |
| Percentage of admissions spending more than 40 percent of income, assets on care | 39 | 35 | 35 | 37 | 39 |
| Target efficiency[c] | | | | | |
| Percentage of insurance expenditures spent on people who otherwise would have incurred catastrophic out-of-pocket costs | . . . | 56 | 57 | 49 | 31 |

SOURCE: Brookings-ICF Long-Term Care Financing Model.
a. These data are based on total out-of-pocket payments for an admission cohort over the entire length of the nursing home stay.
b. The numerator is equal to the out-of-pocket contribution to nursing home care for the entire length of stay; the denominator is equal to income during the stay plus nonhousing assets.
c. These data are based on total private insurance expenditures for an admission cohort for the entire length of stay. Total insurance expenditures are $23.7 billion under SPENDASSETS, $21.1 billion under SPEND7PCT, $13.3 billion under SPEND5PCT, and $4.0 billion under SPEND3PCT.

assets in 2018 declines from 39 percent in the base case to 35 percent for SPENDASSETS; the proportion for SPEND5PCT is 37 percent.

Another issue regarding catastrophic costs relates to the "target efficiency" of private insurance; that is, the extent to which private insurance payments are concentrated on patients who would otherwise incur catastrophic out-of-pocket costs (as measured by spending more than 40 percent of their income and assets on nursing home care in the base case). Even though private insurance expenditures are concentrated on upper-income elderly, table 3-3 suggests that nursing home costs are so high that all of the options, except SPEND3PCT, will expend almost half or more of their insurance payments on individuals who otherwise would have incurred catastrophic out-of-pocket costs.

## Employer-Sponsored Long-Term Care Insurance

Since 1987 a small, but expanding market of employer-sponsored insurance for long-term care has developed. This market's potential lies in the fact that if people buy long-term care insurance when they are younger, especially through employer groups, then premiums could be significantly lower and therefore more affordable. Moreover, proponents contend that the purchasing power of and attention from employers will result in better quality products. The underlying assumption is that long-term care policies sold to groups, particularly through employers, would enjoy many of the same advantages associated with group medical policies.

In addition, many employers now play a major role in providing retirement income security and medical benefits for the elderly through pensions and supplements to the medicare program. Presumably, employers might also help meet the long-term care needs of their retired employees by offering private insurance, because the need for long-term care can quickly unravel all the careful planning for retirement that employers help their employees do.

## THE CURRENT MARKET

As of the end of 1992, a total of 350,000 policies had been sold through 566 employers.[22] About 32 percent of all long-term care policies sold in 1992 were through employers; that was up from nearly zero in 1987 and represented growth of more than 80 percent over 1991.

Employers who offer long-term care insurance to their employees tend to be very large and to include a disproportionate number of insurance companies. In a key difference from acute care policies, where most employers pay a large portion of the cost of the insurance, virtually all employer-sponsored long-term care policies are offered on an employee-pay-all basis.

## POTENTIAL ADVANTAGES OF EMPLOYER-SPONSORED INSURANCE

Theoretically, employer-sponsored plans offered to the nonelderly provide several advantages over those purchased individually. First, premiums for younger policyholders can be substantially lower than those for older policyholders because younger policyholders pay premiums over a longer period of time and because earnings on premium reserves have more time to build. For example, we estimate that the premium for a 42-year-old will be approximately one-quarter to one-third of the premium for a 67-year-old.[23]

Although lower premiums are tied to the age of the purchaser and not necessarily to the fact that the policy is employer-sponsored, the nonelderly are easiest to reach through their place of employment. As noted above, the workplace is where most health, life, and disability insurance is purchased and most retirement savings through pensions are established.

Lower administrative and marketing costs offer another potential source of savings over individual policies. Administrative and marketing costs are high in individual policies because sales have to be made one at a time. Group markets are able to achieve lower costs through certain economies of scale. Moreover, employers bear many of the costs of administering the policy, such as collecting premium payments through payroll deductions. Employers may also elect to assume part of the costs of marketing the plan to their employees.

It should be noted, however, that group long-term care insurance is unlikely to achieve the administrative savings of large group acute care health insurance. This is partly because enrollment rates are low (see the discussion below). That means marketing material and efforts must be developed and directed at a large number of people who will not purchase the policy, a cost that must be built into the premium. In addition, recognizing that the vast majority of people who purchase employer-sponsored long-term care insurance will not use the policy until far into the future, virtually all policies allow individuals to retain coverage even if they change employers. If the new employer does not offer exactly the same policy, however, the insurance company must assume the costs of billing the insured. Informal discussions with in- surance actuaries suggest that most assume only a ten percentage point difference in the anticipated loss ratio between individual and group plans.[c] Thus, although administrative savings are desirable and not triv- ial, they will not dramatically lower premiums.

Enrolling people at younger ages through the workplace also reduces the risk of adverse selection and therefore the need to medically under- write. Disability, especially of the type likely to result in a need for services provided in long-term care insurance policies, is relatively rare at younger ages.[24] Consequently, the stringency of the underwriting process varies among both insurers and employers. Typically, but not universally, companies offer employees the opportunity to enroll once without a review of their health status.[25] Thereafter, employees may enroll during an annual open enrollment period only after they submit

c. The loss ratio is the percentage of the premium that is for benefits rather than administration and other overhead. Many companies assume a loss ratio of 60 percent for individual policies and 70 percent for group policies.

proof of insurability. Spouses, parents, and retirees are almost always medically screened, even in the first offering. Although these practices are an improvement in access over the universally strict underwriting required for purchase of individual insurance policies, most disabled persons with significant disabilities are not in the work force and would not, therefore, be eligible for these policies.[26]

Finally, advocates of employer-sponsored insurance argue that the quality of policies should improve through the involvement of company benefit managers. Large groups have more market power than individuals to negotiate with insurance carriers for less restrictive policies with richer benefits and lower prices. Employers are more apt than individuals to have the time and expertise necessary to find the plan that offers the highest quality for the money.

In general, the quality of policies offered in the employer market is quite good, especially in providing home care benefits. Employers, however, are not exempt from having to trade off benefits against costs. Most policies have inadequate inflation protection, and the insured must purchase additional coverage from time to time to compensate for inflation, but at the new older age and therefore at a higher premium. To avoid losing purchasing power, both nominal and inflation-adjusted premiums must increase dramatically over time. (See chapter 5 for a discussion of this issue.)

## IMPEDIMENTS TO AN EMPLOYER-SPONSORED STRATEGY

Despite the potential advantages of selling to the nonelderly population through employer groups, the employer-sponsored market may not expand enough to play a significant role in financing long-term care. Specifically, employers are reluctant to offer the policies, and employees are reluctant to purchase them.

The uncertain tax status of long-term care insurance, especially whether employer contributions are tax deductible, has no doubt prevented some employers from offering long-term care insurance policies to their employees. (The tax status of private long-term care insurance and its implications for employer contributions are discussed in chapter 4.) To date, employee demand has not played a large role in the decision of companies to add long-term care insurance to their benefit package. The desire to maintain a company's image as a leader in employee benefits or a personal sensitivity to the problem by a senior officer or employee benefit manager have been larger factors. Nonetheless, surveys of large employers suggest the possibility of a large future increase in the number of companies offering policies.[27] Furthermore, some observers argue that employers will need to offer long-term care insurance as a fringe benefit to help attract and retain an aging and increasingly female work force.[28]

These factors notwithstanding, the future of employer-sponsored private long-term care insurance is likely to be overwhelmed by the financial problems facing employer-sponsored health plans for retirees, both early retirees and those who are eligible for medicare. In brief, employers have incurred hundreds of billions of dollars in unfunded liabilities for retiree health benefits, a situation likely to make them unwilling to take on another major health benefit for retirees. (For a discussion of the potential impact of the unfunded liability for retiree health benefits on employers' willingness to contribute to the cost, see chapter 4.)

Although they acknowledge the problems associated with unfunded retiree health benefits, advocates of group long-term care insurance see a different dynamic operating. They posit that as companies cut back on the acute care benefits they offer their retirees, they will look for something to offer employees to soften the blow. In this scenario employer-sponsored, but employee-paid, private long-term care insurance becomes an ideal benefit. It addresses a major financial problem facing retired employees but involves no additional employer contributions.

The other side of the coin is that employees have been reluctant to purchase insurance. The Health Insurance Association of America estimates that, depending on how the universe of eligibles is defined, only 5.3 to 8.8 percent of those offered employer-sponsored long-term care insurance have purchased it.[29]

Several factors limit employee demand. First, although premiums for policies without inflation adjustments are quite low at younger ages, they may cost more than many people are willing to pay voluntarily.[30] Moreover, a high quality long-term care insurance policy with a level premium, inflation protection, and nonforfeiture benefits purchased at age 50 can cost more than $1,000 a year.[31] In a survey of nonpurchasers of employer-sponsored policies offered by two major insurers, LifePlans, Inc., reported that 82 percent of respondents felt that the fact that "the policy costs too much" was either "very important" or "important" in their decision not to purchase a policy.[32] Even though most economists contend that increased employer contributions for fringe benefits are offset by reduced wages, 90 percent of respondents in this survey said they would be more willing to purchase a policy if their employer contributed to the cost.[33]

In addition, middle-age workers usually must contend with other, more immediate expenses, such as child care, mortgage payments, and college education for their children. In the LifePlans, Inc., survey, 80 percent of nonpurchasers stated that the fact that they had "more important things to spend money on at this time" was either "very important" or "important" in their decision not to purchase a policy.[34] The risk of needing long-term care is too distant to galvanize many people into buying insurance.

Finally, selling to the nonelderly population raises difficult considerations of pricing and product design. As discussed earlier in this chapter, an actuary pricing a private long-term care insurance product for a 45-year-old must predict what is going to happen forty years into the future, when the insured is age 85. To say the least, this is difficult. Ironically, although one of the advantages commonly claimed for private insurance is its flexibility to respond to the needs and wants of consumers, policyholders who buy insurance at younger ages are locked into the existing model of service delivery decades before they use services.[35] Who knows what the optimal delivery system will be a half century from now?

**SIMULATION ASSUMPTIONS AND RESULTS**

To evaluate the potential effect of selling to the nonelderly population and also selling through employer-sponsored plans, we simulated two different plans. The first option—YOUNGINS—simulated purchase of individually sold policies beginning at age 40. The second option— GROUPINS—simulated purchase of group policies beginning at age 40. For comparison purposes, data are also presented on purchase of insurance by the elderly, who are assumed to buy the policy if it costs no more than 5 percent of the purchaser's income and if the purchaser has a minimum of $10,000 in nonhousing assets—SPEND5PCT. The detailed simulation assumptions for YOUNGINS and GROUPINS are presented in figure 3-5.

In both cases, individuals purchase a policy that covers either two or four years each of nursing home care and home care, has an indemnity level that increases at a rate of 5.5 percent a year compounded annually, and has a relatively low lapse rate. Premiums for YOUNGINS and GROUPINS are calculated with 70 and 80 percent loss ratios, respectively. Thus, premiums for GROUPINS are somewhat lower than for YOUNGINS.

Although initial premiums vary by age of initial purchase, these policies treat inflation differently from most policies currently on the mar-

FIGURE 3-5. **Simulation Assumptions for Individual Private Long-Term Care Insurance and Group Policies Sold to the Nonelderly**

- People buy one of two policies: the first covers four years of nursing home care after a sixty-day deductible and four years of home care after a thirty-visit deductible; the second covers two years of nursing home care after a sixty-day deductible and two years of home care after a thirty-visit deductible. Home care benefits are limited to persons with two or more problems with the activities of daily living or cognitive impairment.[a]

- The payment rate in 1986 is $60 a day for nursing home care and $30 a visit for home care. Benefits are increased annually by 5.5 percent.

- YOUNGINS: Initial annual premiums vary from $343 at age 40 to $4,687 at age 84 for the four-year individual policy, from $239 at age 40 to $2,991 at age 84 for the two-year policy.

- GROUPINS: Initial annual premiums vary from $301 at age 40 to $4,038 at age 84 for the four-year group policy, from $209 at age 40 to $2,617 at age 84 for the two-year policy.

- YOUNGINS AND GROUPINS: Premiums for insureds aged 40 to 64 increase by 5.5 percent a year. In addition, initial premiums are increased by 5.5 percent a year to reflect nursing home and home care inflation.

- All individuals and couples between ages 40 and 49 buy insurance if it costs no more than 2 percent of their income, those between ages 50 and 59 buy it if it costs no more than 3 percent of their income, and those between ages 60 and 66 buy it if it costs no more than 4 percent of their income. Elderly individuals and couples between ages 67 and 84 purchase policies if they have at least $10,000 in nonhousing assets and if the policy costs no more than 5 percent of their income. Couples purchase only one policy if they cannot afford two.

- Elderly individuals who have problems with the activities or instrumental activities of daily living may not purchase policies.[b] Social Security Disability Insurance beneficiaries are also excluded.

- Individuals drop policies if the premium exceeds 20 percent of their income.

- Demand for nursing home care is assumed to increase by 20 percent and covered home care use by 80 percent for people with four-year policies. Nursing home use is assumed to increase by 15 percent and covered home care use by 80 percent for insureds with two-year policies.

---

a. The activities of daily living are eating, bathing, dressing, getting in and out of bed, and toileting.

b. The instrumental activities of daily living comprise a range of activities, including handling personal finances, meal preparation, shopping, traveling, doing housework, using the telephone, and taking medications.

ket. After initial purchase, premiums increase by 5.5 percent a year for people between ages 40 and 64. At age 65, premiums stop increasing and thereafter remain constant in nominal terms. The assumption is that, as working-age people gain seniority and more responsible positions, their incomes probably will continue to increase until they retire, when their incomes are likely to remain relatively level. Thus, this strategy attempts to avoid the problem of level premiums for inflation-adjusted policies, which are expensive to purchase at age 40 but affordable at age 55. This approach attempts to establish a middle ground between a level premium that requires the nonelderly to fund their inflation protection with expensive current dollars and the completely unindexed approach that requires the insured to buy all additional coverage at the higher age when coverage is more expensive.

In the simulations, people buy policies if they cost no more than 2 percent of income at ages 40 to 49, 3 percent at ages 50 to 59, and 4 percent at ages 60 to 66. Individuals aged 67 to 84 buy insurance if it costs no more than 5 percent of income, and if they have at least $10,000 in nonhousing assets. In positing that consumers are willing to pay a significant portion of their income for insurance and that significant numbers of employers are willing to offer policies, these assumptions are fairly generous to private insurance. Moreover, affordability is assumed to be the only barrier to purchasing the insurance, although, as discussed earlier, there are several other significant barriers to purchase. Thus, these assumptions represent an upper bound on the potential market and its effect on financing. Actual experience is almost certain to be less.

The proportion of elderly who might have long-term care insurance in 2018 is dramatically higher if policies are sold widely to the nonelderly population than if they are sold primarily to the elderly (figure 3-6). Although the proportion of elderly who might have private insurance under SPEND5PCT is 20 percent, that proportion increases to 66 and 76 percent for YOUNGINS and GROUPINS, respectively. These rates are comparable to the proportion of elderly with medicare supplemental policies. Note that the key difference in affordability is purchase by the nonelderly, rather than the efficiencies obtained by the lower administrative costs in the group market.

Assuming that the market grows along these lines, private insurance could eventually play a greater role in the financing of long-term care (figure 3-7). By 2018 insurance geared to initial purchase by the non-

FIGURE 3-6. **Elderly Participation in Private Long-Term Care Insurance Options Sold to the Elderly and Nonelderly, Selected Periods**

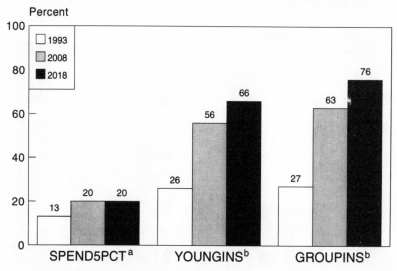

SOURCE: Brookings-ICF Long-Term Care Financing Model.
    a. Aged 67 and older. The population aged 67 and older is 28.6 million in 1993, 33.2 million in 2006, and 42.1 million in 2018.
    b. Aged 65 and older. The population aged 65 and older is 32.7 million in 1993, 38.2 million in 2006, and 49.2 million in 2018.

elderly might pay 31 to 35 percent of total nursing home expenditures and between 23 and 25 percent of total home care expenditures, almost four times the proportion paid by policies purchased by the elderly alone (table 3-4).

Because premiums for YOUNGINS and GROUPINS are much more affordable, the income distribution of private insurance payments for nursing home care is relatively close to that of the overall nursing home population (figure 3-8). It is, however, still somewhat skewed toward the upper-middle- and upper-income population. In 2018 the proportion of private insurance expenditures for nursing home care on behalf of patients with incomes greater than $40,000 is 29 to 33 percent; in the base case only 20 percent of expenditures are devoted to that income group (not shown).

By 2018 YOUNGINS and GROUPINS could have a moderate effect on medicaid expenditures for nursing homes, decreasing them by 22 to 28 percent, compared with the base case (table 3-5). That is at least ten times the reduction obtained by policies geared toward purchase by the

FIGURE 3-7. **Insurance Expenditures as a Proportion of Total Long-Term Care Spending under Private Insurance Options Sold to the Elderly and Nonelderly, Selected Periods**

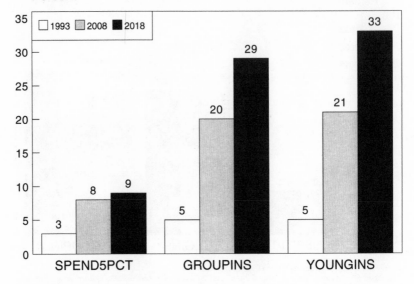

Percent

SOURCE:: Brookings-ICF Long-Term Care Financing Model.

TABLE 3-4. *Total Expenditures for Nursing Home and Home Care, by Source of Payment, Base Case and Private Insurance Options Sold to the Elderly and Nonelderly, 2018*
*Billions of 1993 dollars*

| Payment source | Base case | SPEND5PCT | YOUNGINS | GROUPINS |
|---|---|---|---|---|
| Total long-term care expenditures | 168.2 | 173.2 | 184.9 | 188.8 |
| Nursing home | | | | |
| Medicaid | 49.0 | 48.0 | 38.3 | 35.3 |
| Medicare | 10.0 | 10.3 | 10.9 | 11.0 |
| Private insurance | 0.0 | 12.5 | 43.3 | 50.4 |
| Family cash | 42.6 | 37.3 | 31.4 | 30.1 |
| Family assets | 26.6 | 23.2 | 17.6 | 17.2 |
| TOTAL | 128.2 | 131.3 | 141.4 | 143.9 |
| Home care | | | | |
| Medicaid | 5.2 | 5.2 | 4.8 | 4.7 |
| Medicare | 19.0 | 19.2 | 20.3 | 20.6 |
| Other payers[a] | 4.3 | 3.9 | 3.1 | 3.0 |
| Private insurance | 0.0 | 2.6 | 9.8 | 11.4 |
| Out-of-pocket | 11.5 | 11.0 | 5.6 | 5.3 |
| TOTAL | 40.0 | 41.9 | 43.5 | 44.9 |

SOURCE: Brookings-ICF Long-Term Care Financing Model.
a. See note a, table 3-1.

FIGURE 3-8. **Insurance Expenditures for Nursing Home Care under Private Insurance Options Sold to the Elderly and Nonelderly, by Income of Patients, 2018**[a]

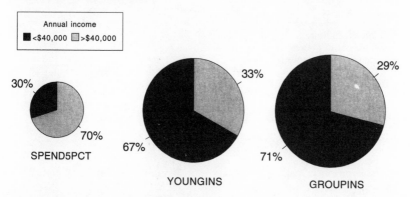

Annual income
■ <$40,000  □ >$40,000

30%
70%
SPEND5PCT

33%
67%
YOUNGINS

29%
71%
GROUPINS

SOURCE:: Brookings-ICF Long-Term Care Financing Model.
a. These data are based on the total payments for an admission cohort over the entire length of their stays in nursing homes. For a person who is admitted to a nursing home in 2018 for a two-year stay, for example, we totaled two years' worth of nursing home expenditures and then calculated the proportion of those expenditures paid by private long-term care insurance.
Total insurance expenditures are $13.3 billion under SPEND5PCT, $46.5 billion under YOUNGINS, and $54.3 billion under GROUPINS.

elderly (SPEND5PCT). That is a significant reduction, but real medicaid expenditures are still projected to increase by as much as 73 percent between 1993 and 2018 (not shown).

What is the effect on catastrophic out-of-pocket costs of policies sold to the nonelderly? Table 3-5 shows that YOUNGINS and GROUPINS manage to achieve a modest, although still significant, reduction in the number of medicaid nursing home patients, compared with the base

TABLE 3-5. *Effect on Medicaid of Private Insurance Options Sold to the Elderly and Nonelderly, Selected Periods*

| Option | Percentage reduction from base case | | |
|---|---|---|---|
| | 1993 | 2008 | 2018 |
| | *In medicaid nursing home expenditures* | | |
| SPEND5PCT | 0.0 | 3.1 | 2.0 |
| YOUNGINS | 1.3 | 11.3 | 21.8 |
| GROUPINS | 0.9 | 12.4 | 28.0 |
| | *In number of medicaid nursing home patients* | | |
| SPEND5PCT | 0.5 | 2.2 | 1.9 |
| YOUNGINS | 1.0 | 8.3 | 13.7 |
| GROUPINS | 0.9 | 7.9 | 15.5 |

SOURCE: Brookings-ICF Long-Term Care Financing Model.

TABLE 3-6. *Effect of Private Insurance Options Sold to the Elderly and Nonelderly on Catastrophic Out-of-Pocket Expenditures for Nursing Home Care, 2018*

| Measure | Base case | SPEND5PCT | YOUNGINS | GROUPINS |
|---|---|---|---|---|
| Absolute expenditure[a] | | | | |
| Average out-of-pocket spending (thousands of 1993 dollars) | 44 | 38 | 29 | 28 |
| Percentage of admissions spending more than $20,000 out of pocket | 33 | 29 | 24 | 23 |
| Relative expenditure[b] | | | | |
| Percentage of admissions spending more than 40 percent of income, assets on care | 39 | 37 | 30 | 29 |
| Target efficiency[c] | | | | |
| Percentage of insurance expenditures spent on people who otherwise would have incurred catastrophic out-of-pocket costs | ... | 49 | 64 | 63 |

SOURCE: Brookings-ICF Long-Term Care Financing Model.
a. These data are based on total out-of-pocket payments for an admission cohort over the entire length of the nursing home stay.
b. The numerator is equal to the out-of-pocket contribution to nursing home care for the entire length of stay; the denominator is equal to income during the stay plus nonhousing assets.
c. These data are based on total private insurance expenditures for an admission cohort for the entire length of stay. Total insurance expenditures are $13.3 billion under SPEND5PCT, and $46.5 billion under YOUNGINS, and $54.3 billion under GROUPINS.

case. Absolute levels of out-of-pocket nursing home expenditures decline considerably under private insurance, but average expenditures remain fairly high (table 3-6). In 2018 YOUNGINS and GROUPINS reduce average out-of-pocket nursing home expenses from about $44,000 in the base case to $29,000 and $28,000, respectively. The proportion of nursing home admissions who incur out-of-pocket expenditures of $20,000 or more falls from 33 percent in the base case to 24 percent and 23 percent for these respective options.

These two private insurance options also appear to have a modest impact on the proportion of income and assets paid out of pocket for a nursing home stay. The percentage of nursing home admissions who spend more than 40 percent of their income and assets declines from 39 percent in the base case to 30 percent for YOUNGINS and 29 percent for GROUPINS.

Because we simulated relatively widespread purchase of private insurance across a fairly wide income distribution, YOUNGINS and GROUPINS have relatively good target efficiency. Almost two-thirds of private long-term care expenditures would be for individuals who otherwise would have incurred catastrophic out-of-pocket costs relative to their income and assets.

## Long-Term Care and Life Insurance

The high number of American households that carry life insurance has stimulated interest in using this mechanism to finance long-term care services.[36] "Accelerated death benefits" represent one way for policyholders—largely those with cash-value life insurance policies—to gain early access to their death benefits in order to pay for long-term care needs.[d] The concept behind accelerated death benefits is quite simple. Since most nursing home patients end their stay because of death, insurers would merely pay benefits a bit earlier than they would otherwise.[37] According to the American Council of Life Insurance, about two hundred companies offered some form of accelerated death benefits in 1991.[38]

There are three major types of benefit riders.[39] The first type pays expenses in the event that the insured needs long-term care, especially nursing home care. The benefit has a maximum amount payable, which is often a specified amount or a percentage (commonly 50 percent) of the death benefit. These policies must meet the regulatory standards for

---

d. There are two basic types of life insurance: simple term policies and cash-value policies. Term life insurance pays death benefits only when the insured person dies within a specified time period, or "term." This type of policy, which is the most prevalent and is often offered as an employee fringe benefit, is characterized by its relative affordability when the insured is young because the risk of death is low. As the person ages, the premiums grow more expensive. Few persons retain term policies past their mid-sixties.

Cash-value policies, such as universal life and whole life, have two parts—a term insurance portion and a built-in savings plan. Early in the life of the policy, when the risk of death is low, the policyholder "overpays" the actuarially required premium, with a large portion of the payment going into the savings component. Later, this cash reserve is partly used to purchase insurance coverage that otherwise would be unaffordable under a simple term policy. Cash-value life insurance policies vary greatly in the way premiums are set, the way interest on the cash reserves is credited, how death benefits are calculated, and if and how dividends are paid to policyholders. The accumulated cash value may be borrowed by the insured.

Life insurance benefits that are paid out under certain circumstances before the actual death of the policyholder are called by various names, including terminal period benefits, living benefits, and accelerated benefits. Here, we will refer to all of these as "accelerated death benefits."

private long-term care insurance. According to the Health Insurance Association of America, forty-five insurers offered this type of accelerated death benefit in 1991, accounting for 141,000 policies.[40] In a "dread disease" (or catastrophic illness) rider, benefits are paid upon diagnosis of a specified dread disease. The benefit is often a single payment, which is a percentage of the policy's death benefit. Finally, "terminal illness" riders pay a benefit upon diagnosis of a specified life-threatening or catastrophic condition that severely limits life expectancy (maximum life expectancy is usually six to twelve months). The benefit may be a single payment or periodic payments.

Some accelerated death benefits are financed through the policyholder's purchase of a rider equal to a small percentage (generally less than 5 percent) of the premium. Others are financed through a reduction in the death benefit that approximates the interest that the insurance company would have earned on the cash reserves had the payment not been made until the death of the policyholder.

## Advantages and Disadvantages of Accelerated Death Benefits

Using accelerated death benefits to finance long-term care needs has two main advantages. First, and most important, although middle-aged consumers are often reluctant to purchase long-term care insurance, many own life insurance policies. Thus, cash-value life insurance may offer a practical (and perhaps more palatable) means of planning for long-term care needs earlier in life. Second, for those in need of long-term care, the cash value of the accelerated death benefits could be greater than the cash value if the policy were cashed in or if a loan were taken out against the policy reserves.

Unfortunately, accelerated death benefits suffer from many of the same limitations associated with regular private long-term care insurance. Many Americans do not have cash-value life insurance.[41] Moreover, most policies have a small face value. In 1991 the average face value was only $26,532.[42] Even more to the point for long-term care is that the average face value of policies for individuals over age 65 was only $8,300 in 1984.[43] Such low face value means that the amount of long-term care that can be purchased with accelerated death benefits is also likely to be small.

People hold cash-value policies with low face values for two reasons.

First, cash-value life insurance is expensive. For example, most whole life insurance policies with a $100,000 death benefit cost between $1,200 and $2,400 a year if purchased at age 45.[44] As a result families tend either to be underinsured or to purchase a significant portion of coverage through less expensive term policies.

Second, as policyholders age, they often fail to increase their coverage to keep pace with inflation, thus eroding the purchasing power of their death benefit. Partly, the failure to increase coverage occurs because most people's need for life insurance declines once they attain a certain age and some of their financial responsibilities lessen. For example, children grow up and become independent, and mortgages are paid off. Increasingly, women have their own sources of income and are not as dependent on their husbands to maintain their standard of living. If policies are not updated to maintain their value against inflation, however, policyholders cannot expect accelerated death benefits to purchase meaningful amounts of long-term care. Thus, life insurance with accelerated death benefits becomes equivalent to private long-term care insurance policies that are not indexed for inflation.

A concern about using life insurance to pay for the needs of the living is whether it undermines the traditional purpose of life insurance—to assure the financial well-being of surviving dependents. Although few elderly in need of long-term care have dependent children, a significant portion are married, and spouses may need the life insurance benefits to maintain an adequate standard of living after the insured's death.[45]

Finally, as with private long-term care insurance, the lapse rate among people who purchase cash-value life insurance policies is high. Only 13 percent of purchasers are likely to keep their policies for twenty years.[46]

## SIMULATION ASSUMPTIONS AND RESULTS

To evaluate the potential impact of life insurance on the financing of long-term care, we simulated an accelerated death benefits policy (ADBENEFITS), in which individuals use their cash-value life insurance to finance their nursing home stay (figure 3-9). They may use 2.5 percent a month of the face amount; thus, a maximum of forty months of care is provided. Following industry practices, nursing home care is not covered until after a six-month deductible period. No home care benefits are simulated.

Ownership of cash-value life insurance and its face value were assigned based on an analysis of the 1984 Survey of Income and Program Par-

FIGURE 3-9.  **Assumptions for Simulation of Accelerated Death Benefit Option**

- Ownership and face value of permanent life insurance is assigned based on data from the 1984 Survey of Income and Program Participation. Amount varies by age, gender, and income. For years after 1984, life insurance values at age 67 are based on the distribution for persons aged 65 to 67, indexing the average face value of life insurance and the income categories by the change in the consumer price index.

- Nursing home care after a six-month deductible. No home care benefits.

- People with life insurance use it to finance their nursing home stays. The amount they may use on a monthly basis is 2.5 percent of the face amount.

ticipation. The average amount varies by age, gender, and income. For each year after 1984, life insurance values at age 67 were based on the distribution for people aged 65 to 67, indexing the average face values of life insurance and the income categories by the change in the consumer price index.

Because the number of people with cash-value life insurance is large, the potential number of elderly with accelerated death benefits could increase substantially (figure 3-10). In 2018, 85 percent of elderly might have accelerated death benefit riders. As a result of the low cash value of these policies, however, accelerated death benefits are likely to finance only 2 percent of nursing home care (table 3-7), and even less of the total long-term care bill (figure 3-11). A substantial portion (69 percent) of these expenditures will be for the nonwealthy population (figure 3-12). The use of accelerated death benefits to finance long-term care also will have only a small effect on catastrophic out-of-pocket costs. The number of medicaid nursing home patients would be reduced by 0.6 percent in 1993, 0.5 percent in 2008, and 0.7 percent in 2018. Average absolute expenditures would drop only $1,000 from the base case in 2018, from $44,000 to $43,000. The proportion of nursing home admissions who spend more than $20,000 on their care would drop from 33 percent in the base case to 31 percent, while the percentage of nursing home admissions who must spend more than 40 percent of their income and assets for care would remain unchanged, at 39 percent.

FIGURE 3-10. **Elderly Participation in Accelerated Death Benefit Option, Selected Periods**[a]

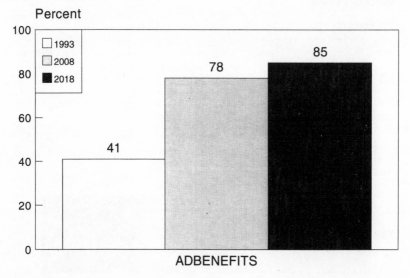

SOURCE: Brookings-ICF Long-Term Care Financing Model.
a. Aged 67 and older. The population aged 67 and older is 28.6 million in 1993, 33.2 million in 2008, and 42.1 million in 2018.

TABLE 3-7. *Total Expenditures for Nursing Home and Home Care, by Source of Payment, Base Case and Accelerated Death Benefit Option, 2018*
*Billions of 1993 dollars*

| Payment source | Base case | ADBENEFITS |
|---|---|---|
| Total long-term care expenditures | 168.2 | 167.8 |
| Nursing home | | |
| Medicaid | 49.0 | 48.4 |
| Medicare | 10.0 | 10.0 |
| Private insurace | 0.0 | 2.1 |
| Family cash | 42.6 | 41.3 |
| Family assets | 26.6 | 26.3 |
| TOTAL | 128.2 | 128.1 |
| Home care | | |
| Medicaid | 5.2 | 5.2 |
| Medicare | 19.0 | 18.8 |
| Other payers[a] | 4.3 | 4.2 |
| Private insurance | 0.0 | 0.0 |
| Out-of-pocket | 11.5 | 11.5 |
| TOTAL | 40.0 | 39.7 |

SOURCE: Brookings-ICF Long-Term Care Financing Model.
a. See note a, table 3-1.

FIGURE 3-11. **Insurance Expenditures as a Proportion of Total Long-Term Care Spending under Accelerated Death Benefit Option, Selected Periods**

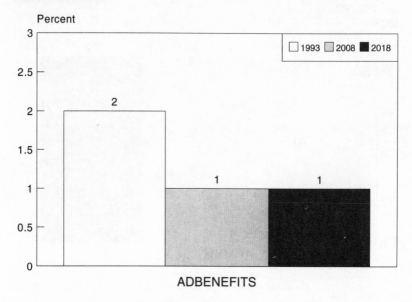

ADBENEFITS

SOURCE: Brookings-ICF Long-Term Care Financing Model.

FIGURE 3-12. **Insurance Expenditures for Nursing Home Care under Accelerated Death Benefit Option, by Income of Patients, 2018[a]**

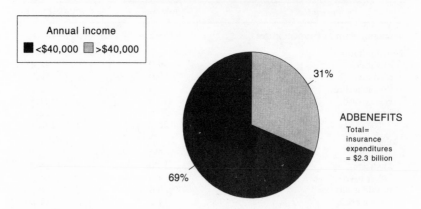

SOURCE: Brookings-ICF Long-Term Care Financing Model.
  a. These data are based on the total payments for an admission cohort over the entire length of their stays in nursing homes. For a person who is admitted to a nursing home in 2018 for a two-year stay, for example, we totaled two years' worth of nursing home expenditures and then calculated the proportion of those expenditures paid by private long-term care insurance.

# Conclusion

Private long-term care insurance is at a crossroads. So long as it is aimed principally at the elderly population, its market penetration and ability to finance long-term care will likely remain limited. Even assuming that the elderly are willing to spend a substantial portion of their income and some of their assets for policies, only a minority are likely to have policies in 2018. Good quality policies are simply too expensive. The dilemma is that when people's interest in purchasing long-term care is greatest—when they are elderly—the policies are unaffordable.

Because of limited market penetration, private insurance bought by the elderly is unlikely to reduce substantially the level of catastrophic long-term care costs. Moreover, private insurance expenditures will be made mostly on behalf of the upper-middle- and upper-income elderly. As a result, private insurance sold to the elderly will have very little effect on public spending through medicaid.

The story would change significantly if employers could be persuaded to offer private long-term care insurance to their active employees and if workers were willing to buy the product. The simulation results clearly suggest that the affordability problem could be largely overcome by selling properly structured policies to the nonelderly. The improvement in affordability derives almost entirely from convincing people to buy policies at a younger age, rather than from the administrative efficiencies obtained through the group insurance market.

Actual experience with employer-sponsored private long-term care insurance is likely to be substantially less favorable than the simulations suggest. Already anxious about their huge unfunded liability for retiree health benefits in particular and the costs of health care in general, employers are unlikely to embrace a major new benefit, even if the employee pays all of the cost. Moreover, selling policies to the nonelderly in large numbers will be extremely difficult. Even when they may think it is a good idea, middle-aged workers are unlikely to purchase voluntarily insurance for an event that will not affect them, if at all, for thirty to forty years. Uncertainty about what will happen to long-term care in the future makes selling policies to the nonelderly a large financial risk for insurers. And finally, the employer-sponsored insurance policies being sold today are not well structured to deal with the critical problem of inflation in the cost of nursing home and home care services. This is a general problem with private long-term care insurance, but it is especially acute for policies sold to the nonelderly. Current policies provide inflation protection either by automatically building it into level premiums, which require purchasers to buy distant coverage with expensive current dollars, or by allowing the insured to buy additional coverage at the new attained age, when premiums are certain to be too expensive for almost everyone.

The introduction of long-term care insurance riders to cash-value life insurance policies is an interesting new development. But the face value of the typical policy is too small, the policies are too often allowed to lapse in late years, and they are too rarely upgraded for inflation to provide a major source of financing for nursing home and home care.

## Chapter Four

# Public Subsidies for Private Long-Term Care Insurance

The limitations of the current market for private long-term care insurance have led to several proposals for public subsidies to promote its purchase. One approach would give employers or individuals a tax subsidy for the purchase of long-term care insurance policies. Another approach would combine tax-advantaged savings accounts with private insurance. Yet another strategy would waive some or all of the medicaid asset-depletion requirements for purchasers of qualified private long-term care insurance policies. The shared intent of these proposals is to induce more people to purchase policies, either by reducing premium costs through tax breaks, enhancing the value of benefits by subsidizing a portion of coinsurance requirements, or guaranteeing publicly funded coverage once privately purchased coverage is exhausted.

All of these options will, no doubt, promote the purchase of private long-term care insurance, but to what extent is unclear. Unless the subsidy is substantial, these strategies are unlikely to make private insurance much more affordable than it is now. By presenting an "endorsement" of private insurance, however, these public subsidies may help overcome the market failure that currently results in only a small proportion of people who can afford policies actually purchasing them. But, with the possible exception of easing access to medicaid for holders of private policies, these strategies are not free to the government. All of them could result in substantial loss of federal revenue—which is spending just as certainly as the direct expenditures of a public insurance program. Thus, a central question is whether promoting private insurance is the wisest way for government to spend additional long-term care dollars.

## The Tax Status of Employer Contributions to Private Insurance

Private long-term care insurance is so new that the federal tax code has yet to acknowledge it specifically in law or regulation. Because of its unique characteristics, long-term care insurance does not fit neatly into the existing tax models of health and accident, life, or disability insurance; pensions; or private annuities.[1] For example, private long-term care insurance relies on a large buildup of reserves, as does whole life or cash-value (not term) life insurance but not health insurance. Receipt of benefits depends on having an underlying medical problem, but individuals may not be "sick," as they must be to receive most health insurance benefits. In addition, long-term care benefits may cover not only health services such as skilled nursing care, but also unskilled care, such as homemaker services, which is intrinsically desirable, whether or not a person has a disability. Indeed, some new private long-term care insurance policies provide cash benefits to individuals who have a specified level of impairment, making these products resemble disability insurance more than health insurance. Table 4-1 summarizes the key tax treatment of these different insurance or retirement income mechanisms.

Ambiguity over its tax status has no doubt slowed the growth of private long-term care insurance, at least somewhat. Its advocates would like the federal tax code to allow tax-deductible premium contributions by employers and perhaps individuals, tax-free accumulation of earnings on reserves,[a] and tax-exempt receipt of benefits.[b] These tax changes are included in President Clinton's long-term care proposal.

a. All private long-term care insurance is based on the buildup of reserves in the early years of the policy. These reserves are then paid out in benefits in later years, when the insured is older and more likely to be disabled. Without reserves, premiums would be unaffordable when the individual is most likely to need services. In a letter ruling (Ruling 89-43), the Department of the Treasury found that interest earnings on long-term care insurance reserves are tax exempt, as they are with life insurance. Although the tax ruling technically applies only to the specific insurer who requested the ruling, presumably other companies are taking advantage of the clarification (198-1 CB213).

b. Although the Internal Revenue Service (IRS) has not ruled on the general taxability of long-term care insurance benefits, it has decided that accelerated death benefits are not taxable. Albert B. Crenshaw, "IRS Proposes a New Rule to Aid the Terminally Ill," *Washington Post*, December 20, 1992, p. H3.

TABLE 4-1. *Current Tax Treatment of Various Insurance and Retirement Funding Arrangements*

| Product | Premium or contribution | Buildup of reserves | Benefits |
|---|---|---|---|
| Health insurance | Tax-deductible for employers; employer contribution exempted from income for employees; employee contribution usually with after-tax income | Not applicable | Tax-free to beneficiary |
| Term life insurance | Tax-deductible for employer; employer contribution up to $50,000 limit exempted from income for employees; beyond limit counted as income | Not applicable | Tax-free to heirs |
| Cash value life insurance | Not deductible for employers; employees use after-tax income | Tax free | Tax-free to heirs |
| Disability insurance | Tax-deductible for employers; employer contribution exempted from income for employees | Not applicable | Taxable to beneficiary |
| Pensions | Tax-deductible for employers; employer contribution exempted from income for employees; employee contribution with after-tax income | Tax free | Employer contribution and interest earned on reserves taxable to beneficiary |
| Private annuities | Not deductible for employers or employees | Tax free | Contributions tax-free, interest earnings taxable to beneficiary |

SOURCE: Based on U.S. Department of the Treasury, *Financing Health and Long-Term Care: Report to the President and to the Congress* (March 1990); and Stephen Kraus, American Council of Life Insurance, personal communication, January 19, 1994.

From a tax perspective, long-term care insurance raises many difficult policy and political questions. According to a report from the U.S. Department of the Treasury on financing health and long-term care:

In practice, tax preferences for almost all forms of health, pension, and annuity income fall under one of these [health and accident, basic pension, or private annuity] models. Almost no expenditures on health care are granted a combination of the benefits of the basic pension model and the employer-provided health insurance model. That is, there are few prefunded health plans that receive the combination of a deduction for deposits into the plan, nontaxation of interest earned on plan deposits as it accumulates, and an exclusion of distributions from the plan. Such generous tax treatment would be almost without parallel anywhere in the Tax Code.[2]

Aside from insurers, the tax implications are important to employers, who are especially unlikely to contribute to the cost of group policies unless they are assured that the contributions are tax deductible and that the tax consequences of receiving long-term care benefits can be clearly explained to their employees. Employer contributions could make long-term care insurance more affordable by reducing the amount that employees have to pay out of pocket and might give employees confidence in the product.[3]

Supporters of private insurance who oppose increased direct federal spending for long-term care face a dilemma regarding the revenue loss inherent in tax clarification. On the one hand, if advocates contend that the revenue loss will be small, they are implicitly admitting that the change will not encourage many employers to contribute. On the other hand, if they say that tax benefits will encourage a great many employers to contribute to the cost of insurance, the potential revenue loss could be large, partly defeating the purpose of relying on private rather than public spending.

Tax factors notwithstanding, the future of employer-paid long-term care insurance is likely to be overwhelmed by the financial problems facing employer-sponsored health benefits for retired employees; these benefits supplement the acute care services of the medicare program. Unlike pensions, virtually all corporations offering postretirement health benefits have financed them on a pay-as-you-go basis rather than prefunding them. Prodded by new accounting rules established by the Financial Accounting Standards Board that require companies to disclose their future financial liability for these benefits, corporations are now aware that, collectively, they have an estimated $187 billion to $400 billion in unfunded liabilities.[4]

As a result, large numbers of employers, concerned about health care costs for both active employees and retirees, are cutting back on retiree benefits or dropping that coverage altogether. For example, in 1991, 41 percent of the employees of medium and large firms with health benefits for retirees aged 65 and older paid none of the insurance cost, down from 55 percent in 1988.[5] In this environment, it seems unlikely that many additional employers will want to contribute to a new, potentially expensive insurance plan that will primarily benefit retirees twenty to thirty years after they have left the company. Indeed, employers are trying to distance themselves as much as they can from such benefits. Health reform may improve prospects for employer contributions, however. President Clinton has proposed to relieve companies of a substantial portion of their obligations for retiree health benefits.[6]

## Tax Incentives to Purchase Private Policies

Another set of options would improve the affordability of private long-term care insurance by offering direct tax incentives to individuals who purchase policies. These tax subsidies would reduce the net price of the policies. Some insurance advocates also argue that tax benefits would have a "sentinel" effect, signaling potential purchasers that the government thinks private long-term care insurance is a worthwhile product.[7]

The type of tax subsidy defines the scope of who can benefit. Allowing taxpayers to deduct all or part of the cost of a private long-term care insurance policy would provide a premium subsidy valued at the marginal tax rate of the household. Because upper-income taxpayers have higher marginal tax rates than lower-income taxpayers, deductions are regressive in nature; that is, they are worth more to upper-income people than to lower-income people. Moreover, for the 60 percent of taxpayers in the lowest tax bracket, a tax deduction would reduce the premium cost by only about one-sixth, probably not enough to motivate very many additional people to purchase polices.[8] The other major drawback is that relatively few taxpayers itemize their deductions—only 29 percent of all tax returns in 1991 included itemized deductions.[9] Not surprisingly, taxpayers who itemize have disproportionately higher income.[10]

The other broad approach is to provide a tax credit, which is a direct reduction in the amount of tax owed, for purchase of policies. In theory, tax credits need not be as regressive as deductions. As a practical matter, however, moderate- and low-income taxpayers may not have the cash on hand to pay premiums during the year and therefore would not be eligible to claim a tax credit at the end of the year. The other problem is that unless the credit is refundable, it is an ineffective policy for people who do not have a tax liability and, therefore, do not file income tax returns.[c] This is especially a problem for the elderly; only about half file returns each year.[11]

The key issue is whether tax incentives are an effective and efficient way to promote the purchase of private long-term care insurance and, thereby, the reform of nursing home and home care financing. Tax incentives may not actually induce very many people to change their behavior and buy private insurance. Tax incentives are also potentially inefficient because benefits may go largely to people who would have bought the policies without the subsidy. Thus the government cost per additional policy sold may be very high.

In addition a tax incentive is, by definition, a revenue loss that will increase the already large federal deficit unless offset by other revenue increases or spending cuts. Most economists believe that our nation's long-run economic health depends on reducing, not increasing, the deficit.[12] Some advocates of tax incentives argue that reductions in government expenditures for medicaid nursing home and home care services will offset the tax loss because some people who will buy private insurance would otherwise be eligible for medicaid.

At least for a very long period of time, these offsets are unlikely for two reasons. First, the tax loss will happen immediately, because the tax incentives are linked to premium payments, but the savings, if any, will not occur until benefits are used, typically many years into the future. This imbalance in timing guarantees short-term tax losses. Second, even with a tax credit, people who buy long-term care insurance are not the same people who are likely to be eligible for medicaid.

## Combining Insurance with Tax-Free Savings Vehicles

Another possible option to increase the attractiveness of private long-term care insurance is to combine it with some type of tax-free savings mechanism.[13] For example, insurance could be sold with a relatively long (say, six-month) deductible period, which would be separately funded through tax-advantaged "individual medical accounts for long-term care."

This approach has three major advantages. The first is that longer deductible periods would mean somewhat lower insurance premiums, making them more affordable. The second is that, for the nonelderly employee who is not yet concerned about long-term care, the tax-

c. Currently, the only refundable tax credit is the earned income tax credit.

advantaged cash accumulation accounts might be more attractive than straight insurance. The funds could always be used for something else, albeit not on a tax-free basis. The third is the meshing of macro-economic and long-term care policy. The United States has a low savings rate, and many economists believe that prospects for economic growth would be enhanced if private savings could be increased and channeled into productive investment. It is appealing to imagine that tax incentives could be used both to expand private savings and to enable older people to finance long-term care more easily.

But this approach would have to overcome several barriers. First, experience with individual retirement accounts (IRAs) suggests that less than one-fifth of all taxpayers are likely to establish any tax-favored savings account.[14] Despite significant tax advantages, only 5 percent of tax returns in 1991 claimed an income adjustment because of a payment to an IRA.[15] Because use of the savings funds would be restricted to long-term care, participation would be expected to be lower than for IRAs, which retirees can spend on anything. Like IRAs before the Tax Reform Act of 1986 reduced their attractiveness, individual medical accounts would most likely be concentrated among higher-income people.[16]

Second, although this strategy reduces the insurance premiums that must be paid, it increases the total amount of money that individuals must put aside each year. For example, we estimate that a group policy that covers four years of nursing home and home care with a sixty-day deductible would cost $524 a year at age 50; the cost of a similar policy with a six-month deductible and a savings component covering the deductible period would require the insured to put aside at least $1,089 a year.[17] This higher "premium" occurs because some of the risk pooling of the insurance is replaced by individual asset accumulation. The problem is that everyone must save quite a lot each year to accumulate enough to pay for the long-term care expenses that only a minority will incur. Indeed, about 60 percent of the elderly will never spend any time in a nursing home.[18] Furthermore, because most nursing home expenses are actually incurred with long lengths of stay, not with short stays, the longer deductible period will not reduce the insurance premium very much.[19]

## Easier Access to Medicaid: A Public-Private Partnership

Changing the tax code has been the most commonly proposed way to subsidize private long-term care insurance, but recent initiatives by

California, Connecticut, Indiana, Iowa, and New York take a substantially different approach.[20] These states provide easier access to medicaid for purchasers of a state-approved private long-term care insurance policy. In essence, these states allow nursing home patients with approved insurance to be eligible for medicaid with substantially higher levels of assets than is normally allowed.[d] In 1993 medicaid allowed unmarried nursing home patients to retain only $2,000 in assets (excluding the home). While employer-paid plans and tax incentives seek to reduce the net cost of insurance, this public-private partnership does the reverse by trying to increase the amount of benefits received for each dollar spent.

The five states link medicaid and private insurance in two different ways. In both cases medicaid acts as a kind of reinsurance for people with limited private long-term care insurance. In the model used by California, Connecticut, Indiana, and Iowa, the level of medicaid-protected assets is tied to the amount that the private insurance policy pays out. For example, if a person buys a policy that pays $100,000 in long-term care benefits, then that individual can keep an additional $100,000 in assets and still be eligible for medicaid.[21] Consumers are able to purchase insurance equivalent to the amount of assets they wish to preserve, potentially reducing the amount of insurance individuals need to buy.[e]

The model used by New York protects an unlimited amount of assets if an individual purchases a policy that meets state standards, including coverage of at least three years of a combination of nursing home and home care, with a minimum indemnity payment of $100 a day.[f] The model does not require an asset test for medicaid coverage because nursing home costs are so high in New York that, over an extended period of time, few individuals can avoid medicaid.[22] Thus, New York

d. Medicaid law allows states great flexibility in determining countable income and assets of medically needy patients—patients with high medical bills in relation to their income. In essence, states using this strategy exclude insurance-related assets from their definition of resources that must be used in determining medicaid eligibility. The Omnibus Budget Reconciliation Act of 1993 (OBRA 1993—PL 103-66), however, severely restricts the ability of additional states to pursue this option by including the insurance-related protected assets in an individual's estate. OBRA 1993 requires states to attempt to recover the cost of institutional care from the estates of medicaid patients. Thus, patients may not be able to pass on these additional funds to their heirs.

e. In both models, nursing home patients must still contribute all of their income toward the cost of care except for a small (usually $30 per month) personal needs allowance.

f. New York's approach resembles the "back-end" public insurance option, where coverage commences after a two- or three-year deductible period (see chapter 7 for a detailed discussion of this option). The main difference is that in New York the public benefits are available only to persons who buy private long-term care insurance.

is targeting a higher-income population, with potentially more assets, than are the other states.

The key observation supporting these public-private approaches is that insurance covering shorter periods of nursing home and home care is cheaper and more affordable than are policies covering longer periods of care.[g] The problem with the current system is that an individual who buys a policy covering, for example, two years of nursing home care but who ends up needing care for five years can still lose all his or her assets. These medicaid initiatives thus make it possible to obtain lifetime asset protection without having to buy an insurance policy that pays lifetime benefits. Proponents of this approach argue that the goal is not to protect assets, per se, but rather to preserve financial autonomy toward the end of life.

Supporters contend that by encouraging purchase of insurance, medicaid expenditures for long-term care may be reduced or, at least, will not increase. This argument is probably stronger for the approach used by California, Connecticut, Indiana, and Iowa, where there is a "dollar-for-dollar" correspondence between the amount the insurance pays and the level of protected assets. In New York the potential for protecting very large amounts of assets weakens this argument. To the extent that these systems are budget neutral, these strategies move toward what economists call "Pareto optimality," that is, making some people better off without making anybody worse off. Insurance dollars are simply substituted for private asset dollars.

This public-private partnership has two other potential advantages. First, because people are eligible for the enhanced asset protection only if they buy approved policies, state regulators can use the initiative as a "carrot" to induce insurance companies to upgrade the quality of their policies.[h] Second, legal and illegal transfers of assets for the purpose of obtaining medicaid eligibility may be reduced because people have a plausible alternative.

Despite these arguments, several concerns have been raised about the

g. The prototype individual private insurance policy that covers four years of nursing home and home care costs $2,337 a year for an insured who purchases it at age 67; a policy that covers only two years of nursing home and home care costs the same insured $1,617 a year.

h. For example, Connecticut requires that indemnity benefits be adjusted for inflation and that the adjustment be compounded annually. In addition, the state requires companies to offer a policy with less extensive coverage to individuals who discontinue their premium payments and let their policy lapse. Connecticut has also mandated training for insurance agents selling certified policies and is requiring the distribution of a consumer booklet that compares insurance policies.

equity and efficiency of this option. The first concern, which has been vigorously pressed by Representative Henry A. Waxman, is whether a means-tested welfare program is an appropriate mechanism to protect the assets of the upper-middle- and upper-income elderly. Indeed, under this approach, it remains an open question how far down the income distribution insurance purchase will go. Simulations presented in chapter 3 suggest that the vast bulk of private insurance expenditures will be for the upper-middle- and upper-income elderly.

The second concern is whether improved asset protection will actually induce substantial numbers of people to purchase long-term care insurance. Although people's motivations for buying insurance are difficult to pinpoint, one recent study of purchasers found that only 14 percent of respondents listed protection of assets as the "most important" reason for buying insurance.[23] In addition, asset protection may have a narrow appeal because most elderly have relatively modest levels of financial wealth.[24]

Furthermore, public support may be weak for a financing reform strategy that emphasizes asset protection. Many people may rightly ask why public medicaid funds are being used to ensure that the well-to-do are able to pass on their private wealth to their children.

Moreover, many elderly do not want easier access to medicaid. Indeed, one of the major reasons people buy long-term care insurance is to avoid having to apply for welfare. The survey of insurance purchasers found that 73 percent of respondents reported that avoiding medicaid was an important reason for buying a policy.[25] Medicaid's relatively low reimbursement rates have led to inadequate access to nursing home care and problems of quality in some nursing homes heavily dependent on medicaid.[26] In addition, upper-middle- and upper-income elderly would probably find the $30 a month medicaid allows for personal needs to be inadequate and would use up at least some of their newly protected assets for daily living expenses. In sum, it is not clear that easier access to medicaid will be sufficient to induce large numbers of additional elderly to purchase private long-term care insurance.

A third concern is whether the public-private partnership will truly be budget neutral. Because most policies probably would be sold to healthy young elderly who are at least ten to twenty years away from needing nursing home care, the effect of the partnership on the public purse will not be known for a decade or two. If additional public expenditures should prove necessary, then one may well ask whether providing asset protection to relatively well-to-do elderly is the best place to put the next long-term care dollar.

To assess the effect on the medicaid budget, it is necessary to establish a comparison level of expenditures.[27] In a world with no private long-term care insurance at all, it is likely, although not certain, that the partnership would be budget neutral. Private insurance does exist, however, and the number of policies sold is likely to continue to grow modestly. In that situation, the partnership needs to attract substantial numbers of additional insurance purchasers; otherwise, medicaid expenditures will actually increase. That is because, under current medicaid rules, purchasers of insurance would have to spend down their assets after their insurance benefits have been exhausted before qualifying for medicaid, something that they would not be required to do under the partnership.

In addition, although supporters argue that the partnership offers a more appealing alternative to transferring assets as a way to avoid medicaid's claim on these resources, it is conceivable that the level of premature asset transfer would actually increase. Current rules forbid people to transfer assets at less than fair market value for three years before applying for medicaid.[28] Once the partnership has encouraged the elderly to look to medicaid as a way to protect their assets, some insurance purchasers will buy only the three years' worth of coverage required to comply with medicaid rules and then legally transfer the remainder of their financial wealth upon entry to a nursing home.

## Simulation Assumptions and Results

To evaluate their potential effects on private long-term care insurance, we simulated five different public subsidy plans. The detailed simulation assumptions are shown in figure 4-1. The first option—TAXFAVINS—provides a 20 percent, income-limited tax credit to purchasers of private long-term care insurance. The second option, modeled on Connecticut's program—CTINS—provides easier access to medicaid for people who buy private insurance and increases the level of protected assets to the amount paid by insurance. In both simulations, purchase is limited to the elderly population.

Three options are simulated that include initial purchase of private long-term care insurance by the nonelderly population. EMPLOYINS simulates the widespread offering of employer-sponsored and largely

FIGURE 4-1. **Simulation Assumptions for Public Subsidies of Private Long-Term Care Insurance**

*All options*
- Individuals purchase policies that cover either two or four years of nursing home and home care, pay $60 a day for nursing home care and $30 a visit for home care in 1986, have inflation-adjusted indemnity levels, and assume relatively low levels of lapse.

*Elderly-oriented options*
- Individuals purchase policies if they have $10,000 or more in nonhousing assets and if premiums cost no more than 5 percent of their income.

- TAXFAVINS: A nonrefundable 20 percent tax credit is available for single elderly persons with income of $40,000 or less and married persons with income of $60,000 or less. The tax credit decreases one percentage point for each $1,000 increase in income for a cap of $60,000 for individuals and $80,000 for married couples. The income limits increase by 5.5 percent annually.

- CTINS: Individuals aged 67 and older who purchase private long-term care insurance have easier access to medicaid. The level of protected assets for nursing home patients with insurance equals the total maximum payout under the insurance policy for nursing home care.

*Nonelderly-oriented options*
- EMPLOYINS: Employees who work for companies with pension plans and their spouses are eligible to purchase employer-sponsored private long-term care insurance. Employers pay half of the costs of the policies; employer contributions are tax deductible. All other persons purchase individual policies.

  Individuals purchase policies if they cost no more than 2 percent of income at ages 40 to 49, 3 percent of income at ages 50 to 59, 4 percent of income at ages 60 to 66, and 5 percent of income at ages 67 to 84. Persons aged 67 and older must have at least $10,000 in nonhousing assets. Premiums after purchase increase 5.5 percent a year until age 65 and then are level.

- INDSAVINS: Individuals may purchase policies that cover two or four years of nursing home and home care after a 180-day deductible. Individuals save the money needed to cover the deductible at age 80 through separate tax-free savings accounts. Total premiums and savings for the two-year product range from $524 at age 40 to $2,399 at age 60; for the four-year product, from $613 at age 40 to $2,738 at age 60.

  Individuals purchase policies if they cost no more than 3 percent of their income at ages 40 to 49, 4 percent of income at ages 50 to 59, and 5 percent of income at ages 61 to 84. Persons aged 67 and older must have at least $10,000 in nonhousing assets. Premiums after purchase increase 5.5 percent a year until age 65 and then are level.

- GRPSAVINS: Same as INDSAVINS except that people purchase a group insurance product with somewhat lower premiums. Total payments for the two-year policy range from $504 at age 40 to $2,328 at age 60; total payments for the four-year policy range from $583 at age 40 to $2,632 at age 60.

FIGURE 4-2. **Elderly Participation in Subsidized Private Long-Term Care Insurance Options, Selected Periods**[a]

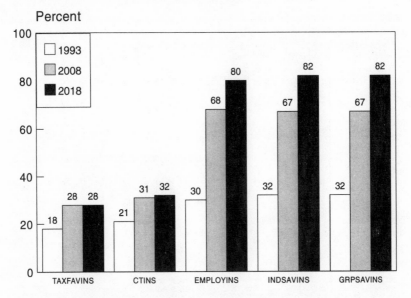

SOURCE:: Brookings-ICF Long-Term Care Financing Model.
Note: In comparison, the percentage of elderly with private insurance under SPEND5PCT is 13 percent in 1993, 20 percent in 2008, and 20 percent in 2018; under GROUPINS, those figures are 27 percent in 1993, 63 percent in 2008, and 76 percent in 2018.
a. Age 67 and older. The population aged 67 and older is 28.6 million in 1993, 33.2 million in 2008 and 42.1 million in 2018. In this and other figures and tables in this chapter, 1993 represents the five-year average for the period 1991–95; 2008, the five-year average for the period 2006–10; and 2018, the five-year average for the period 2016–20.

employer-paid private long-term care insurance. The other two options—INDSAVINS AND GRPSAVINS—explore the combination of insurance and retirement savings. Working age individuals can buy long-term care insurance with 180-day deductible periods for nursing home care instead of the 60-day deductible period we simulate in the other policies. These individuals then cover the 180-day deductible period with funds accumulated in a tax-free savings plan established at the same time as the policy. In INDSAVINS, people purchase individual insurance policies; in GRPSAVINS, people purchase group policies.

As a result of these public subsidies, the proportions of elderly with insurance are somewhat, but not dramatically, higher than they would be without the subsidies (figure 4-2). For example, in 2018, 28 percent of the elderly might have private insurance under TAXFAVINS, compared with 20 percent under SPEND5PCT. Under CTINS, 32 percent of the elderly might have private insurance, assuming that the elderly

TABLE 4-2. *Total Expenditures for Nursing Home and Home Care, by Source of Payment, Base Case and Subsidized Private Insurance Options, 2018*[a]
Billions of 1993 dollars

| Payment source | Base case | TAXFAVINS | CTINS | EMPLOYINS | INDSAVINS | GRPSAVINS |
|---|---|---|---|---|---|---|
| Total | 168.2 | 174.7 | 175.7 | 194.8 | 184.2 | 184.5 |
| Nursing home | | | | | | |
| Medicaid | 49.0 | 47.4 | 46.8 | 33.3 | 37.1 | 37.0 |
| Medicare | 10.0 | 10.3 | 10.4 | 11.1 | 10.9 | 10.9 |
| Private insurance | 0.0 | 17.4 | 19.4 | 55.9 | 47.9 | 48.3 |
| Patient's cash | 42.6 | 34.6 | 35.5 | 29.9 | 27.4 | 27.4 |
| Patient's assets | 26.6 | 22.3 | 20.6 | 16.0 | 17.3 | 17.3 |
| TOTAL | 128.2 | 132.1 | 132.7 | 146.2 | 140.6 | 140.9 |
| Home care | | | | | | |
| Medicaid | 5.2 | 5.2 | 5.2 | 4.7 | 5.2 | 5.2 |
| Medicare | 19.0 | 19.4 | 19.4 | 20.8 | 20.4 | 20.4 |
| Other payers[b] | 4.3 | 3.7 | 3.6 | 2.8 | 3.3 | 3.3 |
| Private insurance | 0.0 | 3.8 | 4.4 | 12.3 | 9.9 | 9.9 |
| Out-of-pocket payment | 11.5 | 10.5 | 10.3 | 8.0 | 4.9 | 4.7 |
| TOTAL | 40.0 | 42.7 | 43.0 | 48.6 | 43.6 | 43.6 |

SOURCE: Brookings-ICF Long-Term Care Financing Model.

a. In comparison, under the SPEND5PCT option, total expenditures would be $173.2 billion, $131.3 billion for nursing home care, $41.9 billion for home care; total expenditures under the GROUPINS option would be $188.9 billion, $143.9 billion for nursing homes, $44.9 billion for home care.

b. Other payers include state and local expenditures, social service block grants, Older Americans Act and Department of Veterans' Affairs home care funds, charity, and out-of-pocket expenditures by people other than the service recipient.

TABLE 4-3. *Effect on Medicaid of Subsidized Private Insurance Options, Selected Periods*

| Option | Percentage reduction from base case | | |
|---|---|---|---|
| | 1993 | 2008 | 2018 |
| | *In medicaid nursing home expenditures* | | |
| TAXFAVINS | 0.4 | 3.4 | 3.3 |
| CTINS | 0.4 | 3.4 | 4.5 |
| EMPLOYINS | 1.3 | 15.3 | 32.0 |
| INDSAVINS | 1.3 | 10.7 | 24.3 |
| GRPSAVINS | 1.3 | 11.0 | 24.5 |
| | *In number of medicaid nursing home patients* | | |
| TAXFAVINS | 0.7 | 1.9 | 2.2 |
| CTINS | 0.2 | 1.5 | 2.3 |
| EMPLOYINS | 1.0 | 9.3 | 16.9 |
| INDSAVINS | 1.2 | 8.4 | 18.1 |
| GRPSAVINS | 1.2 | 8.5 | 18.4 |

SOURCE: Brookings-ICF Long-Term Care Financing Model.

would be willing to spend a higher percentage of their income to purchase insurance. As was observed in earlier simulations, the key to more widespread affordability is convincing the nonelderly population to buy policies. For EMPLOYINS, INDSAVINS, and GRPSAVINS, 80 percent or more of the elderly could afford private insurance in 2018.

Because the subsidies produce relatively small increases in the number of policies purchased, it is not surprising that the results on other dimensions, including the proportion of long-term care expenditures paid by insurance, the effect on medicaid nursing home expenditures, percent of private insurance expenditures spent on the upper-income population, and catastrophic costs, show relatively small changes compared to the unsubsidized simulations (see tables 4-2 to 4-4), and figures 4-2 to 4-4). In general, the results for INDSAVINS and GRPSAVINS are quite similar to subsidized and unsubsidized group insurance—EMPLOYINS and GROUPINS.

Not only do the subsidies fail to entice large additional numbers of people to purchase policies, but all of the options except CTINS result in substantial revenue losses to the federal government (CTINS produces small savings compared with the base case). As shown in figure 4-5, revenue losses for TAXFAVINS, EMPLOYINS, INDSAVINS, and GRPSAVINS are not offset by public savings at any time during the simulation period. Net revenue losses are particularly large for INDSAVINS and GRPSAVINS, potentially reaching as high as $34 billion in 2018. Tax losses for EMPLOYINS exceed public savings throughout most of the simulation period but come close to breaking even in 2018.

TABLE 4-4. *Effect of Subsidized Private Insurance Options on Catastrophic Out-of-Pocket Expenditures for Nursing Home Care, 2018*

| Measure | Base case | TAXFAVINS | CTINS | EMPLOYINS | INDSAVINS | GRPSAVINS |
|---|---|---|---|---|---|---|
| **Absolute expenditure**[a] | | | | | | |
| Average out-of-pocket spending (thousands of dollars) | 44 | 35 | 35 | 27 | 27 | 26 |
| Percentage of admissions spending more than $20,000 out of pocket | 33 | 28 | 27 | 23 | 24 | 24 |
| **Relative expenditure**[b] | | | | | | |
| Percentage of admissions spending more than 40 percent of income, assets on care | 39 | 36 | 35 | 28 | 28 | 28 |
| **Target efficiency**[c] | | | | | | |
| Percentage of insurance expenditures spent on people who otherwise would have incurred catastrophic out-of-pocket costs | . . . | 56 | 57 | 67 | 63 | 63 |

SOURCE: Brookings-ICF Long-Term Care Financing Model.

a. These data are based on the total out-of-pocket payments for an admission cohort over the entire length of the nursing home stay.

b. The numerator is equal to the out-of-pocket contribution to nursing home care for the entire length of stay; the denominator is equal to income during the stay plus nonhousing assets.

c. These data are based on total expenditures for an admission cohort for the entire length of stay. Total insurance expenditures are $18.4 billion under TAXFAVINS, $21.1 billion under CTINS, $60.4 billion under EMPLOYINS, $52.5 billion under INDSAVINS, and $52.8 billion under GRPSAVINS.

FIGURE 4-3. **Insurance Expenditures as a Proportion of Total Long-Term Care Spending under Subsidized Private Insurance Options, Selected Periods**

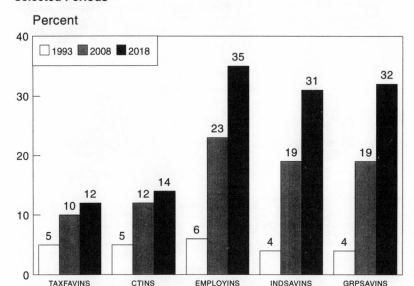

Percent

SOURCE: Brookings-ICF Long-Term Care Financing Model.
Note: In comparison, the percentage of total long-term care expenditures covered by private insurance under SPEND5PCT is 3 percent in 1993, 8 percent in 2008, and 9 percent in 2018; under GROUPINS, those figures are 5 percent in 1993, 20 percent in 2008, and 29 percent in 2018.

Moreover, because most of the tax expenditures go to people who would have purchased policies anyway, the subsidies are very costly ways to promote private insurance. In the TAXFAVINS and EMPLOYINS simulations for 1993, for example, it costs the federal government $1,700 and $11,300, respectively, in lost revenue per additional policy sold, compared with the unsubsidized simulations (table 4-5).

TABLE 4-5. *Public Cost for Each Additional Purchaser of Subsidized Private Long-Term Care Insurance, Selected Periods*[a]
*Thousands of 1993 dollars*

| Selected period | TAXFAVINS | EMPLOYINS |
| --- | --- | --- |
| 1993 | 1,700 | 11,300 |
| 2008 | 1,700 | 7,000 |
| 2018 | 1,900 | 7,900 |

SOURCE: Brookings-ICF Long-Term Care Financing Model.
a. Public cost is equal to the tax loss from providing public subsidies divided by additional purchasers.

FIGURE 4-4. **Insurance Expenditures for Nursing Home Care under Subsidized Private Insurance Options, by Income of Patients, 2018[a]**

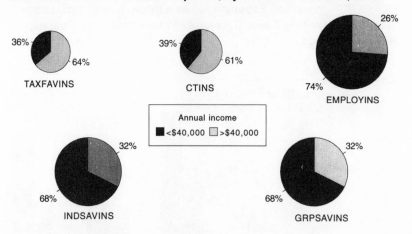

SOURCE:: Brookings-ICF Long-Term Care Financing Model.
   Note: In comparison, in 2018, 70 percent of the $13.3 billion in insurance expenditures under SPEND5PCT would go to people with incomes greater than $40,000; under GROUPINS, only 29 percent of the $54.3 billion private insurance expenditures would be made on behalf of this upper-income group.
   a. These data are based on the total payments for an admission cohort over the entire length of their stays in nursing homes. For a person who is admitted to a nursing home in 2018 for a two-year stay, for example, we totaled two-years' worth of nursing home expenditures and then calculated the proportion of those expenditures paid by private long-term care insurance.
   Total insurance expenditures are $18.4 billion under TAXFAVINS, $21.1 billion under CTINS, $60.4 billion under EMPLOYINS, $52.5 billion under INDSAVINS, and $52.8 billion under GRPSAVINS.

FIGURE 4-5. **Comparison of Public Long-Term Care Savings with Tax Loss under Subsidized Private Insurance Options, Selected Periods**

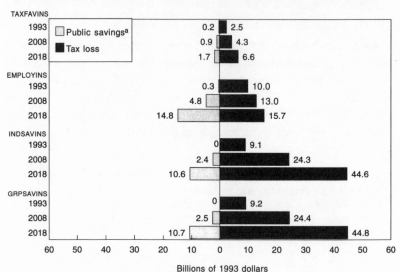

SOURCE: Brookings-ICF Long-Term Care Financing Model.
   a. Net reduction from base case in medicaid and medicare spending for nursing home care, and medicaid, medicare, and other payer spending for home care.

# Conclusion

Limitations on the affordability of private long-term care insurance for the elderly and the lack of employer contributions in the group market have led to a range of proposals to provide public subsidies as a way to expand the market. This chapter examined five options.

One strategy would clarify the tax code to encourage employers to contribute to the cost of private long-term care insurance for their employees. The unprecedented combination of tax advantages that advocates seek makes many tax experts uncomfortable, however. Moreover, even with tax incentives, most large corporations face a large unfunded liability for acute care benefits for their retirees and are unlikely to want to contribute to yet another benefit for this group.

Another option would improve the affordability of private long-term care insurance by offering tax deductions or credits to individuals who purchase policies. This strategy is likely to be highly inefficient, with most of the benefits going to those who would have bought the policies without the subsidy. Moreover, at most levels of subsidy, this strategy is not likely to reduce the price enough to improve affordability significantly for the elderly.

A third option would combine high-deductible insurance with tax-advantaged savings accounts. Proponents of this approach hope that the cash accumulation component will be more attractive than pure insurance to the nonelderly. Unfortunately, because of the reduction in risk pooling, the amount of money that would have to be put aside is fairly high, reducing the affordability advantage of selling policies to the population under age 65.

A final option would provide easier access to medicaid for people who purchased approved private long-term care insurance policies. Those people would be able to retain a higher level of assets than is normally permitted and still be medicaid eligible. This approach can provide a lifetime level of asset protection without requiring people to buy expensive policies with unlimited coverage. It is not clear, however, whether many people want easier access to medicaid, which is, after all, a welfare program, even if it allows greater asset protection. Moreover, a government program that protects inheritances raises political problems.

Simulation results suggest that these approaches are moderately effective in improving the affordability of private long-term care insurance, compared with the unsubsidized options. Common sense dictates that private insurance is more likely to achieve these simulation results with a subsidy than without it. The simulations are relatively generous, however, because affordability is assumed to be the only barrier to purchasing insurance, when in reality there are several other impediments. These approaches would also result in significant tax losses to the federal government. Thus policymakers must decide whether they wish to put additional spending into direct funding of services or into promoting private insurance.

## Chapter Five

# High-Quality Private Insurance: Can We Get There from Here?

Because private long-term care insurance is likely to play a larger, if limited, role in the future, it is critical that products and agents be properly regulated.[1] Issues include how to protect consumers without stifling a relatively new and developing market, and which level of government—state or federal—should regulate private insurance?

Although the quality of long-term care policies has improved greatly in the last few years, problems remain. Inflation protection is inadequate, lapse rates are high, few policies offer nonforfeiture benefits, activities of daily living are not uniformly defined and measured, and agent and marketing abuses are not uncommon. The problem is not that high-quality policies are unavailable; they are. Instead, the difficulty is that current regulations also allow lower-quality policies to be sold.

Concerns of consumer advocates about the quality of private long-term care insurance have prompted President Clinton to propose federal intervention. The federal government could take any number of approaches to the problem, but instituting mandatory standards substantially higher than the current model standards of the National Association of Insurance Commissioners (NAIC) may prove the most effective way to improve the quality of policies on a nationwide basis.

## Evolving Policies and Regulations

Long-term care insurance products have changed dramatically from the so-called "first generation" policies. Faced with great uncertainties and lacking actual experience with an insured population, companies initially tried to protect themselves against financial loss by imposing severe restrictions on the services they covered and the eligibility of the insured for reimbursement. The net effect was to lessen substantially the probability that a person with a policy who used nursing home or home care would actually receive insurance benefits.[2] With good reason, these first generation policies were roundly criticized by consumer groups and researchers.[3]

The newer policies have improved substantially. Although the average policy in force still has restrictions, newer policies provide significantly better coverage.[4] In particular, prior hospitalization requirements have been eliminated, policies are guaranteed renewable, Alzheimer's disease is explicitly covered, all levels of nursing home care and more home care are covered, indemnity levels are sometimes indexed for inflation, and a few policies provide some residual benefits to people who terminate their policies. These changes were made largely in response to strengthened state regulatory requirements and market demand. It is still true that few insurers have meaningful payment experience under insurance.

Historically, the states have regulated the insurance industry. When the federal government does intervene, the issues often involve market imperfections unresolvable at the state level. For example, the federal government now regulates flood, mail-order, and medicare supplemental ("medigap") insurance.[5]

The NAIC plays a prominent intellectual role by providing state regulators with a variety of support services, including research, model legislation and regulations, and standardized administrative functions. As the private long-term care insurance market has grown, so has regulatory activity, much of it revolving around the NAIC Model Act and Regulation. Inevitably, however, the influence of the NAIC depends on the regulatory climate peculiar to each state.

State insurance regulators must strike a balance between protecting consumers and nurturing a new product. Proponents of strict regulation fear that without tough standards, consumers will not be protected against inferior products and fraudulent sales practices. They recall the scandals that resulted from the failure to set minimum standards for medigap policies. Opponents of strict regulation argue that the government has neither enough information nor experience to regulate intelligently. Moreover, they argue that it is difficult for the government to provide the flexibility needed to encourage innovation.

## Consumer Protection Issues

Regulatory advances, although considerable, have not been uniform. Some states have not adopted the NAIC standards, and some of the NAIC standards are too lax.

### THE VANISHING BENEFIT: THE NEED FOR ADEQUATE INFLATION PROTECTION

It is no secret that health care prices are increasing rapidly. According to the Health Care Financing Administration, daily nursing home revenue—a rough proxy for price—increased, on average, more than three percentage points above the consumer price index between 1977 and 1990.[6] Unlike acute health care insurance, which links benefits to costs or charges, almost all private long-term care insurance provides fixed indemnity benefits ($60 a day for nursing home care, for example). Without adequate inflation adjustment, the benefits may not be sufficient to cover long-term care costs and thus may offer the policyholder little relief from asset depletion or reliance on medicaid.[7] As of 1990 most newly purchased policies lacked any, let alone adequate, inflation protection.[8] Current NAIC model regulations require only that insurers offer the option to purchase a policy where the indemnity value increases at least 5 percent a year compounded annually or that the insured be given the right to increase benefit levels periodically without providing evidence of health status or insurability so long as the policyholder had not declined this option for the previous period.[9] The model regulation does not prohibit the sale of policies that do not increase the benefit level over time. As of July 1992, thirty-one states had adopted this standard or some variant on it.[10]

Insurers typically deal with the inflation issue in one of four ways. First, virtually all policies allow consumers to buy additional coverage in the future at the new, attained age, but only if they provide evidence of good health. This approach puts the onus on the individual to monitor long-term care prices and to make periodic adjustments. Obviously, it also prevents policyholders who have become disabled from upgrading their policies. As discussed below, this approach is also extremely expensive.

Second, many companies offer policies where the insured can periodically purchase increased indemnity benefits—called attained age pieces—without medical underwriting. This additional coverage is purchased, however, at the new attained age and will cost more—perhaps dramatically more—than if the coverage had been bought when the insured was younger. For example, if a person buys a policy at age 62 that pays $60 a day in nursing home benefits and if inflation is 33 percent during the next five years, then the insured can buy additional coverage of $20 a day to compensate for the inflation but at the price charged 67-year-olds, not 62-year-olds. We estimate that to retain purchasing power, the premiums at age 82 would be approximately ten times, in nominal dollars, what they were at age 62. Even after adjusting for general inflation, premiums at age 82 are likely to be more than four times higher than they were when the insured was age 62.[11]

The premiums will skyrocket, but the incomes of the elderly will not. Income and assets of the elderly tend to decline as they age, because private pensions are not indexed for inflation, because surviving spouses do not usually receive full pension benefits after the pension-earning spouse dies, and because the elderly slowly use up their savings as they age. Thus, to maintain the policy's purchasing power, the elderly will have to use a sharply higher percentage of their incomes. This "attained age piece" approach is particularly problematic because it makes an adequate benefit appear far less expensive than it actually will be.

Third, some companies offer "simple" inflation adjustments, where the benefit level increases by a fixed amount each year, usually 5 percent of the initial indemnity value, for some period of time, often twenty years. For example, a policy that initially pays $60 per day for nursing home care will increase $3 a year, which represents a declining percentage increase with every passing year.

Although many consumers undoubtedly confuse simple adjustments with increases that are compounded annually, the benefits are dramatically different. For a person who purchases a policy at age 55, a simple inflation adjustment of 5 percent for thirty years will increase the benefit level by only 150 percent by age 85. In contrast, if the price of long-term care services increases at a compound rate of 5 percent per year, it will have increased by 332 percent during that thirty years. Thus policies that use "simple" inflation adjustments do not adequately adjust for the rising cost of nursing home or home care. This approach is less common than it was a few years ago.

Finally, insurers are offering compound inflation adjustments, generally 5 percent a year. Compound inflation adjustment substantially increases premiums, compared with unindexed policies. For example, Wiener and others estimate that a four-year, unindexed policy covering both home and nursing home care with nonforfeiture benefits would cost $1,195 if the purchaser were between the ages of 65 and 69.[12] A similar policy with indemnity benefits compounded at 5.5 percent a year for the life of the policyholder would cost $2,607. Despite the substantial increase in cost, the deleterious effects of increases in long-term care costs make inflation protection the single most important benefit that should be mandated by regulators.

These high costs can be somewhat offset by reducing the minimum benefit level. The elderly with good incomes and substantial assets have little reason to buy insurance that covers the full cost of nursing home care. Indemnity levels set at the full cost of care will result in nursing home patients' saving virtually all of their social security and pension income, thus "making money" by being institutionalized. Thus, purchase of lower indemnity levels that increase with inflation would be a preferable strategy.

Opponents of mandatory compound inflation protection contend that many consumers do not want this feature and that it will make policies unaffordable.[13] It is likely, however, that few consumers understand how devastating inflation is to a policy's purchasing power. Anecdotal evidence suggests that consumers want very high initial indemnity values but then do not purchase inflation protection. But it is illogical to have the best financial protection when one is young (or at least younger), healthy (after being medically underwritten), and with a lower risk of needing long-term care services, and the worst financial protection when one is very old, possibly disabled, and with a higher risk of needing nursing home or home care.

## THE VANISHING INSURED: HIGH LAPSE RATES AND NONFORFEITURE BENEFITS

If long-term care insurance is purchased at age 65, premiums may have to be paid for twenty years or more until death. If insurance is purchased at younger ages, the insured will have to pay premiums for even longer periods. For a variety of reasons, not all those who initially purchase a policy will make premium payments until death. Although not many data are available, the insurance industry commonly assumes that, not counting the insured who die, approximately half of all insured people will drop their policies within the first five years of purchase and approximately 70 percent will drop their policies within fifteen years.[14] In pricing their premiums, some companies assume even higher lapse rates (that is, voluntary nonpayment of premiums). The number of policyholders who drop their policies in order to switch to other policies, which have fewer restrictions or may be cheaper, is unknown.

The public policy problem is that virtually all policies have level premiums, designed to build up substantial reserves in the early years for payout in the later years. Consumers who decide not to renew their policies will have overpaid in terms of the actuarially fair cost of the protection actually received during the early period when the policy was in effect. With no way to receive back any portion of the premiums they paid in, they will, in effect, be subsidizing the premiums of those policyholders who maintain their policies.

In addition, some actuaries have argued that some companies are assuming very high lapse rates in order to lower prices and gain market share. The higher the insurer's lapse rate assumptions, the lower the premiums will be because fewer benefit payments will be made on behalf of purchasers. If actual lapse rates do not meet expectations, then premiums must be raised, which will in turn result in lapses by insured who do not want or cannot afford to pay more.[15] Although policies sold on a level premium basis do not have scheduled premium increases, insurance companies universally reserve the right to raise premiums for all persons in a class, if necessary. Under these circumstances, companies could make windfall profits and the insured would be left both overcharged and without coverage.

Although data are not available, a portion of the lapses may occur among moderate- and low-income elderly who bought policies without fully realizing the financial burdens. In a study for the Health Insurance Association of America, LifePlans, Inc., found that nearly one-fifth of private long-term care insurance purchasers in 1990 had annual incomes of less than $15,000.[16] Moreover, the U.S. General Accounting Office has found that insurance agents make little effort to ensure that prospective policyholders will be able to continue making payments over the long run.[17]

Lapse rates would be a less significant consumer protection issue if insurance policies had nonforfeiture benefits, which allow policyholders who drop their policies to finance a residual benefit with a portion of their accumulated reserves. Nonforfeiture benefits are required in prefunded life insurance products, but few long-term care insurance policies have them.

It is important, however, to distinguish between short-term and long-term lapses. To date, most of the adverse publicity concerns lapses within the first five years after purchase. Short-term lapses may be better addressed by establishing higher overall standards so that policies are not being constantly changed by insurers and by restructuring commissions paid to sales agents so that they have an incentive to keep policyholders insured. Nonforfeiture benefits are most appropriate for people who have paid premiums for a substantial period of time—at least five to ten years. Only at that point will consumers have built up enough reserves to finance a meaningful nonforfeiture benefit.

In June 1993 the NAIC voted to amend its model statute to make nonforfeiture benefits mandatory, although the exact form of the benefit is still to be worked out.[18] In opposing the move, the insurance industry argued that mandatory nonforfeiture benefits would raise premiums, especially for people who would otherwise have kept their policies.[19]

Ultimately, the dilemma is this: If lapse rates are low, then nonforfeiture benefits can be added at little cost. If lapse rates are high, then nonforfeiture benefits are an essential element of consumer protection, even though they may add substantially to premiums. Private long-term care insurance simply cannot be taken seriously as a mechanism for financing nursing home and home care if half or more of initial purchasers end up without coverage when it comes time to use services.

## GETTING IN THE DOOR: MEASURING DISABILITY

Every insurance policy, public or private, must have criteria to determine who qualifies for benefits. Many insurance policies now use inability to perform the activities of daily living (ADLs), such as bathing, dressing, and eating, as a trigger for paying benefits, especially home care. This approach has substantially replaced the older criteria of prior hospitalization, need for skilled care, or a doctor's certification of medical necessity. Although the use of ADLs is a positive development, policies do not use a standard set of ADL elements, nor do they generally describe how ADLs are assessed. For example, some companies omit bathing as an ADL or combine it with another activity; others include continence or ability to take medications as ADLs. This is a serious problem because differences in defining and measuring ADLs can result in great differences in the number of people who qualify for benefits.[20] A key assessment issue is whether individuals are considered disabled if they need "supervision or standby help" (providing cues and reminders) or mechanical assistance or only if they require "active human assistance." Using the latter, more restrictive definition of disability can reduce the number of elderly qualifying for benefits by as much as two-fifths.[21]

Moreover, although policies specifically provide coverage for people with Alzheimer's disease, consumers may erroneously believe that people with the condition automatically qualify for benefits, regardless of their level of disability. This is not the case. Alzheimer's disease is degenerative, with a very wide range of impairment. To receive insurance benefits, persons with Alzheimer's disease must meet disability screens generally designed to provide benefits only to the severely cognitively impaired. Not all policies, however, have separate eligibility criteria for the cognitively impaired. A substantial portion of demented persons do not have serious ADL limitations, especially if limitations are narrowly defined to include only those persons needing active human assistance. According to one study, nearly 40 percent of the elderly with moderate to severe cognitive impairment received no active human assistance in any of five ADLs.[22]

Regulators currently are considering whether to standardize how ADLs and cognitive impairment should be measured and what elements should be included. The rationale for this standardization is not that there is "one true" measure and that regulators know what it is. But without standardization, a consumer has no conceivable way to make comparisons across policies. Without a computer and several large national surveys, a consumer cannot know whether a policy that provides benefits when the insured has deficiencies in four of seven ADLs is stricter or more generous than one that provides benefits when an individual has deficiencies in two of five ADLs.

## AGENT AND MARKETING ABUSES

Although regulatory activity has centered on benefits and other policy characteristics, stories of agent abuses have focused attention on the marketing side of long-term care insurance. Reports by the U.S. House Select Committee on Aging, Families USA, and Consumers Union allege a variety of unethical practices, including misrepresentation of products and product endorsements, failure to provide an outline of coverage, high-pressure tactics, sales of multiple policies to a single individual, encouraging current policyholders to switch policies unnecessarily, and falsifying medical histories.[23] In general, insurance companies and agents have dismissed these charges, saying that a few agents may have engaged in such behavior but that it is not at all typical.[24]

The NAIC Model Act and Regulation already includes several provisions to ensure that marketing abuses do not occur. These include a requirement that prospective purchasers be given a shopper's guide and an outline of coverage, that agents demonstrate knowledge of long-term care insurance, and that insurers establish marketing procedures to assure fair and accurate comparisons of products.[25] A survey for the Health Insurance Association of America found that very few states had adopted these provisions as of July 1992.[26]

Additional proposals to curb marketing abuses have been made. Many of these, such as more training of agents, including long-term care in the exam that agents must take to be licensed to sell general life and health insurance, and even increasing criminal penalties for violation of marketing standards, have relatively wide support.[27] Both the current NAIC standards and these proposals are hard to enforce, however, because they attempt to control behavior that occurs in private between the agent and the potential policyholder.

The most controversial proposal would limit the amount of the commissions agents could receive on sales of new policies, most commonly to 200 percent of renewal commissions. In an analysis of five insurance companies accounting for 50 percent of the individual private long-term care insurance market, the General Accounting Office found that the average commission on a new policy was about 60 percent of the premium, with a range from 45 to 70 percent.[28] Advocates of restructuring agent commissions argue that the existing structure creates strong incentives for agents to make inappropriate first-year sales and to be indifferent to subsequent renewals.[29] Agents maximize their income by having policyholders switch policies frequently, even though insureds may have to pay higher premiums because they are older. Opponents of regulatory controls argue that the difficulty of selling private long-term care insurance warrants a high commission and that agents simply will not be motivated to sell this product without substantial compensation.[30] Although the number of policies sold might decline, a modest restructuring is probably desirable to address the problem of short-term lapses.

## OTHER ISSUES: FINANCIAL STATUS OF COMPANIES AND POLICY UPGRADES

Two other important regulatory issues are the financial status of insurance companies and the availability of insurance policy upgrades. Selling long-term care insurance is a financially risky venture, with a potential for losses that may be substantial and not apparent for many years into the future. The question is whether companies are capable of accepting the financial risk.

An analysis by the Health Insurance Association of America of companies selling private long-term care insurance suggests that these companies are, on average, in good financial condition.[31] More than a quarter of these companies had financial holdings of less than $25 million in 1991, however, raising the question whether these insurers could survive if their claims experience turned sour. Although company solvency is a general concern of state insurance commissioners, regulations that specifically address the financial status of companies selling long-term care insurance are lacking.

In addition, as policies have evolved, a significant issue is how to protect consumers who bought policies containing restrictions that are now or will soon be outmoded. Some companies do offer policyholders the chance to upgrade policies without further medical underwriting, but regulators have not yet addressed whether all consumers should have the right to upgrade to a better policy without reassessment.

## Federal Regulation of Long-Term Care Insurance

There is debate over which level of government—state or federal—should set standards for long-term care insurance. On one hand, the federal government can set stricter standards and reduce variation in state regulation. Despite regulatory progress, the current NAIC model embodies relatively minimal standards, which do not guarantee high-quality policies. In addition, there is no guarantee that individual states will incorporate the NAIC standards into their own requirements. For example, according to one analysis, twenty-two states had adopted fewer than twelve of the fifteen key NAIC provisions as of July 1992.[32] Proponents of federal regulation also argue that it is inefficient for insurers to modify policies to meet individual state requirements. Long-term care insurance is provided mostly by large companies who sell in more than one state. Finally, the regulation of medigap policies sets a precedent for federal regulation of insurance products marketed to the elderly.

On the other hand, federal intervention may create its own problems. The federal government may prove more rigid than the NAIC in adapting to inevitable changes in regulatory issues. For example, lapse rates and differences in ADL measures were barely perceived as serious problems just a few years ago. Further, the development of federal standards does not guarantee that more adequate resources for enforcement will be made available at either the state or federal level. The result of federal intervention may be a set of impressive standards with uneven compliance and enforcement.

Despite possible drawbacks, federal regulation of long-term care is probably an inevitable by-product of the strong likelihood of national standards for acute care insurance. There are three broad options for federal involvement. First, the federal government could adopt a voluntary certification strategy with standards much like the current NAIC Long-Term Care Model Statute and Regulation. This approach, similar to the original medigap regulatory strategy, would not impose substantial new requirements, but it would bring all policies up to minimally acceptable levels.[33] The advantage of this approach is that some states would upgrade their requirements and some insurers might upgrade their policies to meet these higher standards, improving the average product. It would also establish the principle of federal involvement, opening the door to raising the minimum standards in the future. This approach, however, could mislead consumers into thinking that policies with the "government stamp of approval" were high-quality policies. In addition, as more states adopt the NAIC Model Act and Regulation, this intervention may not add a great deal to what would have occurred under the current state-run system.

Second, the federal government could adopt a voluntary certification strategy that set such stringent standards that few policies currently on the market could meet them. Under this scenario, policies not meeting this standard could still be sold so long as they met state regulatory standards, but they could not claim to deserve a "government seal of approval." The advantage of this approach is that any policies that met the standards would truly deserve recognition as high-quality products. The standards would send a strong message to consumers and insurers about what constitutes a good policy. If, however, the voluntary standards are set so high that they are considered irrelevant by insurers, they may not have much of an influence on policy design.

Finally, the federal government could strengthen the NAIC standards substantially and then require all insurers to meet them; states could exceed these minimum standards if they wished. This is the approach President Clinton has proposed, and it is similar to the medigap regulatory strategy embodied in the Omnibus Budget Reconciliation Act of 1990. Its advantage is that all policies will be of good quality. Some in the insurance industry will regard the upgraded standards as unduly intrusive, but the bulk of the necessary additions are critical to making sure that benefits are not illusory. The risk of this approach is that insurers might decide that the compliance costs are too high and drop out of the market altogether. In addition, some consumers may find the cost of the improved policies too high, and lower-cost (and lower-quality) policies would no longer be available. Additional problems may arise if a good mechanism is not provided for modifying the regulations as new issues arise.

## Conclusion

Companies that write private long-term care insurance and the state insurance regulators who regulate it are handicapped by lack of experience with how the insured and the long-term care delivery system will respond to insurance. Both companies and regulators face a trade-off between protecting consumer interests and encouraging a financially risky product.

During the last five years the quality of private long-term care insurance policies has improved markedly, as has the stringency of state regulation of these policies. Unfortunately, many states have failed to upgrade their regulations to protect consumers. The private long-term care insurance market is now mature enough so that more than bare bones national standards should be adopted. Proper resolution of almost all of the principal regulatory issues discussed in this chapter is essential to ensuring that consumers actually get the benefits they think they are purchasing. With the exception of inflation protection, the proposal offered by the Clinton administration addresses all of these issues.

## Chapter Six

# Public Strategies: Liberalized Medicaid

Medicaid, the federal-state health care program for the poor, is the predominant source of financing for long-term care services in the United States. Approximately 35 percent of the more than $75 billion spent on nursing home and home care for the elderly in 1993 was paid by the medicaid program.[1] One third of all medicaid spending goes for long-term care, and much of that is spent on nursing homes, where the program finances at least part of the care for approximately three-fifths of all nursing home residents.[2]

Several reforms would improve the operation of the medicaid program in behalf of the elderly while retaining its basic character as a welfare program. Desirable changes include expanding coverage of nonmedical home care, increasing the amount of income and assets that patients and their spouses can retain and still be eligible for medicaid, and increasing reimbursement rates. These "liberalizing" reforms, all of which were proposed by the U.S. Bipartisan Commission on Comprehensive Health Care (Pepper Commission),[3] need not be introduced all at once but could be phased in gradually.

Although medicaid reform could stand alone, it is also a necessary complement in all but the most comprehensive public long-term care insurance program. Several proposals to cover long-term care through social insurance leave at least some nursing home and home care use uncovered. For upper-income and some middle-income patients, either private long-term care insurance or personal resources might fill the gaps. Others must continue to rely on medicaid. If the personal needs allowance and asset tests of medicaid are not liberalized, the goal of preventing people from impoverishing themselves when they require nursing home or home care would be defeated. Easing the means test, however, will expand the fraction of long-term care users who will be touched by the welfare system.

## The Existing System

Many policymakers and analysts decry the large role that long-term care plays in the medicaid budget, saying it was unintended. That role, however, is consistent with the program's historical antecedents and legislative intent. Federal support for nursing home care for the elderly poor actually predates medicaid, going back to the Social Security Amendments of 1950. The direct antecedent of medicaid was the Kerr-Mills medical assistance program, which was developed in 1960 specifically to provide medical care to the "deserving elderly."[4] In fact, the House-Senate conference report for the 1965 social security amendments establishing medicaid refers to the program as a means to provide a "more effective Kerr-Mills medical assistance program for the aged and to extend its provisions to additional needy persons."[5]

Medicaid represents a state-federal partnership, where each shares in both the financing and policymaking.[6] On the financing side, the federal government's percentage of expenditures is based on the state's per capita personal income relative to the nation as a whole, with the federal government picking up at least 50 percent of total expenditures.[7] Overall the federal government pays about 57 percent of the total medicaid bill.[8] Although states determine the methods and rates of reimbursement (within certain federal guidelines), most states use prospective payment mechanisms for both nursing homes and hospitals, and rate schedules for physicians.[9]

To receive matching funds from the federal government, states are required to provide a basic package of acute and long-term care services to federally determined populations.[10] The mandatory services include nursing home care and home health care for those who require nursing home-level care. At their option, however, states can also extend a more comprehensive set of services to a broader population and still receive matching funds. There is considerable variation across states in the kinds of optional long-term care services that are available.[11]

Medicaid eligibility requirements for long-term care are extremely complex and differ depending on whether the applicant resides in a nursing home or in the community. The nursing home eligibility criteria are remarkably uniform across states. Whether they need services at home or in a nursing home, unmarried people are not eligible for medicaid if they have more than $2,000 in assets, generally not counting the value of the home.[12] The asset limits for married couples, one of whom still lives at home, were liberalized under the Medicare Catastrophic Coverage Act of 1988; a spouse of a nursing home resident may now keep substantially more of the couple's income and assets than was previously permitted.[13] Meeting the asset limits by transferring assets to other parties at less than market value is strictly prohibited.

Nursing home patients who meet the asset test must contribute all of their income toward the cost of care, after deducting a small allowance (usually $30 a month) to pay for personal items. Only then will medicaid help pay the bills. Most states permit people with relatively high incomes to qualify for medicaid if they meet the asset test and if their medical expenses exceed their income. In some states, however, individuals with income above a set amount—usually 300 percent of the supplemental security income (SSI) level, which was $1,302 a month in 1993—are ineligible, regardless of how high their medical expenses may be.[14] SSI is the cash welfare program for the aged, blind, and disabled.

Elderly living on their own or with friends or family generally become eligible for medicaid in two ways. First and most common, people whose income and assets are low enough to qualify for the SSI program also qualify for medicaid, although the so-called 209(b) states may apply stricter eligibility requirements.[15] Second, most states have "medically needy" programs that allow people with higher levels of income to qualify for medicaid if, after deducting their medical expenses, their incomes are below the "medically needy income level."[16] Relatively few noninstitutionalized elderly qualify for medicaid this way.[17]

## Rationale for a Means-Tested Program

Several arguments can be made for continuing to rely on the means-tested medicaid program to finance long-term care rather than turn to more comphensive public social insurance programs. First, undergirding the historical use of means-tested programs is the belief that individuals (and their families), not society at large, should bear the responsibility for taking care of their own long-term care needs.[18] In this formulation, the principal virtue of means-tested strategies is their ability to target the most needy. Second, the correspondingly lower relative government costs resulting from this targeting will also have fewer negative economic effects than non-means-tested public programs. The third major advantage of staying with a means-tested approach is that it may be more politically feasible to liberalize gradually an already existing program than to enact new, more comprehensive (and expensive) strategies.

## TARGETING THE MOST NEEDY

The most compelling argument for means-testing is that it targets expenditures to those people with the greatest financial need. Distributing additional public monies to populations who are most "at risk" is the most cost-effective strategy in times of high budget deficits and scarce public resources.[19] Indeed, advocates of limiting government financing of long-term care to means-tested approaches argue that it is inequitable to tax low- and moderate-income nonelderly to pay for benefits provided to upper-income elderly.[20] No legitimate government interest, they argue, is served by using public dollars to protect the financial assets and incomes of people who can afford to pay for services on their own.

Moreover, there is little need to preserve assets to help finance future community living because so few nursing home patients ever return home.[21] Supporters of a medicaid strategy contend that protecting the financial assets of the elderly so that they can be passed on to adult children is not a health policy issue but an estate planning issue that is more appropriately addressed through private insurance rather than public sector programs.[22] This is especially true given the myriad competing demands for state and federal funds.

Proponents of a means-tested approach also note that medicaid's institutional bias ensures that those receiving publicly financed care are predominantly the severely disabled and those without family support. Additionally, because medicaid covers primarily nursing home care and not home care, the risk of uncontrolled demand is lessened. It has been argued that the demand for the less medical, more social components of home care, if provided under any insurance scheme (public or private), would be so great that the use and costs of these services would be hard to control.[23] Medicaid provides only a moderate level of home care services.

## LOWER RELATIVE COSTS

As previously noted, medicaid-sponsored nursing home residents must contribute virtually all of their assets and income toward the cost of care before medicaid begins paying. This stringent eligibility criterion means that a medicaid-centered approach to financing long-term care is the least expensive of all public strategies. Liberalizing the medicaid program could be accomplished at a relatively low additional cost to taxpayers—at least compared with social insurance proposals. The more modest cost of these changes makes the new taxes or spending cuts necessary to pay for the changes, as required by the Budget Enforcement Act of 1990, more politically palatable.[24] In addition, this strategy would be expected to have fewer negative effects on economic growth or national savings.[25] Proponents of a medicaid strategy argue that, by keeping public costs down, private savings can be encouraged in various ways and that long-term care is precisely the type of activity for which savings should be used.

**BUILDING ON AN EXISTING SYSTEM**

Finally, as an incremental change, medicaid liberalization has a greater chance of being enacted than does more comprehensive reform.[26] That is, there is significant room for reform between the abject poverty currently necessary to qualify for medicaid and the most comprehensive social insurance program. Improvements in medicaid can be passed incrementally, with the support of advocates of both public and private insurance.[27] For example, although opposed to social insurance for long-term care, the Health Insurance Association of America supports raising the level of protected assets for medicaid nursing home patients.[28]

Moreover, because medicaid reform would build on an existing administrative system, implementation of most of the proposed liberalizations would be relatively easy and could be put in place quickly. Long-term care is primarily the responsibility of the states; administration and policymaking expertise is located at the local level. States, much more than the federal government, regulate the supply and quality of care, set reimbursement rates, and process the claims of nursing homes and home care agencies. Furthermore, by utilizing state-level agencies, local preferences, circumstances, and styles of care can be more easily accommodated.

## Drawbacks of a Means-Tested Program

Although improvements to medicaid would make it a more humane program, relying exclusively on a welfare-based reform strategy has several disadvantages. First, because medicaid helps to fund care only for those people who have already depleted much of their income and assets, it cannot prevent the elderly from incurring catastrophic costs. Second, because many elderly cannot afford the costs of a nursing home stay, medicaid has become a welfare program on which the majority, rather than the minority, rely. Third, some stigma may attach to receipt of medicaid long-term care, as it does to the receipt of benefits under other welfare programs. Fourth, public support for means-tested programs is usually no more than lukewarm. Fifth, partly because of the political unpopularity of welfare programs, politicians are always trying to hold down the costs of medicaid to the taxpayer. This in turn perpetuates a two-class system of long-term care, with medicaid recipients having inferior access to care of highly variable quality. Finally, because benefits are available only to the impoverished, a perverse incentive exists to hide or dispose of wealth in order to qualify.

## INABILITY TO PREVENT CATASTROPHIC OUT-OF-POCKET COSTS

Because medicare, supplemental private insurance, and the acute care medicaid program cover most expenses associated with acute illness, the principal causes of catastrophic out-of-pocket expenses for the elderly are long-term care and prescription drugs.[29] In 1981, for example, prescription drugs accounted for more than half of the total health care expenses incurred by disabled elderly persons who spent more than 10 percent of their income on out-of-pocket health care expenses. Nursing home expenditures represented between 20 and 30 percent of total out-of-pocket spending for this group.[30] The proportion of spending on nursing home care grew as the financial burden of out-of-pocket health expenditures increased. Medicaid cannot prevent these catastrophic costs because, by definition, individuals are not eligible for medicaid until they have incurred catastrophic out-of-pocket expenses that they can no longer pay.

## THE MANY, NOT THE FEW

An underlying assumption of American welfare programs, such as SSI and aid to families with dependent children (AFDC), is that only a relatively small proportion of the population will need public assistance. To avoid large-scale dependence on welfare for income security and acute health care for the elderly, American society has turned to social insurance programs—social security and medicare. Consequently, in 1993 only an estimated 6.7 percent of the elderly received income assistance from SSI,[31] and less than 13 percent of the elderly relied on medicaid to help pay for their medical care.[32] Yet, when it comes to long-term care, the elderly routinely end up on welfare in the form of medicaid. Indeed, in January 1987, 61 percent of nursing home residents were receiving medicaid.[33] On average nursing home care costs almost $37,000 a year, a sum that relatively few elderly can afford to pay solely out of current income.[34]

Thus, the need for nursing home services will force a significant number of people who have been financially independent all their lives to depend on welfare.[35] The elderly beneficiaries of medicaid include the middle class as well as the very poor.

## WELFARE STIGMA

Proponents of universal social insurance programs for long-term care often argue that means-tested strategies result in an undeniable welfare stigma. Even with more liberal income and asset standards, they assert, medicaid is still welfare, and welfare almost always includes some stigma for the recipient. Welfare stigma manifests itself in two ways: recipients may lack self-respect, or others may have little respect for recipients.[36]

Although welfare stigma undoubtedly applies to some degree to long-term care patients who receive medicaid, the actual extent of the problem is unknown. Surprisingly little empirical research has been done on welfare stigma in general and, to our knowledge, none at all on the use of medicaid long-term care services.[37] Based on fragmentary evidence on other programs for the elderly, it seems likely that less stigma is associated with medicaid and long-term care than is often assumed.

First, among recipients of means-tested benefits, programs for the aged and disabled appear to be less stigmatizing than those for working-age people with no disabilities. Indeed, most welfare stigma applies to AFDC and, to a lesser extent, food stamp recipients.[38] SSI is conceptually no different from AFDC, yet, based on public opinion surveys, less stigma appears to attach to receipt of SSI than AFDC.[39] Society does not hold people responsible for conditions felt to be beyond their control—such as aging and disability. Conversely, welfare dependence among people of working age is often felt to be a personal failure and to reflect a lack of effort rather than circumstances beyond a person's control.[40]

Second, less stigma is associated with programs such as medicaid that provide in-kind benefits than with cash assistance programs such as AFDC. Fewer Americans accept the concept of a right to income than support the right to the necessities income might buy.[41] Furthermore, the public's belief that a significant amount of fraud and abuse occurs in cash assistance programs contributes to the negative characteristics ascribed to recipients.[42]

Third, the fact that some people may actually transfer or shelter assets in order to become eligible for medicaid suggests that the stigmatizing effects of receipt of medicaid long-term care may not be significant. Finally, as many as 45 percent of the elderly in nursing homes and 28 percent of disabled elderly in the community suffer from Alzheimer's disease or other cognitive impairments and consequently have limited awareness of where or who they are, let alone the nature of who pays for their services. This potentially reduces the importance of welfare stigma, although it may be of great concern to relatives and friends of the disabled person.[43]

### LIMITED PUBLIC SUPPORT

An issue perhaps more important than welfare stigma is whether means-tested programs such as medicaid can garner the public and political support needed to sustain them. Ironically, although "enactability" is supposed to be a strong suit of proposals that would make incremental changes in the medicaid program, public opinion polls suggest only meager support for means-tested approaches, especially when compared with the broader social insurance programs.[44] Programs such as medicaid, AFDC, and food stamps—all means-tested programs aimed at lower-income, largely nonelderly people—enjoy little public support.[45] Moreover, a review of several hundred public opinion surveys conducted over the last half century suggests that Americans consistently show less support for welfare-based health programs than for health care programs with broad coverage.[46] As one observer noted, "the more public programs are perceived by members of the wider society as benefiting only certain groups, the less support those programs receive."[47]

Any efforts to improve the long-term care component of the medicaid program also may be impeded by what has been described as America's misunderstanding about welfare.[48] The one program that most Americans generally equate with "welfare"—AFDC—accounts for only 12 percent of all means-tested aid. Yet the public has transferred its general misgivings and misperceptions about this program to other means-tested programs.[49] Thus, the policies for expanding public financing of long-term care that are potentially the easiest to enact because they are the least costly are the ones that have the least public support.

## COMPETING PROGRAMS AND UNDEDICATED FUNDING

Medicaid is the most politically vulnerable vehicle for financing long-term care because it must compete with other programs for general revenues at both the federal and state levels. States must constantly struggle to balance the federal mandates for expanded medicaid coverage against no new federal funds for the program and the need to fund a wide range of other state programs.[50] In the 1980s medicaid was the fastest-growing state program, accounting for about 14 percent of all state spending in 1990, up from 9 percent in 1980.[51] Critics of an expanded medicaid program for long-term care also question whether dedicating such a large portion of the nation's antipoverty budget to medical care might not jeopardize the effectiveness of other programs intended to improve the well-being of welfare recipients.

## INCENTIVE TO APPEAR POOR

In the last few years, policymakers and the media have focused attention on the growing number of middle- and upper-income elderly who transfer, shelter, and underreport assets in order to appear poor and therefore gain medicaid eligibility for nursing home care.[52] Although this practice has allegedly been going on for years, many now believe that it has reached epidemic proportions. Federal law and regulation specifically prohibit transfer of assets at less than market value for thirty-six months before one applies for medicaid benefits, but these restrictions can be circumvented in numerous ways.[53]

Debate over the propriety of these transfers has been quite strident. Defenders of the practice insist that transferring or sheltering assets to qualify for medicaid is morally indistinguishable from using the tax code to avoid paying estate taxes.[54] Moreover, the disabled elderly who do not want their life savings totally destroyed by the costs of long-term care and who want to leave some inheritance to their spouse and children have few alternatives.

Opponents of transfers respond that medicaid is meant only for those who really need it and that manipulating loopholes to gain eligibility is a perversion of the program's intent.[55] Moreover, they argue that money that goes to artificially eligible nursing home patients is money that cannot be spent on medicaid services for low-income children and non-elderly adults. Some observers also worry that publicity about asset transfers will negatively affect the "moral color" of the debate on long-term care reform. After all, if long-term care reform is only about protecting the assets of the well-to-do, then there is not likely to be much of a constituency for change.

While the debate rages over the morality and legality of these asset transfers, there are few data on which to judge the size of the problem. Did a substantial portion of the roughly 1.4 million elderly medicaid nursing home patients transfer substantial amounts of assets in order to prematurely qualify for medicaid? This question cannot be answered definitively, but the available data suggest that the answer is no.

The only direct quantitative study of asset transfer was done in Massachusetts by the U.S. General Accounting Office (GAO). Massachusetts was chosen, in part, because asset transfers were thought to be widespread there. GAO found that about one in every eight applicants in their sample transferred assets within the time period prohibited by medicaid. About one-third of all these transfers totaled $10,000 or less. Moreover, in about half the cases, medicaid eligibility was denied so there was no cost to the government.[56]

More indirect evidence also suggests that asset transfer is not as widespread as commonly thought. First, the disabled elderly population overall has disproportionately low income and little in the way of financial assets to transfer.[57] Some do have substantial housing assets, but these are generally excluded from medicaid financial eligibility criteria. According to data from the Survey of Income and Program Participation, among the disabled population aged 75 and older, who constitute a large majority of nursing home patients, 86 percent have less than $15,000 in annual per capita income and about 57 percent have less than $10,000 in financial assets (in 1989 dollars).[58] In fact, less than 10 percent have the level of financial assets ($100,000 or more) considered typical of estate planners' clients.

Second, if an increasing number of the elderly are transferring their assets to qualify for medicaid benefits, then the number of medicaid nursing home recipients should be rising rapidly. In fact, the number grew by less than 2 percent a year between 1984 and 1992, a rate consistent with the growth in the nursing home population.[59] Moreover, the liberalization of medicaid eligibility in 1988 for married nursing home patients could account for virtually all of the increase. Thus, while the transfer of assets has undoubtedly been increasing, it is apparently not increasing as much as is generally assumed.

## REDUCED ACCESS AND QUALITY

Lack of broad political support for medicaid and for the spending increases it has required puts states under constant pressure to hold down medicaid expenditures for long-term care.[60] Because medicaid helps pay for the care of three-fifths of nursing home residents, states have considerable influence over the supply of and reimbursement rates for nursing home beds and other services. Both influence the degree to which medicaid patients have access to services and the quality of the care they receive.

Nursing homes generally give admission preference to private-pay over medicaid patients,[61] in large part because medicaid payment rates are 18 to 30 percent below the rates that private patients pay.[62] Most nursing homes are for-profit businesses and maximize their profits by admitting medicaid patients only after all private-pay patients have been served. The nursing home industry contends that medicaid reimbursement rates are so low that the very viability of the industry is threatened.[63] In addition, the medicaid payment process is often slow and the paperwork and regulatory requirements burdensome.[64] Some observers speculate that certain social characteristics of medicaid clients might also make them less desirable to providers.[65]

Although medicaid patients have less ready access to services than do private-pay patients, it does not follow that they have no access. Indeed, approximately 35 percent of nursing home entrants are eligible for medicaid at admission.[66] Moreover, some analysts argue that the inferior access available to medicaid patients motivates people to avoid welfare and to buy private insurance.[67]

The care medicaid patients receive is also widely believed to be of inferior quality, especially in homes where medicaid supports a large percentage of the residents. The assumption is either that medicaid payments are insufficient to pay for high-quality care or that quality suffers when homes are not competing for the more lucrative private patients.[68]

Despite these widespread beliefs, the empirical evidence to prove them is less clear cut. A review of the literature by the Institute of

Medicine suggests that, issues of measuring quality aside, the relationship between quality and payment policy is "highly variable and somewhat unpredictable."[69] There is even disagreement about whether private-pay clients receive the same or better care than medicaid patients in the same nursing home.[70]

The issue of the adequacy of medicaid reimbursement rates (and concomitant concerns about access and quality) has not gone totally unaddressed by policymakers. For example, federal law establishes a theoretical floor on medicaid rates for nursing homes, requiring that they be "reasonable and adequate to meet the costs of efficiently and economically operated facilities."[71] Recent amendments require that states take into account the cost of services necessary to provide the "highest practicable" well-being of its residents.[72] In addition, in 1990 the Supreme Court made clear that providers can sue states over the adequacy of medicaid reimbursement rates.[73] Since then providers in more than a dozen states have brought lawsuits challenging the adequacy of medicaid reimbursement rates for nursing homes.[74]

## Simulation Assumptions and Results

To understand the effects that liberalizing the existing medicaid program would have, we modeled a program that retains medicaid's basic structure but makes changes in financial eligibility standards (income and assets), personal needs allowance, and service coverage (figure 6-1).

Under this liberalized medicaid system, the level of protected assets would be increased to $30,000 for individuals and $60,000 for married couples, and the personal needs allowance would be set at $100 a month.[75] The income allowance for the community-based spouse of a nursing home patient would be set at 200 percent of the poverty level for couples. Otherwise, medicaid nursing home benefits would be unchanged.

State medicaid programs would be expanded to cover a broad array of nonskilled services. People who meet the asset requirements for nursing home patients would be eligible for these services if their income is not greater than 150 percent of the poverty level, an increase over the exisiting eligibility rules. To qualify for these benefits, a person would have to meet the financial requirements and have two or more deficiencies in the activities of daily living or have substantial cognitive impairment. Private insurance would be available to those who can afford it.

FIGURE 6-1.  **Simulation Assumptions for Liberalized Medicaid**

MEDICAID

- *Nursing home eligibility.* The personal needs allowance is increased to $100 a month. The level of protected assets is increased to $30,000 for individuals and $60,000 for couples excluding the home, which is always a protected asset. The income allowance for a spouse in the community is set at 200 percent of the poverty level for couples.

- *Home care eligibility.* Individuals qualify if their income is 150 percent of the poverty level. The level of protected assets same as for nursing home care.

- *Home care benefits.*[a] Benefits are unlimited with no cost-sharing for severely disabled.[b] Benefits for less disabled are the same as medicaid benefits under current system.

PRIVATE INSURANCE[c]

- People buy what they can afford. Affordability is age-related and is based on premiums as a percentage of income and minimum financial assets. The policy lapses if premiums exceed 20 percent of income.

- Persons with IADL or ADL problems cannot purchase private insurance.

- Policies are available covering two or four year each of nursing home and home care with a sixty-day deductible for nursing home care, and a thirty-visit deductible for home care.

MEDICARE AND OTHER PROGRAMS

- Existing skilled nursing home and home care benefits under medicare are retained.

- Home care under social services block grant, state-only funding, and other programs is retained.

a. Home care demand is assumed to increase at least 20 percent.
b. "Severely disabled" is defined as two or more ADL deficiencies or cognitive impairment.
c. For people with private insurance, induced demand is assumed to be 25 percent for nursing home care and 90 percent for home care.

Medicare nursing home and home health benefits would not change, nor would other government home care programs.

Table 6-1 and figure 6-2 show that medicaid liberalization would cost federal and state governments an additional $6.0 billion in 1993 and $4.3 billion in 2018. Despite the efforts to bring more balance to the delivery system, this medicaid liberalization strategy would not improve the ratio of public spending for home care to nursing home care, but would actually worsen it slightly.[a] Because this reform strategy is, by definition, means-tested, it is not surprising that the vast majority of incremental expenditures would go to the low-income population.

a. Presumably, a better balance could be obtained either by lowering the medicaid income and asset protection levels or by expanding the population eligible for home care.

TABLE 6-1. *Total Expenditures for Nursing Home and Home Care, by Source of Payment, Base Case and Medicaid Liberalization, Selected Periods*
Billions of 1993 dollars

| | 1993 | | | 2018 | | |
|---|---|---|---|---|---|---|
| Payment source | Base case | Liberalized medicaid | Percentage change | Base case | Liberalized medicaid | Percentage change |
| Total long-term care expenditures | 75.3 | 76.8 | 2 | 168.3 | 174.7 | 4 |
| Nursing home | | | | | | |
| Medicaid | 22.4 | 26.4 | 18 | 49.0 | 52.5 | 7 |
| Medicare | 4.3 | 4.3 | 1 | 10.0 | 10.0 | 0 |
| Private insurance | 0.0 | 1.3 | . . . | 0.0 | 15.6 | . . . |
| Family cash | 17.0 | 14.3 | −16 | 42.6 | 33.9 | −20 |
| Family assets | 11.0 | 7.7 | −30 | 26.6 | 19.9 | −25 |
| TOTAL | 54.7 | 54.0 | −1 | 128.2 | 131.9 | 3 |
| Home care | | | | | | |
| Medicaid | 3.6 | 6.1 | 67 | 5.2 | 6.7 | 30 |
| Medicare | 9.4 | 9.4 | 0 | 19.0 | 19.0 | 0 |
| Other payers[a] | 2.2 | 1.7 | −23 | 4.3 | 3.6 | −16 |
| Private insurance | 0.0 | 0.5 | . . . | 0.0 | 2.5 | . . . |
| Out-of-pocket | 5.5 | 5.1 | −8 | 11.6 | 10.9 | −6 |
| TOTAL | 20.7 | 22.7 | 10 | 40.1 | 42.7 | 7 |

SOURCE: Brookings-ICF Long-Term Care Financing Model. In this and other tables and figures in this chapter, 1993 represents the five-year average for the period 1991–95; 2018 represents the five-year average for the period 2016–20.

a. Other payers include state and local expenditures, social service block grants, Older Americans Act and Department of Veterans' Affairs home care funds, charity, and out-of-pocket expenditures by people other than the service recipient.

Nearly two-thirds of incremental public nursing home expenditures in 1993 and 30 percent in 2018 would be spent on patients with incomes below $20,000 (table 6-2). Virtually all of the incremental expenditures in 1993 and 90 percent in 2018 would be for patients with incomes under $40,000.

Medicaid liberalization allows long-term care users to keep more of their income and assets, but at the price of having more persons rely on welfare. Compared with the base case, the number of medicaid nursing home patients would increase by 7.1 percent in 1993 and 10 percent in 2018 (figure 6-3).

Table 6-3 shows that average out-of-pocket expenditures for nursing home care under medicaid liberalization would decrease from approximately $44,000 in the base case to $35,000 in 2018, and the proportion of nursing home admissions who spend more than $20,000 out of pocket for nursing home care would decrease from 33 percent to 28 percent. Moreover, the proportion of nursing home admissions who spend more than 40 percent of their income and financial assets on nursing home care would decline from 39 percent to 31 percent in 2018.

FIGURE 6-2. **Annual Public Expenditures for Long-Term Care, Base Case and Medicaid Liberalization, Selected Periods**[a]

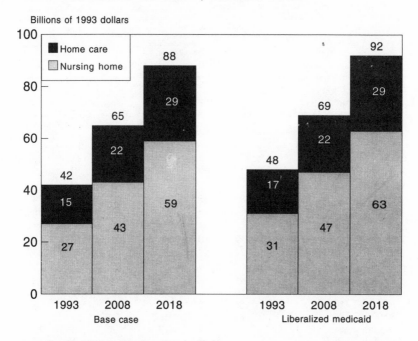

Billions of 1993 dollars

SOURCE:: Brookings-ICF Long-Term Care Financing Model.
   a. Here and in figure 6-3, the year 2008 represents the five-year average for the period 2006–10.

Finally, medicaid liberalization is very target-efficient, with 76 percent of incremental public expenditures being spent on persons who would have incurred catastrophic out-of-pocket costs under the existing system of financing.

## Conclusion

Despite the fiscal constraints of federal and state budgets, medicaid makes good use of its public funding. It meets the most urgent needs of the low-income disabled population at the lowest possible public cost. Although targeted to the poor, medicaid also provides a safety net for middle-income people with high long-term care expenses. The cost of medicaid expansion to taxpayers is comparatively small, with spend-down requirements ensuring that the program finances only that part of the care that is beyond the resources of the elderly. The institutional bias guarantees that persons receiving publicly financed care are pre-dominantly the severely disabled and those without family support. And

TABLE 6-2. *Public Expenditures for Nursing Home Care, by Demographic and Income Groups, Base Case and Medicaid Liberalization, Selected Periods*[a]
*Percent unless otherwise noted*

| | 1993 | | | 2018 | | |
|---|---|---|---|---|---|---|
| | | Liberalized medicaid expenditures | | | Liberalized medicaid expenditures | |
| Patient characteristics | Base case | Total | Incremental | Base case | Total | Incremental |
| Public nursing home expenditures (billions of 1993 dollars)[b] | 33.6 | 37.8 | 4.2 | 64.2 | 68.5 | 4.2 |
| Age | | | | | | |
| 65–74 | 20 | 20 | 20 | 15 | 17 | 33 |
| 75–84 | 34 | 35 | 42 | 32 | 33 | 48 |
| 85 and older | 46 | 45 | 39 | 52 | 50 | 19 |
| Marital status | | | | | | |
| Married | 33 | 35 | 45 | 30 | 33 | 74 |
| Unmarried | 67 | 65 | 55 | 70 | 67 | 26 |
| Gender | | | | | | |
| Men | 29 | 30 | 39 | 30 | 32 | 55 |
| Women | 71 | 70 | 61 | 70 | 68 | 45 |
| Income (dollars) | | | | | | |
| Under 7,500 | 31 | 28 | 11 | 19 | 18 | 6 |
| 7,500–14,999 | 40 | 39 | 28 | 33 | 32 | 18 |
| 15,000–19,999 | 11 | 12 | 24 | 14 | 13 | 6 |
| 20,000–29,999 | 13 | 15 | 28 | 20 | 21 | 39 |
| 30,000–39,999 | 3 | 3 | 7 | 7 | 8 | 20 |
| 40,000–49,999 | 1 | 1 | 1 | 3 | 4 | 11 |
| 50,000 and above | 2 | 2 | 0 | 4 | 4 | −1 |

SOURCE: Brookings-ICF Long-Term Care Financing Model.
a. These data are based on the public expenditures on behalf of an admission cohort over the entire length of the nursing home stay.
b. Public expenditures are medicare and medicaid.

home care services, although not as widespread as many would like, are moderately available. In addition, the entitlement nature of medicaid means that expenditures rise with need and are not limited arbitrarily by the appropriation process.

Continued use of the medicaid system would also take advantage of states' knowledge and experience in long-term care and would permit flexibility in fashioning a system most suitable to unique state populations and communities. In addition, because it is a currently operating program already heavily involved in long-term care, medicaid is a reasonable vehicle for making incremental changes. Aside from whether a means-tested strategy is the best policy, there is the question of political feasibility. Modest medicaid reform is far less costly to the public purse than any social insurance proposal and, therefore, more likely to be considered affordable.

FIGURE 6-3. **Number of Medicaid Nursing Home Patients, Base Case and Medicaid Liberalization, Selected Periods[a]**

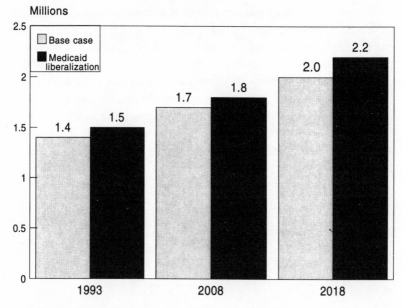

SOURCE:: Brookings-ICF Long-Term Care Financing Model.
a. Nursing home patients who are financed by medicaid at any time during the year.

TABLE 6-3. *Effect of Medicaid Liberalization on Catastrophic Out-of-Pocket Expenditures for Nursing Home Care, 2018*

| Measure | Base case | Medicaid liberalization |
|---|---|---|
| Absolute expenditure[a] | | |
| Average out-of-pocket spending (thousands of 1993 dollars) | 44 | 35 |
| Percentage of admissions spending more than $20,000 out of pocket | 33 | 28 |
| Relative expenditure[b] | | |
| Percentage of admissions spending more than 40 percent of income, assets on care | 39 | 31 |
| Target efficiency[c] | | |
| Percentage of incremental spending for people who would otherwise have incurred catastrophic out-of-pocket costs | . . . | 76 |

SOURCE: Brookings-ICF Long-Term Care Financing Model.
a. These data are based on the total out-of-pocket payments for an admission cohort over the entire length of the nursing home stay.
b. The numerator is equal to the out-of-pocket contribution to nursing home care for the entire length of stay; the denominator is equal to income during the stay plus nonhousing assets.
c. These data are based on incremental public expenditures for an admission cohort for the entire length of stay. In 2018 incremental public spending for medicaid liberalization is $4.2 billion.

These are powerful arguments for staying with medicaid as the primary public program for financing long-term care. But there are serious drawbacks as well. Even if all the improvements that have been suggested were made, medicaid would still be a means-tested program that places the burden of needing care on the individual. Most of the medicaid program's problems are directly related to the fact that it is a welfare program.[76] At a minimum, fixing all that is wrong with medicaid would be costly, and to be eligible recipients would still have to impoverish themselves (albeit to a lesser extent) or hide assets in order to appear poor. Even in an improved form, medicaid would lack dedicated funding and perhaps broad political support, and it would likely perpetuate a two-class system.

## Chapter Seven

# Public Strategies: Social Insurance

Another broad strategy for reforming long-term care is to cover part of its costs under a social insurance program. Indeed, most of the risks of growing older are addressed through these types of universal non-means-tested programs: income support through social security, and acute health care through medicare. The basic premise behind social insurance is that, under the auspices of the government, people are enabled or required to pool their risks for some future costly event such as medical care or retirement. Under a social insurance program, everyone pays something into the program's fund (usually through an insurance premium, an earmarked tax, or both) and then earns the right to or is entitled to benefits under specified conditions without regard to financial need. Although contributory financing and entitlement to benefits are the hallmarks of most social insurance strategies, wide variations in the design of the program are possible.

## The Rationale for Social Insurance

A social insurance approach to financing long-term care offers several advantages, including universal coverage, protection against catastrophic out-of-pocket costs, broad political support, the ability to develop a more balanced delivery system, reduction of the current two-class system of care, and the market power to negotiate favorable payment rates.

### UNIVERSAL COVERAGE

Social insurance is the only approach that guarantees universal or near-universal coverage. Social insurance covers the able-bodied and the currently disabled, the young and the old, and people of all levels of income and wealth. For example, in 1990, the social security system covered 94 percent of all employees and medicare covered 97 percent.[1] In this way, social insurance avoids the adverse selection that plagues private insurance for long-term care.[a] By including virtually everyone in the risk pool, social insurance has the ability to spread the cost over the widest possible revenue base, thereby reducing the burden any one person has to bear. Only government is big enough to socialize the risk associated with long-term care.

One key question for policymakers is how long they are willing to wait before making major changes in the way the elderly pay for their nursing home and home care. The harsh reality is that fewer than 5 percent of the elderly currently have any private long-term care insurance.[2] As a result, reliance on private insurance is a very long-range strategy that will never guarantee universal coverage. Even if all people who turned 65 in 1993 bought private long-term care insurance, this population would not require much long-term care for another twenty years. Reliance on employer-sponsored insurance, while a desirable development, would take even longer to affect who pays for nursing home and home care. Putting aside the question of whether it could actually be enacted in the near term, the social insurance approach could provide universal coverage relatively quickly in comparison with private insurance.

## PUBLIC SUPPORT FOR UNIVERSAL PROGRAMS

Because social insurance programs benefit everyone, they enjoy broad political support. Social security is overwhelmingly supported by Americans regardless of age, race, income, or political party.[3] Even though the public's confidence in the future of the social security system declined somewhat in the early to mid-1980s,[4] public support for the program has been consistently strong since its inception in the 1930s.[5] Medicare enjoys equal if not greater public favor.

---

a. Adverse selection occurs when a disproportionate number of people most in need of services buy insurance, driving up use and cost of services beyond expectations and thereby making the policy unprofitable for insurers. Private insurers try to avoid this problem by employing stringent medical underwriting criteria to screen out potentially high-cost purchasers—the group that needs coverage the most. Although insurers can reduce (but not eliminate) adverse selection by selling private insurance to people at younger ages when they tend to be healthier, only social insurance can offer coverage to the nonelderly disabled who would otherwise be prevented from obtaining private insurance.

Ironically, social security, like some of the less popular means-tested programs, redistributes money from higher-paid to lower-paid workers, but it does so in a more subtle way and without the appearance of charity.[b] Moreover, the public is more willing to believe that society as a whole benefits from social security than it is willing to believe that society benefits from income support, medical care, and food given to low-income families.[6]

Social insurance programs garner both broad political and public support owing in part to the inclusion of middle-class beneficiaries. Middle-class beneficiaries, who feel they have earned benefits because they have made contributions to the program, generally have more political power than do the poor. The magnitude of the political power wielded by middle-class constituents is most evident when issues of making cuts to any number of middle-class programs are raised.

Although cuts in the social security program have been proposed frequently since its inception, few have been made. Indeed, the history of the program is characterized by frequent increases in the benefits.[7] Even after the social security "crisis" of the early 1980s, the most significant changes had only small effects on current beneficiaries, and the the other changes, such as increases in the retirement age, were scheduled to be implemented far in the future.

Public opinion polls also show that Americans generally favor a social insurance approach to long-term care. For example, in a 1993 survey commissioned by the American Association of Retired Persons, 69 percent of those interviewed preferred a "government program of long-term care similar to medicare or social security that would provide coverage for all and be financed by everyone." Only 25 percent preferred "leaving it up to individuals to pay for private insurance, with the government providing coverage only for the very poor."[8] A Los Angeles Times poll reported that nearly two-thirds still support a social insurance strategy even when the question was couched in more specific terms of whether the program would be available to everyone regardless of wealth.[9] Support may stem, however, not from a philosophical preference, but from the recognition that only government can provide what people want at the price they are willing to pay.[10]

Public opinion polls also show a strong support for long-term care

b. The social security benefit formula is redistributive because it provides a greater return on contributions for low-salaried workers.

as one of several federal government spending priorities, even if it means higher taxes or an increased budget deficit.[11] As a rule, people appear willing to pay some additional taxes if they can see tangible benefits. Gauging what level of additional taxes Americans are willing to pay is difficult, however, and they may not be so willing to pay the necessary amount.[12] The American public does not have a good understanding of what a public long-term care insurance program would cost.

## A MORE BALANCED DELIVERY SYSTEM

Social insurance can also be used deliberately to create a more balanced delivery system by providing broad coverage of home care. Both the elderly and their families show a strong preference for home care.[13] In a recent poll, families preferred, by a large margin, that their disabled relatives remain at home, receiving care from a combination of paid providers, family, and friends.[14] Even when faced with the prospect of around-the-clock care, more than two-thirds of the respondents wanted their disabled family members to receive care in their own homes rather than go to a nursing home.[15] In a 1993 survey, when asked to choose among potential new benefits for the elderly as part of health care reform, respondents chose home care over nursing home care by about two to one.[16] This expressed preference for home care is strong even if increased home care were to raise overall program costs.[17] All of the major proposals for public long-term care insurance, including President Clinton's, offer broad coverage of home care services.[18]

## IMPROVEMENTS IN ACCESS AND QUALITY

Public long-term care insurance should mitigate the access and quality problems affecting the current financing and delivery system. Obviously, coverage of a broader range of home care services would help improve access to long-term care. Access for low-income patients would also improve because social insurance would reduce the preference providers tend to give to private-pay patients.[19] From the provider's perspective, all income classes would be economically equivalent sources of revenue. Although access by disadvantaged groups would improve under either medicaid liberalization or social insurance, the extent of the improvement would depend on the program adopted. The greater the role left for private payments, the greater the likelihood a two-class system would continue.

A potential threat to improved access would be an inadequate supply of services. Any new funding for services and reductions in the out-of-pocket cost of services to the elderly are certain to increase demand. If growth in service does not keep pace with increase in demand, improved access for lower-income and care-intensive patients could be accompanied by reduced access for other groups, such as patients who are easier to care for.

Overall quality of care should improve under a social insurance model of long-term care. This program would cover all the elderly, not just the poor. Middle- and upper-income beneficiaries are expected to have the clout to demand higher quality. That would require payment rates higher than those under medicaid so that nursing homes would have the funds necessary to upgrade services. As a result, the number of low-quality facilities should decline.

An entirely public system could, however, result in some leveling in quality of care. Extremely high-quality, high-cost facilities might move toward the average if the payment rate necessary to sustain that level of care is deemed excessive by the social insurance program. Moreover, because nursing homes would receive the same reimbursement rate for most patients, facilities would have little incentive to provide high-quality care simply to attract higher-paying private-pay patients.[20]

As the primary purchaser of long-term care services under almost any combination of social insurance and medicaid, the government would have a very large market share. Consequently, the government should use its monopsony power to negotiate favorable reimbursement rates, and providers would have little choice but to comply.[21] Whether this power to set rates would adversely affect quality of care would depend on the fiscal pressure that government agencies faced.[22]

## Arguments against Social Insurance

Opponents grant that social insurance would dramatically change the way long-term care is financed and delivered, but they argue that the benefits of such a program are not worth the cost. They make five arguments: First, social insurance programs are too expensive and will become more so with the aging of the population. Second, it is unfair to younger generations to provide another major program for the elderly. Third, because of the universal coverage, social insurance provides benefits to upper-income people who can afford to pay for their own care. Fourth, a primarily government-based program can be inflexible.

And, finally, providing health care to the uninsured is more important than providing additional long-term care to the elderly and disabled.

## SOCIAL INSURANCE IS TOO EXPENSIVE

The primary disadvantage of all of the social insurance approaches to long-term care is their expense. The relatively modest recommendations of the Pepper Commission, for example, were estimated to cost $43 billion a year in new federal spending.[23] Adding to this are the public's fears of an uncertain national economic future and the costs associated with a rapidly aging population.

Hand in hand with issues of a program's cost are the taxes that will have to be raised to pay for it. Americans do not like taxes, and politicians are regularly elected and defeated according to whether they promise to reject new taxes. As a result, the United States has one of the lowest tax rates of any of the industrialized countries.[24] Opponents of social insurance argue that there is some fixed level beyond which Americans will not tolerate new taxes. In this view, increasing taxes for long-term care consumes available taxing capacity that might otherwise go for deficit reduction, education, research, public infrastructure, foreign aid, or services for the poor. Evidence suggests that this may not be the case. (For a more complete discussion of this issue, see chapter 9.)

## GENERATIONAL INEQUITIES

Critics also contend that it would be unfair to create yet another program—in addition to social security and medicare—that benefits mostly the elderly but is financed mostly by the nonelderly. They argue that allocating more federal resources for the elderly would be "generationally inequitable" because it would leave insufficient resources for other worthwhile goals that benefit the nonelderly, such as improving education.[25] Central to this view of social policy is the widely held perception that the economic status of the elderly has improved markedly, while the rate of poverty among children has grown substantially.[26] The growing proportion of elderly in the population, the declining relative size of the work force, and the impact of the federal debt on the country's economic future are all cited to support the argument that maintaining even the current programs for the elderly, let alone adding new ones, will be very difficult.[27]

Debates over equity are ultimately a matter of value preferences, but there are at least four responses to generational equity concerns about social insurance for long-term care. First, although the financial status of the elderly has improved substantially during the last three decades, most elderly still have quite modest levels of income and assets (see chapter 2 for details). The elderly have the highest poverty rate of any adult group, and subgroups of the elderly (widows, minorities, ages 85 and older) have even higher poverty rates than the elderly as a whole.[28] Between 30 and 40 percent of the elderly aged 75 and older have incomes below 150 percent of the federal poverty level.[29] Roughly 60 percent of the impaired elderly live at or below 150 percent of the poverty level.[30]

Second, and most important, proponents of "generational equity" miss the extent to which long-term care affects everyone, regardless of age. Most social insurance proposals would provide benefits to both the nonelderly and elderly disabled populations as beneficiaries. Although disability rates are much higher for the elderly, at least a quarter of the disabled people who have trouble performing the activities of daily living but who still live in the community are under age 65.[31] And, because family care is the backbone of community-based long-term care, middle-aged caregivers would benefit from an expanded federal home care program. Although most research suggests that families would continue to provide almost as much care as they would have without publicly paid home care services, family caregivers would receive needed respite and benefit from being able to arrange their hours and tasks more efficiently.[32]

Third, generational equity concerns are based on a narrow, cross-sectional perspective of benefits and tax payments at one moment in time rather than over a lifetime.[33] Indeed, because those currently under age 65 are likely to live longer than their parents, they are more likely to need long-term care than the current generation of elderly. Like the long-run benefits of public education for children, public financing of long-term care is a response to a need that exists across the course of life and thus benefits all groups.

Finally, it is naive to assume that reduced spending on the elderly would automatically lead to greater spending on children. The two sets of programs have sharply different political dynamics and constituencies, and there is little reason to believe that cuts in social security benefits, for example, would translate into an increase in aid to families with dependent children or elementary education. Indeed, when asked, a large majority of Americans reject the notion of expanding services to the young by cutting services to the elderly.[34] As one observer noted, an "attempt to impose trade-offs [between the elderly and children] would be a supremely daring political act."[35]

## TARGET INEFFICIENCY

By definition, social insurance provides benefits for all people without regard to income. Consequently, critics of social insurance strategies argue that they are not target efficient; that is, they provide benefits to the upper-income elderly who could otherwise afford to pay for long-term care themselves.[36]

Upon closer examination, this problem turns out to be small, remediable, and, as has been discussed above, a source of political strength. First, the amount of resources that would go to the upper-income population is not that large.[37] Long-term care is used principally by the very elderly, disabled population. This population has extremely modest income and assets. A recent examination of the distribution of public expenditures under various social insurance approaches shows that only about a third of incremental public expenditures and about 15 percent of total government spending under public long-term care insurance would be for elderly with family income of $30,000 or more in 1990.[38] (For additional and somewhat lower estimates, see the simulation results for this chapter.) Thus, the bulk of both incremental and total expenditures would be for people whose financial status is decidedly modest.[c]

Second, people may disagree about how much public funding would go to the well-off, but it is nonetheless correct that upper-income elderly will receive some benefits under a social insurance plan. That is also true for medicare and social security, but few critics suggest that these programs be dismantled and the elderly made to rely primarily on private insurance and welfare for acute care and retirement income. The key point is that including both the rich and poor in a single program has enormous political advantages for the poor. As was argued above, this has been the principal reason for the political success of the medicare and social security programs and would be a critical element in maintaining support for a public long-term care program.

Third, to the extent that a social insurance program redistributes income from the lower- to the upper-income population, those funds

c. Although $30,000 does represent the upper reaches of the income distribution of disabled elderly, few would allege that persons at this income level are well heeled, especially when the costs of nursing home care are considered. Indeed, $30,000 represents about 80 percent of the average cost of a year in a nursing home.

can and should be recouped through the tax system. Programs should not, on balance, take from lower-income workers to give to the upper-income elderly. Hence, taxes to support social insurance should at least be proportional if not progressive. This strategy would guarantee that the upper-income population will pay more, at least in absolute terms. Private insurance, whatever its other virtues, is inherently regressive because premiums do not vary with income.

## LACK OF FLEXIBILITY AND CHOICE

Opponents of social insurance, or any other strategy that is government-based, assert that public programs lack the flexibility desirable in a long-term care system.[39] Traditional social insurance programs offer a single benefit package, regardless of the specific needs or preferences of the beneficiary. Likewise, social insurance programs typically do not offer a range of premiums or cost-sharing to the beneficiary. Because long-term care is so intimately connected to quality-of-life concerns, consumer choices are especially important.

There are at least two responses to this concern. First, private long-term care insurance policies, although improving, are sometimes rigid in the range of services they will reimburse. Moreover, because individuals must buy policies years before they will use services, the insured run the risk of locking themselves into the current model of service delivery. Second, properly structured public programs need not be rigid. Indeed, experience with home- and community-based services funded by medicaid has shown that government programs can be quite creative and flexible. (For further discussion of how a social insurance program might be structured to ensure flexibility, see chapter 8.)

## THE GREATER IMPORTANCE OF HEALTH CARE FOR THE UNINSURED

Strong public policy and moral considerations argue for addressing health care for the uninsured first, before long-term care. It is a national disgrace that more than 38.5 million Americans have no health insurance at all.[40] Ironically, public support for health care reform increases significantly when coverage for long-term care is included. In a recent public opinion survey, 57 percent of respondents indicated that they were either "much more likely" or "somewhat more likely" to support the Clinton health care reform plan knowing that long-term care is included in the package.[41] More generally, respondents were asked the extent to which they favored health care reform plans that do and do not include coverage of long-term care. Only 46 percent said they would "somewhat favor" or "strongly favor" a plan that covered only hospital and doctor care. When asked about a plan that covered long-term care, as well as hospital and doctor care, those in favor increased to 83 percent.[42] Similarly, about 90 percent of respondents to another survey said that long-term care services should be included in a "national health care program."[43]

The strong support for long-term care is partly related to benefits middle-class Americans perceive they will gain from health care reform. Although many middle-class Americans are anxious about their ability to maintain their health insurance, for the overwhelming majority of people, lack of acute care coverage is still mostly somebody else's problem. More people are losing benefits under their private insurance policies or are finding private health insurance unaffordable, but 83 percent of the nonelderly population and 99 percent of the elderly population had acute care health insurance in 1992.[44] The situation is totally reversed in long-term care. Because almost no one has insurance coverage for it, expanding long-term care provides new benefits to virtually everyone and thus appeals to a broad population.

In the current political environment, acute care and long-term care reform need each other. Health care for the uninsured needs long-term care to give the otherwise well-insured a reason to support health care reform. And long-term care needs health care for the uninsured to diffuse concerns about generational equity. The dilemma is that these two issues need to be joined together for each to muster substantial political support, but the taxes necessary to finance both may be more than Congress can afford—politically and financially—to approve.[45]

## Four Social Insurance Prototypes

Several specific social insurance proposals have been introduced in Congress to cover long-term care. Similar in many ways—they all provide for extensive home care—these proposals are generally differentiated by the type and duration of nursing home coverage they provide. There are "home care coverage only" bills with no new nursing home coverage, "front-end" plans with first dollar coverage of limited duration, "back-end" coverage with lengthy deductible periods, and "comprehensive" models with little or no deductible periods and unlimited duration of coverage.

**HOME CARE ONLY**

Unlike other major strategies, a proposal by President Clinton and another by the late Congressman Claude Pepper offer a wide array of in-home services but no new nursing home benefits.[46] The primary purpose of these proposals is to make a bold financing shift away from nursing home care and toward home care. One clear advantage is that access to home care services would improve, thus creating a more balanced delivery system. In 1993 only 28 percent of total long-term care expenditures for the elderly and only 36 percent of government spending for long-term care were estimated to be for home care services.[47] By providing more formal home care, the overall amount of home care (including informal care) would increase, resulting in fewer unmet needs among the disabled elderly.[48] More than one-third of the elderly with disabilities in activities of daily living reported some unmet daily needs.[49] Increased availability of paid home care would also provide some relief to family, friends, and other informal caregivers. At the very least, expanded home care coverage should give caregivers some increased flexibility in their schedules.[50] Also, because more than one-quarter of the $20.8 billion spent on home care in 1993 was financed by out-of-pocket expenditures, expanded home- and community-based services would reduce direct financial burdens on the elderly and their families. By leaving the institutional aspects of long-term care untouched, this is the least expensive social insurance strategy.

Weighing in against "home care only" is the fact that nursing home care, not home care, is the major cause of catastrophic long-term care costs and welfare dependency among the elderly.[51] Expanding home care would do little or nothing to address these problems or to correct the access and quality problems of nursing home care.

**HOME CARE AND FRONT-END NURSING HOME COVERAGE**

A second strategy would similarly cover comprehensive home care but also provide public insurance for the first part, or "front end," of nursing home stays. Proposals by Senator Edward Kennedy and former Social Security Commissioner Robert Ball would cover the first six months of nursing home care.[52] The Pepper Commission proposed coverage of three months of nursing home care.[53] More recently, Democratic leaders in both the House and Senate have introduced legislation based on the Pepper Commission's 1990 proposals, except that two six-month episodes of nursing home care would be covered.[54]

The rationale for providing front-end coverage is that, in a time of limited public resources, incremental public expenditures should be concentrated on people who are either in the community or who have the greatest probability of returning to the community after a nursing home stay. Some 55 percent of all nursing home patients have short stays (six months or less) and half of these return to the community.[55] These are the people who have the greatest need for income and asset protection, because they will rely on these resources when they are back in the community. The Pepper Commission and Democratic leadership proposals supplement nursing home coverage by liberalizing the amount of income and assets that medicaid patients are allowed to keep.[56] Those looking for asset protection beyond this level can buy private long-term care insurance.

A front-end coverage option is politically attractive for several reasons. First, the greatest number of patients are covered because, by definition, it is available to everyone who enters a nursing home. Second, even six months in a nursing home (especially if it occurs in conjunction with an acute care illness) can be financially devastating for many people, costing $18,000 or more; front-end coverage protects a patient's resources so those who do return home will retain their financial independence. Third, it is the cheapest of the options that provide some coverage for nursing home care because most nursing home expenditures are associated with long stays. And, last, it is a logical and modest expansion of the skilled nursing facility benefit in medicare—a program that is both popular and politically entrenched.[57]

Despite its appeal, front-end coverage has several limitations. First, the "half-empty" message of covering only the first part of a nursing home stay is that 50 percent of the short-stay patients are not discharged alive. Resource protection for these patients benefits heirs rather than the elderly themselves. In addition, many of those discharged alive are later readmitted and never again return to the community. Second, this approach does little to help people with very large nursing home bills. Patients with long stays in nursing homes typically incur the largest bills and greatest out-of-pocket costs, yet, under the front-end proposals, these patients would remain uncovered for the bulk of their stay. Third, front-end coverage overlooks the fact that some people can afford to finance short nursing home stays, especially through private insurance. Fourth, a front-end strategy would only modestly equalize access because once public coverage had ended, nursing homes would be likely to continue their preference for patients with considerable income and assets or with private insurance.

## HOME CARE AND BACK-END NURSING HOME COVERAGE

Another strategy would offer comprehensive home care, but provide nursing home coverage only after a long deductible period (the so-called "back end" of a nursing home stay). For example, legislation proposed by Senator George Mitchell would provide public insurance only for nursing home patients who stay two years or more.[58]

The major assumption attached to this approach is that private insurance would be more affordable (and far more widely purchased) if the coverage was only for a limited duration. Here, in theory at least, private and public insurance are neatly combined into a package where public insurance offers a backstop to private coverage. If it were promoted as a seamless system, this approach could actively encourage the sale of private insurance, in the same way that medicare fostered the sale of supplemental private insurance (medigap) to the elderly.[d]

The strongest argument for back-end coverage is that the government would pay only for the unquestionably catastrophic costs of long nursing home stays, a role that many feel is most appropriate for a public program. Private insurance is less likely to be able to deal with the uncertainty associated with very long stays. From the perspective of a private insurer, there is a big cost difference between a beneficiary who spends five years in a nursing home and one who needs ten years of coverage.

This reliance on a vast expansion of private sector insurance makes back-end coverage a high-risk strategy: few elderly currently have any kind of private coverage in force, and the many impediments to the widespread availability and purchase of private insurance are likely to persist under this option.[59] On the demand side, the overall price of insurance might be reduced, but still be unaffordable to the older buyer and unavailable to buyers with existing disabilities or chronic conditions. We estimate that premiums for a policy that covered only the first two years of a nursing home stay, bought at ages 67 and 77, would cost $1,054 and $1,910, respectively.[60] On the supply side, insurance com-

---

d. In some ways, this proposal is similar to the public-private partnerships being tried in California, Connecticut, Indiana, Iowa, and New York (see chapter 4). The three differences are that the social insurance approach would include home care as a benefit, the backstop program would be medicare or some new social insurance program rather than medicaid, and new nursing home benefits would be available to all, even if patients had not purchased private insurance.

panies still might not be willing to offer policies to a broad population. If the assumptions about the supply or demand for insurance are wrong, nursing home residents would face upward of $74,000 (the approximate cost of two years in a long-term care facility) in out-of-pocket costs before receiving any public insurance benefits.

Another disadvantage is that few of the long-stay patients targeted by such an approach are discharged alive.[61] Thus, back-end coverage provides asset protection for heirs—arguably a less appropriate role for government. In addition, like the front-end strategy, back-end coverage does little to equalize access because not everyone will be able to purchase private insurance and those who do (along with others who have considerable assets and income) will be preferred by providers over the low-income population.

Finally, it is a long-run strategy rather than one that offers immediate results because it relies on the young-elderly purchasing insurance and then not using the benefits right away. Most of the population aged 75 and older, the primary users of long-term care, will be unable to afford private insurance or to pass the medical screening. Even if a back-end nursing home care proposal were put in place tomorrow, at least twenty years are likely to pass before a significant number of nursing home patients have insurance to cover the deductible period. The likely profusion of stories about nursing home patients, unable to buy private coverage, who impoverished themselves during the deductible period, only then to have their care paid for by public insurance, may make the program politically unsustainable.

## HOME CARE AND COMPREHENSIVE NURSING HOME COVERAGE

A fourth strategy, introduced in two different forms by Representatives Henry Waxman and Fortney "Pete" Stark, would provide comprehensive coverage for nursing home and home care after relatively short deductible periods.[62] This strategy seeks to solve the problems of long-term care within the structure of the government program, without relying on private insurance or medicaid to fill the gaps. Consequently, assuming an appropriate program design, it is sure to accomplish the task of financing needed care and providing strong protection against catastrophic costs. This approach would make the government the single payer, thus enabling it to control reimbursement rates and how services are delivered. Of all the options, a comprehensive strategy would be best at equalizing access to nursing home care because the homes would have no financial incentive to prefer patients with higher income and assets.

The costs of a comprehensive program, however, would be by far the highest of all the social insurance approaches, and other spending priorities might be squeezed. Also, certain disadvantages could arise from fashioning a program that is totally dependent on government financing. For example, the bureaucratic system implemented to administer the program could become overly rigid. In addition, because the government would be the sole payer, no other payer could absorb costs in the event of budget cutbacks. Finally, some suggest that competition for the better-paying private-pay patients drives quality in nursing homes.[63] If that is true, then quality may suffer in a system where every patient is publicly sponsored.

## Simulation Assumptions and Results

To assess public insurance options, we simulated four prototype programs using the Brookings-ICF Long-Term Care Financing Model. These are similar to, but not exactly the same as, proposals that have been introduced in Congress. Table 7-1 summarizes our simulation assumptions. All options are modeled as if they were fully implemented immediately, with no phase-in period. All four options impose a moderate 20 percent copayment on home care and nursing home care when covered. Varying assumptions are made to account for the increased demand for services that typically follows the availability of additional monies for services.

Because all but the most comprehensive public insurance program leave at least part of the nursing home stay uncovered, private long-term care insurance is available to complement the public benefits. In addition, to protect low-income elderly against catastrophic out-of-pocket costs as a result of even modest levels of coinsurance, all of these simulations also include liberalization of the medicaid program. (Simulation results without liberalization of the medicaid program are presented in appendix C.) Except where indicated, other public programs for nursing home and home care remain unchanged.

The first option, HOME CARE ONLY, adds a comprehensive home care benefit for people with two or more problems with the activities of daily living or cognitive impairment but makes no changes in nursing home benefits (other than medicaid liberalization). People who meet the affordability criteria purchase private long-term care insurance to

TABLE 7-1. *Eligibility Criteria, Benefits, and Program Characteristics of Public Long-Term Care Insurance Options*[a]

| Option | Nursing home benefits | Home care benefits | Medicaid and medicare benefits | Private insurance[b] |
|---|---|---|---|---|
| Expanded home care only | Existing medicaid and medicare benefits only. | For severely disabled,[c] broad coverage of unlimited duration; 20 percent coinsurance; for less disabled, current medicaid and medicare benefits. | Medicaid improved: 150 percent of poverty income eligibility standard for home care; $30,000 (individual), $60,000 (couple) protected assets; $100 a month personal needs allowance; home care coinsurance paid for low-income severely disabled. Medicare benefits unchanged. | People buy what they can afford; two- or four-year nursing home policies after sixty-day deductible period; no home care benefits; age-based affordability criteria include premiums as a percentage of income and minimum financial assets; annual premiums range from $1,145 to $4,021;[d] people with ADL or IADL problems cannot buy; policies lapse if premium exceeds 20 percent of income. |
| Front-end | First six months of nursing home stay covered for everyone. | For severely disabled,[c] broad coverage of unlimited duration; 20 percent coinsurance; for less disabled, current medicaid and medicare benefits. | Medicaid improved: 150 percent of poverty income eligibility standard for home care; $30,000 (individual), $60,000 (couple) protected assets; $100 a month personal needs allowance; home care coinsurance paid for low-income severely disabled. Medicare benefits unchanged. | People buy what they can afford; two- or four-year nursing home policies after six-month deductible period; no home care benefits; age-based affordability criteria include premiums as a percentage of income and minimum financial assets; annual premiums range from $1,064 to $3,738;[d] people with ADL or IADL problems cannot buy; policies lapse if premium exceeds 20 percent of income. |

| | | | |
|---|---|---|---|
| Back-end | Nursing home stay covered for everyone after two-year deductible period. | For severely disabled,[c] broad coverage of unlimited duration; 20 percent coinsurance; for less disabled, current medicaid and medicare benefits. | Medicaid improved: 150 percent of poverty income eligibility standard for home care; $30,000 (individual), $60,000 (couple) protected assets; $100 a month personal needs allowance; home care coinsurance paid for low-income severely disabled. Medicare benefits unchanged. | People buy what they can afford; two-year nursing home policy after 60-day deductible period; no home care benefits; age-based affordability criteria include premiums as a percentage of income and minimum financial assets; annual premiums range from $1,145 to $2,525;[d] people with ADL or IADL problems cannot buy; policies lapse if premium exceeds 20 percent of income. |
| Comprehensive | First-day, unlimited nursing home coverage for everyone. | For severely disabled,[c] broad coverage of unlimited duration; 20 percent coinsurance; for less disabled, current medicaid and medicare benefits. | Medicaid improved: 150 percent of poverty income eligibility standard for home care; $30,000 (individual), $60,000 (couple) protected assets; $100 a month personal needs allowance; home care coinsurance paid for low-income severely disabled. Medicare benefits unchanged. | No private insurance. |

a. All options include liberalized medicaid benefits.
b. People do not purchase private long-term care insurance until age 67.
c. "Severely disabled" defined as two or more problems with the activities of daily living or cognitive impairment.
d. Premiums depend on initial age at purchase and length (two or four years) of nursing home coverage.

finance their nursing home stays. The model assumes that, under the HOME CARE ONLY option, people without private insurance will increase their demand for nursing home services by 5 percent (due to the medicaid liberalization); for those with private insurance a 25 percent increase in nursing home use is assumed. Under all four options, utilization of home care by the eligible population is assumed to double.[64]

A second option, FRONT-END, adds coverage for the first six months of a nursing home stay for all disabled elderly to the HOME CARE ONLY option. People who meet the affordability criteria purchase private long-term care insurance to finance any nursing home stay that exceeds the six-month public insurance benefit. Demand for nursing home care is expected to increase by 25 percent among those with private insurance and by 15 percent among people who do not have it.

The third option, BACK-END, is the reverse of the FRONT-END option, covering nursing home benefits after a two-year deductible period in addition to comprehensive home care benefits. People who meet the affordability criteria purchase private long-term care insurance to cover the two-year deductible period. Because of the long deductible period, no induced demand for nursing home care is assumed for people who do not purchase insurance; for people with insurance, utilization is assumed to increase 25 percent.

The final option, COMPREHENSIVE, provides first-dollar, unlimited nursing home coverage to severely disabled elderly, in addition to the same expanded home care benefits extended under the other three options. Supplemental private insurance is not needed.[e] Nursing home use is assumed to increase 25 percent.

Table 7-2 presents public and private nursing home and home care expenditures for 1993 and 2018. Figure 7-1 estimates what public expenditures on long-term care would be if any of the various reform strategies were initiated. Currently, government spends $27 billion public dollars on nursing home care and $15 billion on home care each year. Without any changes to the existing system, these expenditures are projected to more than double in twenty-five years, with $59 billion in public monies going to nursing home care and $29 billion to home care (in 1993 dollars).

The HOME CARE ONLY strategy would increase public expenditures by $21 billion over the BASE CASE in 1993. The FRONT-END

e. Private insurance could fill in the coinsurance levels (as medigap policies do for medicare), but that would undermine the utilization control that coinsurance is supposed to supply.

TABLE 7-2. *Total Expenditures for Nursing Home and Home Care, by Source of Payment, Base Case and Public Insurance Options, Selected Periods*[a]
*Billions of 1993 dollars*

| Payment source | Base case | Expanded home care only | Front-end nursing home and expanded home care | Back-end nursing home and expanded home care | Comprehensive nursing home and expanded home care |
|---|---|---|---|---|---|
| | | | *1993* | | |
| Total long-term care expenditures | 75.5 | 92.8 | 93.0 | 98.0 | 107.5 |
| Nursing home | | | | | |
| Medicaid | 22.4 | 26.4 | 22.5 | 12.9 | 3.8 |
| Medicare | 4.3 | 4.3 | 4.3 | 4.3 | 4.3 |
| Public insurance | 0.0 | 0.0 | 6.3 | 25.2 | 50.9 |
| Private insurance | 0.0 | 1.8 | 1.8 | 1.5 | 0.0 |
| Family cash | 17.0 | 14.1 | 13.1 | 10.8 | 9.5 |
| Family assets | 11.0 | 7.6 | 6.4 | 4.7 | 0.4 |
| TOTAL | 54.7 | 54.2 | 54.4 | 59.4 | 68.9 |
| Home care | | | | | |
| Medicaid | 3.6 | 2.3 | 2.3 | 2.3 | 2.3 |
| Medicare | 9.4 | 9.4 | 9.4 | 9.4 | 9.4 |
| Other payer | 2.2 | 0.9 | 0.9 | 0.9 | 0.9 |
| Public insurance | 0.0 | 19.4 | 19.4 | 19.4 | 19.4 |
| Private insurance | 0.0 | 0.0 | 0.0 | 0.0 | 0.0 |
| Out-of-pocket | 5.5 | 6.7 | 6.7 | 6.7 | 6.7 |
| TOTAL | 20.7 | 38.7 | 38.7 | 38.7 | 38.7 |
| | | | *2018* | | |
| Total long-term care expenditures | 168.3 | 207.0 | 209.9 | 218.3 | 236.0 |
| Nursing home | | | | | |
| Medicaid | 49.0 | 52.5 | 45.2 | 24.0 | 7.3 |
| Medicare | 10.0 | 10.0 | 10.0 | 10.0 | 10.0 |
| Public insurance | 0.0 | 0.0 | 16.6 | 59.9 | 119.4 |
| Private insurance | 0.0 | 15.6 | 15.2 | 13.1 | 0.0 |
| Family cash | 42.6 | 33.9 | 31.6 | 24.8 | 22.8 |
| Family assets | 26.6 | 19.9 | 16.3 | 11.3 | 1.3 |
| TOTAL | 128.2 | 131.9 | 134.9 | 143.1 | 160.8 |
| Home care | | | | | |
| Medicaid | 5.2 | 5.0 | 5.0 | 5.0 | 5.0 |
| Medicare | 19.0 | 19.0 | 19.0 | 19.0 | 19.0 |
| Other payer | 4.3 | 1.7 | 1.7 | 1.7 | 1.7 |
| Public insurance | 0.0 | 34.5 | 34.5 | 34.5 | 34.5 |
| Private insurance | 0.0 | 0.0 | 0.0 | 0.0 | 0.0 |
| Out-of-pocket | 11.6 | 14.9 | 14.9 | 14.9 | 14.9 |
| TOTAL | 40.1 | 75.1 | 75.1 | 75.1 | 75.1 |

SOURCE: Brookings-ICF Long-Term Care Financing Model. In this and other tables and figures in this chapter, 1993 represents the five-year average for the period 1991–95; 2018 the five-year average for the period 2016–20.
a. With medicaid liberalization.

FIGURE 7-1. **Annual Public Expenditures for Long-Term Care, Public Insurance Options, Selected Periods**[a]

Billions of 1993 dollars

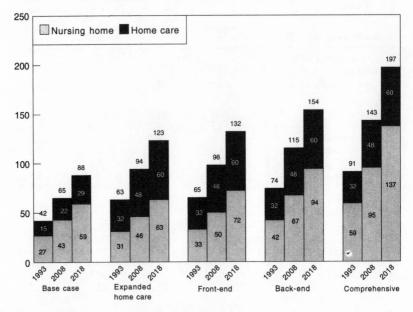

SOURCE:: Brookings-ICF Long-Term Care Financing Model.
a. With medicaid liberalization. Here and in figure 7-3, the year 2008 represents the average for the five-year period 2006–10.

and BACK-END options increase public expenditures by $23 and $32 billion, respectively. As expected, the COMPREHENSIVE strategy is substantially more expensive than other options; for 1993 public costs under this option would increase by $49 billion. Because all of the home care benefits were modeled identically in the social insurance prototypes, differences in public expenditures among the social insurance options are attributable to differences in nursing home coverage. By 2018, the incremental public costs of all of the options roughly double in constant dollar terms.

Although opponents argue that social insurance would provide benefits largely to the well-to-do, tables 7-3 and 7-4 and figure 7-2 suggest that this would not be the case.[f] The overwhelming majority of total and incremental public nursing home and home care spending in 1993 and 2018 would go to persons with incomes under $40,000. In 2018

f. The HOME CARE ONLY option is not included in tables 7-2 and 7-3 because under this strategy, no new social insurance expenditures go toward nursing home care.

TABLE 7-3. *Public Expenditures for Nursing Home Care, by Demographic and Income Groups, Base Case and Public Insurance Options, Selected Periods*[a]
Percent unless otherwise noted

| Patient characteristics | Base case | Front-end nursing home | Back-end nursing home | Comprehensive nursing home |
|---|---|---|---|---|
| | | *1993* | | |
| Public nursing home expenditures (billions of 1993 dollars) | 33.6 | 39.2 | 50.9 | 70.5 |
| Age | | | | |
| 65–74 | 20 | 20 | 20 | 20 |
| 75–84 | 34 | 35 | 34 | 35 |
| 85 and older | 46 | 45 | 46 | 45 |
| Marital status | | | | |
| Married | 33 | 34 | 35 | 32 |
| Unmarried | 67 | 66 | 65 | 68 |
| Gender | | | | |
| Men | 29 | 30 | 31 | 29 |
| Women | 71 | 70 | 70 | 71 |
| Family income (1993 dollars) | | | | |
| Less than 7,500 | 31 | 28 | 25 | 25 |
| 7,500–15,000 | 40 | 38 | 37 | 35 |
| 15,000–20,000 | 11 | 12 | 13 | 13 |
| 20,000–30,000 | 13 | 14 | 16 | 15 |
| 30,000–40,000 | 3 | 3 | 4 | 5 |
| 40,000–50,000 | 1 | 1 | 1 | 1 |
| More than 50,000 | 2 | 2 | 5 | 6 |
| | | *2018* | | |
| Public nursing home expenditures (billions of 1993 dollars) | 64.2 | 77.8 | 105.1 | 150.2 |
| Age | | | | |
| 65–74 | 15 | 17 | 17 | 17 |
| 75–84 | 32 | 34 | 31 | 32 |
| 85 and older | 52 | 49 | 52 | 51 |
| Marital status | | | | |
| Married | 30 | 31 | 31 | 29 |
| Unmarried | 70 | 69 | 69 | 71 |
| Gender | | | | |
| Men | 30 | 32 | 32 | 32 |
| Women | 70 | 68 | 68 | 68 |
| Family income (1993 dollars) | | | | |
| Less than 7,500 | 19 | 17 | 15 | 12 |
| 7,500–15,000 | 33 | 31 | 28 | 27 |
| 15,000–20,000 | 14 | 13 | 12 | 13 |
| 20,000–30,000 | 20 | 21 | 20 | 20 |
| 30,000–40,000 | 7 | 8 | 9 | 10 |
| 40,000–50,000 | 3 | 4 | 5 | 6 |
| More than 50,000 | 4 | 6 | 10 | 12 |

SOURCE: Brookings-ICF Long-Term Care Financing Model.
a. With medicaid liberalization. These data are based on the public expenditures for an admission cohort over the entire length of the nursing home stay.

TABLE 7-4. *Incremental Public Expenditures for Nursing Home Care, by Demographic and Income Groups, Public Insurance Options, Selected Periods*[a]
Percent unless otherwise noted

| Patient characteristics | Front-end nursing home | Back-end nursing home | Comprehensive nursing home |
|---|---|---|---|
| | | *1993* | |
| Public nursing home expenditures (billions of 1993 dollars) | 39.2 | 50.9 | 70.5 |
| Incremental public nursing home expenditures (billions of 1993 dollars) | 5.6 | 17.3 | 36.9 |
| Age | | | |
| 65–74 | 20 | 21 | 20 |
| 75–84 | 40 | 34 | 36 |
| 85 and older | 40 | 45 | 45 |
| Marital status | | | |
| Married | 39 | 38 | 31 |
| Unmarried | 61 | 62 | 69 |
| Gender | | | |
| Men | 36 | 33 | 29 |
| Women | 64 | 67 | 71 |
| Family income (1993 dollars) | | | |
| Less than 7,500 | 10 | 15 | 19 |
| 7,500–15,000 | 28 | 30 | 31 |
| 15,000–20,000 | 22 | 16 | 15 |
| 20,000–30,000 | 21 | 21 | 16 |
| 30,000–40,000 | 11 | 7 | 7 |
| 40,000–50,000 | 9 | 1 | 2 |
| More than 50,000 | 5 | 10 | 9 |
| | | *2018* | |
| Public nursing home expenditures (billions of 1993 dollars) | 77.8 | 105.1 | 150.2 |
| Incremental public nursing home expenditures (billions of 1993 dollars) | 13.6 | 40.9 | 85.9 |
| Age | | | |
| 65–74 | 24 | 19 | 19 |
| 75–84 | 40 | 29 | 31 |
| 85 and older | 36 | 52 | 50 |
| Marital status | | | |
| Married | 36 | 32 | 29 |
| Unmarried | 64 | 68 | 71 |
| Gender | | | |
| Men | 38 | 34 | 34 |
| Women | 62 | 66 | 66 |
| Family income (1993 dollars) | | | |
| Less than 7,500 | 8 | 8 | 8 |
| 7,500–15,000 | 21 | 19 | 22 |
| 15,000–20,000 | 12 | 10 | 12 |
| 20,000–30,000 | 26 | 21 | 20 |
| 30,000–40,000 | 14 | 14 | 13 |
| 40,000–50,000 | 6 | 9 | 8 |
| More than 50,000 | 13 | 19 | 18 |

SOURCE: Brookings-ICF Long-Term Care Financing Model.
a. With medicaid liberalization. These data are based on the public expenditures for an admission cohort over the entire length of the nursing home stay.

FIGURE 7-2. **Annual Public Expenditures for Expanded Home Care, by Income Distribution, Selected Periods**[a]

Billions of 1993 dollars

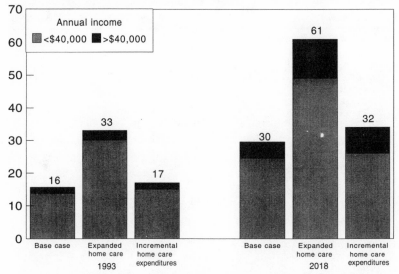

SOURCE:: Brookings-ICF Long-Term Care Financing Model.
a. With medicaid liberalization.

only 24 percent of new spending for HOME CARE ONLY would go to people with incomes above $40,000. For nursing home care, the percentage of new public spending for people with incomes above $40,000 ranges from 19 percent to 28 percent.

Table 7-5 shows the effect the various public options would have on catastrophic costs in 2018. Absolute out-of-pocket spending under the base case would average $44,000 in 2018, and approximately 33 percent of all nursing home patients would spend more than $20,000 out of pocket. Although each of the public options reduces the absolute out-of-pocket expenditures substantially, only the COMPREHENSIVE option has a dramatic impact. Even under the COMPREHENSIVE option, 22 percent of nursing home admissions would still pay more than $20,000 out of pocket. Under the base case in 2018, 39 percent of all persons spend more than 40 percent of their income and assets for a nursing home stay. The various public options reduce this proportion to between 18 and 30 percent.

Policymakers are also concerned about how well additional public dollars target those people who currently face high out-of-pocket spend-

TABLE 7-5. *Effect of Public Insurance Options on Catastrophic Out-of-Pocket Expenditures for Nursing Home Care, 2018*

| Measure | Base case | Expanded home care only | Front-end | Back-end | Comprehensive |
|---|---|---|---|---|---|
| **Absolute expenditure[a]** | | | | | |
| Average out-of-pocket spending (thousands of 1993 dollars) | 44 | 33 | 31 | 21 | 14 |
| Percentage of admissions spending more than $20,000 out-of-pocket | 33 | 26 | 25 | 25 | 22 |
| **Relative expenditure[b]** | | | | | |
| Percentage of admissions spending more than 40 percent of income, assets on care | 39 | 30 | 27 | 26 | 18 |
| **Target efficiency[c]** | | | | | |
| Percentage of incremental spending for people who would otherwise have incurred catastrophic out-of-pocket costs | ... | ... | 57 | 74 | 71 |

SOURCE: Brookings-ICF Long-Term Care Financing Model.
a. These data are based on the total out-of-pocket payments for an admission cohort over the entire length of the nursing home stay.
b. The numerator is equal to the out-of-pocket contribution to nursing home care for the entire length of stay; the denominator is equal to income during the stay plus nonhousing assets.
c. These data are based on incremental public expenditures for an admission cohort for the entire length of stay. In 2018 incremental public spending for front-end care is $13.6 billion, for back-end care $40.9 billion, and for comprehensive care $86 billion.

ing for nursing home care. In 2018 roughly three-quarters of the marginal public spending for nursing home care in the BACK-END and COMPREHENSIVE strategies is projected to go for people who currently spend more than 40 percent of their income and nonhousing assets on nursing home care. Because the catastrophic costs of nursing home care generally result from longer stays, the FRONT END strategy does not fare as well in this test, although the majority of incremental expenditures are for this group.

One reason for creating a social insurance program is to shift not only numbers of people but expenditures away from the medicaid program. Figure 7-3 suggests that reducing medicaid expenditures would be easier than reducing the number of medicaid nursing home patients. Any reductions in the number of medicaid nursing home patients appears to be largely offset by liberalizing medicaid financial eligibility

FIGURE 7-3. **Change in Number of Medicaid Nursing Home Patients from Base Case Public Insurance Options, Selected Periods**[a]

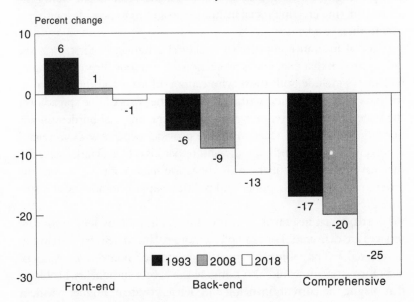

SOURCE:: Brookings-ICF Long-Term Care Financing Model.
  a. With medicaid liberalization.

rules and by increased nursing home use because of improved third-party coverage. Indeed, the FRONT-END strategy would result in a slight increase in the number of nursing home patients dependent on medicaid in 1993 and 2008 and would only produce slight reductions in 2018. Under the COMPREHENSIVE strategy, the number of medicaid nursing home patients would decrease 17 percent in 1993 and 25 percent in 2018. In addition, given the relative low-income status of the disabled elderly and the fact that nursing home prices are increasing faster than general inflation, even a 20 percent coinsurance rate may be too high for many people to avoid needing help in paying for care.

## Conclusion

A social insurance approach to financing long-term care offers coverage to everyone regardless of financial and health status. This approach explicitly recognizes long-term care as a normal risk of growing old and of life. Advocates of social insurance see no cogent reason why long-term care should be financed primarily through a welfare program, while acute health care and income support for the elderly are financed through the social insurance programs of medicare and social security. Recognizing this incongruity, at least two states (Hawaii and Vermont) are considering creating social insurance programs to provide long-term care to their residents.[65]

A social insurance approach has several advantages. First, it is the only approach that guarantees protection for everyone. Private insurance will always exclude both those who cannot afford it and those who fail the tests of medical underwriting. Second, the costs can be spread over the largest possible revenue base, reducing the financial burden on any one individual. Third, social insurance provides benefits without regard to income. Consequently, middle-and upper-class beneficiaries who feel they have earned benefits because they have made contributions to the program bring valuable public and political support to any social insurance program.

Fourth, social insurance offers advantages in the way long-term care services are delivered. For example, a more balanced delivery system can be created by providing for broad coverage of home care. A social insurance strategy would also mitigate the access and quality problems that plague the current financing and delivery system. Higher payment rates in the public program combined with universal coverage would reduce the importance of higher-paying private patients, thus reducing the existing two-class system of care.

Despite the various financing and delivery advantages that social insurance offers, there are drawbacks. Most important, opponents argue that the large increase in public costs would more than outweigh the benefits. Inevitably, people will argue that the taxes necessary to pay for the costs of the program might be better used to reduce the deficit, provide health care for the uninsured, or fund any number of other important programs. A social insurance approach also will provide some benefits to upper-income people. In addition, creating another program that primarily benefits the elderly and is financed mostly by the non-elderly raises issues of generational equity. Finally, some argue that a primarily government-based financial system is less responsive to consumers' desire for choice and flexibility to use alternative modes of care.

## Chapter Eight

# Social Insurance: Design and Administrative Issues

If more long-term care is to be financed through a social insurance program, many questions about the program's design and administration must be addressed. In several aspects, a public long-term care insurance program should diverge from the traditional social insurance models of medicare and social security, with their open-ended entitlement, to strictly defined benefits and centralized federal administration.

## Role of the States

Currently, the lion's share of publicly funded long-term care is available through the medicaid program. Although both federal and state governments are involved in the financing and policymaking, operational responsibility for managing the system is primarily the province of the states. States regulate the supply and quality of care, set reimbursement rates, write contracts with providers, process claims, and coordinate the care of clients.

President Clinton's proposal for expanded home care would rely heavily on states to design, administer, and partly finance the new program. This is a departure from previous social insurance proposals—including those by Senators George Mitchell and Edward Kennedy, Representatives Henry Waxman and Pete Stark, and the Pepper Commission—which specified very limited roles for the states. Although these earlier proposals depended on states for administration, the federal government was to control policymaking and financing. That arrangement is a natural extension of the current medicare and social security programs, in which states have no role, but there are several reasons why designers of a public long-term care program should fully involve the states.

First, states have the substantive experience in developing long-term care delivery systems, so giving them a strong role would capitalize on the creativity and expertise available there. A state-administered approach would also allow any new program to be implemented more quickly.

Second, long-term care is a local issue; the planning and delivery of services is greatly influenced by the local circumstances and particular norms of the area. For example, a thoughtfully designed care plan in rural Alabama would not make sense in New York City because resources, service delivery patterns, and life-styles vary so greatly between these locations. Any strategies to design a new delivery system must take into account the preferences of the local elderly population, their caregivers, and providers.

Third, states will not feel that they have a real stake in this program unless they have some financial responsibility for it. Programs that are entirely federally funded give states little reason to be prudent fiscal managers. If the program is financed through a federal-state matching formula, an inevitable problem will be the variation in states' willingness to fund the program. A high federal match rate, however, should make the program financially attractive to the states. Requiring states to incur some of the costs and the risks of a public insurance program will necessitate giving them a role in policymaking. Giving the states a policy role raises the specter of the interstate variation that plagues the medicaid program, and it will undoubtedly complicate the decision-making process, but the alternative is a more rigid, federally determined program.

## Expenditure Controls

To date, efforts to enact public insurance programs for long-term care have failed largely because of fears about costs. Policymakers have two concerns. The first is the absolute level of expenditures required. All public insurance programs will require substantial additional public expenditures.

The second concern involves the uncertainty inherent in the expenditure estimates. The fear is that no matter how honest the estimates may be, they will prove to be too low. No lawmaker wants to wake up one day and find that the actual costs of a new long-term care financing program are twice what was originally projected. Indeed, part of the folklore of health policy in Washington is that the costs of the medicaid and medicare programs turned out to be far higher than initially calculated. Similarly, the constant upward revision in the estimated costs of the Medicare Catastrophic Coverage Care Act of 1988 hastened the almost complete repeal of that law. The recent explosive growth in medicare home health expenditures, which increased from $2.5 billion in 1989 to $8.2 billion in 1992, has added to worries about the level of future expenditures.[1]

This concern about the accuracy of projected costs is not unwarranted. Most disabled elderly who might qualify for paid services do not currently receive any, and, although the reluctance of the elderly to enter nursing homes reduces the likelihood of a large increase in nursing home use even if universally covered, the inherent desirability of some home care services, such as homemaker and chore services, is certain to increase their use substantially if covered by public insurance.[2] Moreover, the principal effect of public (or private) insurance is to reduce the net cost of a service to the recipient. People tend to buy more of a service when it costs less out of pocket.

Uncontrolled increases in the demand for long-term care have been a persistent worry for policymakers, yet it is difficult to know the extent to which this potential for increased demand will come to pass. For example, some provinces in Canada that pay for long-term care through social insurance–like systems have not experienced unacceptable increases in use.[3] In the United States national cost estimates based on the Channeling demonstration experience, where a wide range of home care services were essentially free, are quite modest.[4] In addition, long-term care use within the social health maintenance organization demonstrations, which provide long-term care on an open-ended, private entitlement basis in addition to acute care services, has not been excessive.[5] In fact, few participants have reached their relatively low benefit ceilings.

Despite (or because of) the uncertainty, the anxiety about potentially runaway costs is so high among policymakers that they are likely to insist upon very strong cost control mechanisms. These mechanisms should include limiting the eligible population to the severely disabled, the use of case management and preadmission screening for nursing home care, cost sharing, strict rate-setting systems, and provision of services through prepaid, capitated arrangements (for example, adding long-term care to the services offered by health maintenance organizations [HMOs], as do social health maintenance organizations [S/HMOs] or

On Lok Senior Health Services in San Francisco and its national replication sites).[a]

Most of the policy discussions about long-term care reforms have been within the context of open-ended entitlement programs such as medicare and medicaid. Yet, open-ended entitlements are under attack in Congress, and acute care is "budgeted" under the Clinton plan.[6] An explicit cap on new public long-term care expenditures would come close to guaranteeing that spending did not exceed a set amount. Expenditures would be set initially through estimates of what it would cost to serve a defined population adequately, which would then be indexed annually to take into account inflation and the growth in the disabled population. Although an approach embodying universal access operating within a fixed budget is common in Europe and Canada, Americans have little experience with this strategy in connection with acute care health programs. In fact, states, which do not rely on medicaid funding, have always run their home care programs under these constraints.

Opponents fear that once capped, expenditures will not rise with inflation, population, experience, or need. The fact is that fixed budget programs lack the automatic engine of spending increases inherent in entitlement programs. Supporters of this approach hope that because services would be provided to persons of all financial means, an effective political constituency would be created to lobby for funding increases. It would also help protect funding levels if financing for the program came primarily from a dedicated revenue source (such as a payroll tax). The reservations about capped programs are serious ones, but policymakers are so frightened by the spending uncertainties that it is doubtful whether major long-term care programs can be enacted without a failsafe mechanism to limit overall financial risk to the government.

## Entitlement and Service Flexibility

Disabled persons, especially the nonelderly, need a very wide range of services. A crucial design issue is how to balance strong cost controls

a. Social health maintenance organizations add a modest amount of long-term care and other services to the more standard acute care benefit package of health maintenance organizations. They attempt to enroll a population that is not disproportionately disabled. On Lok provides a broad range of acute and long-term care services on a prepaid, capitated basis. Only people who are very severely disabled may enroll. The National Chronic Care Consortium is an organization, principally of hospitals and nursing homes, committed to finding ways to integrate acute and long-term care services.

such as expenditure caps with the desire to provide a flexible set of services and still retain an "entitlement" to services. An "entitlement" implies a legal obligation on the part of government to provide services to individuals who meet established criteria, regardless of the cost to the government. The basic dilemma is that the more flexible the set of services provided, the more difficult it is to provide services on an entitlement basis and still keep expenditures within the appropriated amount. The broader the range of available services, the more likely persons will use them, raising overall expenditures.[7] At issue is whether the concept of a "capped entitlement program" makes sense in long-term care or whether it is an oxymoron.

This dilemma could be resolved in at least three ways. First, expenditures could be limited by covering only a narrow set of services but providing them on an entitlement basis. This strategy is similar to the approach private insurers and medicare have traditionally used to limit expenditures. For example, the home care benefit could be limited to personal care services. From a regulatory perspective, it may be difficult to ensure that the home care worker performs only those services that are covered. From the individual client's perspective, this approach limiting the services covered does not explicitly address the range of services that the disabled population needs, which may include homemaker and chore services, respite care, and nutrition counseling. In addition, if the number of people seeking services turns out to be larger than anticipated, it would be difficult to stay within budget.

A second option is to divide the program into two parts. The first part would establish a minimum benefit that would be provided on an entitlement basis—for example, $400 a month of personal care services. The second part of the program would provide a wider range of home care services, but on a nonentitlement basis. Thus, an individual would be entitled to the minimum benefit and could also receive additional services to the extent that funds are available.

This approach aims to provide a middle ground between an open-ended entitlement and an appropriated program. Although more flexible than an open-ended entitlement, it still has significant problems. Again, if the number of people applying exceeds expectations, the minimum benefit might end up consuming more of the budget than anticipated, reducing the funds available for the flexible portion of the program. For the beneficiaries who use a large quantity and broad array of services, the minimum benefit could be well below what they need. At the other end of the spectrum, a minimum benefit could provide more services than needed to at least a portion of the eligible population. Finally, the nonentitlement portion of the program would be financially vulnerable to inadequate appropriation increases over time.

The third option is to entitle persons to an assessment, a plan of care, and government-provided services on a funds-available basis. The notion here is "full funding" rather than an entitlement to a specific set of services. Under full funding, the budget is established by assuming a high level of participation by the eligible population and a substantial level of service provided to each participant. Of the three possible solutions, this option provides federal and state governments with the greatest protection against out-of-control expenditures and gives states the greatest degree of flexibility to design programs that meet individual needs. Because it is not an entitlement program and because its funds must be appropriated, this option avoids the automatic expenditure increases inherent in the medicare program, where the government is legally required to pay the costs of services received by eligible persons. Moreover, even though the federal contribution to the new program would likely be very high, states cannot be forced to contribute more than they are willing or able to pay.

## Integration of Acute and Long-Term Care

During the last decade, awareness of the lack of coordination between acute and long-term care has steadily grown. Under the present configuration of financing, the federal medicare program is the dominant player in acute care for the elderly, while long-term care services are primarily organized and funded by state-run medicaid programs. By emphasizing the state role in long-term care, an undesirable by-product of reform may be to increase the disjuncture between acute and long-term care.

A few efforts, including the S/HMOs, San Francisco's On Lok and its Program of All-Inclusive Care for the Elderly (PACE) national replication sites, and the members of the National Chronic Care Consortium, are attempting to remedy the existing split by bringing the two types of care into one integrated system. The premise underlying these programs is that better coordination of service delivery and integrated financing of care would give the elderly higher-quality, more cost-effective acute and long-term care.

These models strive to avoid both the functional decline that can result from unmet needs and the unnecessary costs associated with overmet needs. At least in theory, this coordinated approach would produce acute care savings because lower-cost outpatient and home-based services could be substituted for more costly inpatient services when appropriate.[8] These acute care savings, in turn, could be used to fund more comprehensive long-term care benefits. Moreover, the fixed-budget, risk-based financing structure of these models creates strong incentives to provide appropriate services at the lowest possible cost.

Some long-term care advocates worry that consolidation with acute care will result in the undesirable medicalization of long-term care. A related concern is that, in an integrated system, acute care will claim the funds budgeted for long-term care, leaving long-term care once again underfunded.

Despite the widespread interest in these coordinated models, several issues must be addressed before they will have more than a small impact. First, S/HMOs provide only modest amounts of long-term care coverage for a deliberately small portion of their covered population.[9] Consequently, they may not provide enough long-term care services to reduce the need for acute care services significantly.

Second, the models have had difficulty generating large enrollments because of the restrictions they place on choice of physician.[10] Indeed, this is a general problem for HMOs. It is difficult to judge whether a large number of elderly can be convinced to exchange limitations in their choice of physicians for expanded coverage of long-term care.[b] Third, and related, the jury is still out about whether these models can achieve substantial savings.[11]

Thus, although the idea of integrated acute and long-term care seems sound, it is not fully tested in practice. In addition, under almost all health reform plans, HMOs will have the prospect of enrolling millions of uninsured persons plus others who will be steered toward them by cost considerations. As a result, it is not at all clear that HMOs will be interested in taking on the elderly and disabled, who are expensive to treat and have needs that HMOs are not used to addressing. Nonetheless, it is important that the new long-term care program be open to experimental approaches to integrating acute and long-term care.

b. This reluctance by the elderly to enroll in HMOs may be a significant problem if, as proposed by President Clinton, home care and prescription drugs are generally available to the elderly population without their having to enroll in health maintenance organizations.

## Integrated Care for All the Disabled

Previous policy debates about long-term care reform have focused solely on the elderly, virtually ignoring the nonelderly disabled. Those days are past. In the current debate, the nonelderly disabled have a seat at the policy table and their views are strongly considered.

This newfound political strength is attributable to two factors. First, exhilarated by their success with the Americans with Disabilities Act, the younger disabled have pushed themselves into the debate. Second, advocacy groups for the elderly have sought to counter arguments about generational equity by promoting the need for long-term care as a problem affecting all age groups, not just the elderly.

As a result, there is substantial policy interest in a single program that would include all disabled persons—the frail elderly, persons with Alzheimer's disease, the mentally retarded, the nonelderly physically disabled, and the mentally ill. The important question is whether all groups will be well served by a single program. Certainly all disability groups need services and share certain similarities, but each group also has substantial differences from the others. These differences exist in the areas of eligibility criteria, breadth of services needed, and desire to control and direct the services.

All programs need criteria to establish who is eligible for services and who is not. The difficulty is that measures—specifically, activities of daily living (ADLs)—that work well for the elderly in distinguishing the severely impaired from the mildly disabled do a relatively poor job for the nonelderly disabled. In particular, they do not "capture" many persons that medicaid is already serving. This is especially true for the mentally retarded and developmentally disabled, many of whom have limitations in the instrumental activities of daily living (IADLs) but not in ADLs.[c] Expanding eligibility to include the IADLs would reach this group, but it would also grant eligibility to very large numbers of elderly, making the program prohibitively expensive.

The breadth of services needed by the elderly and the nonelderly disabled is also different. Most programs for the elderly provide a relatively narrow range of services, primarily personal care and homemaker

c. The term "activities of daily living," or ADLs, refers to the basic tasks of everyday life, such as eating, bathing, dressing, toileting, and getting in and out of bed. "Instrumental activities of daily living," or IADLs, capture a more complex range of activities necessary for independent living in the community, including handling personal finances, preparing meals, shopping, traveling, doing housework, using the telephone, and taking medications.

services. The range of services used by the nonelderly disabled is far broader, especially for the mentally retarded, who use everything from personal care to vocational training. This much broader range of services reflects not only broader needs, but also different expectations. Most people find it acceptable for a disabled elder to live with her daughter and to spend most of her time at home (that acceptance may wane as the "baby boomers" age). This is not true of the nonelderly disabled population who want to live independently and to participate fully in all the same activities open to the nondisabled. The notion of "home" care threatens to imprison these individuals within the narrow physical structure of their houses.

Finally, the elderly and nonelderly disabled have different views concerning who hires and directs the services.[12] The overwhelming majority of home care services for the elderly are provided through an agency, which is responsible for the performance of its employees. In contrast, the nonelderly disabled often want to be able to hire their own "personal attendant" and decide when, where, and what they will do. For persons familiar with elderly programs, this approach raises troublesome issues of quality assurance. It also raises administrative questions of who is responsible for paying social security, unemployment compensation, and (after health care reform) health insurance premiums.

## Conclusion

Although financing is the thorniest problem policymakers must confront when they consider reforming long-term care for the elderly, they must also think through the design and administrative issues that need to be addressed in implementing a new program. These include how expenditures will be controlled, what services will be available, whether there will be a legal entitlement to these services, the role of the states, how acute and long-term care services will be integrated, and how the program will meet the needs of the nonelderly as well as elderly disabled. This chapter has argued for a new approach to social insurance, one that emphasizes capped rather than open-ended funding, "full funding" rather than an entitlement to services, and a broad array of services to be defined by the states rather than a federally specified list of covered services.

These departures from conventional entitlement programs such as medicare and social security come at a price. Politically, it is hard to explain what people would get from such a program because the answer clearly depends on what the state decides to provide. To many, state flexibility makes the benefits ephemeral. Despite these problems, this approach best fits the government's need for fiscal control and the disabled's need for service flexibility.

## Chapter Nine

# Paying for a Public Program

To be seriously considered, any proposal for increasing funding for public programs must be accompanied by an acceptable financing strategy.[1] For example, the Pepper Commission was sharply criticized in the press and elsewhere because it did not offer a specific proposal for raising the revenue necessary to pay for its otherwise sound proposals.[2] To avoid adding to the federal budget deficit, even modest public insurance options will require substantial additional revenue or shifts from other government programs. Possible sources of revenue include broad-based taxes, such as payroll, income, and consumption taxes; taxes that fall more heavily on beneficiaries, such as premiums or estate taxes; and redirected funds from programs benefiting the elderly, such as medicare or social security.

## Comparing Tax Options

Every tax source has its own politics and economics, and any tax increase will be controversial among certain groups. For purposes of comparison, tax proposals are commonly evaluated against several broad, sometimes competing, objectives: equity, economic neutrality, efficiency, and simplicity.[3]

### EQUITY

The equity principle tends to dominate discussions of tax policy, but having people contribute their "fair share" to the cost of government is complex because fairness has many different definitions. One approach considers the benefit derived from the public service. Here, each taxpayer contributes in line with the benefits he or she receives. In the context of financing long-term care, applying a strict benefit standard of equity is unworkable and undesirable.[a] There is no way to know who will receive long-term care benefits until the need is actually present and the costs large. Having the tax burden fall on the relative few who end up in nursing homes or need extensive home care is no better than the current system, where long-term care recipients pay a large portion of costs out of pocket. Further, beneficiaries of a long-term care program will include middle-aged family caregivers, as well as the disabled individual. From this perspective, the nonelderly should also help pay for the program.

Another definition of tax equity relates to an individual's ability to pay. Under this definition, people with more income and assets should pay proportionately more than those with less income and assets. Assessment of whether a tax structure is progressive, regressive, or proportional surrounds the concern that taxes reflect an individual's ability to pay.[b] Thus, federal financing for medicaid passes the ability-to-pay test because it is funded primarily by federal income taxes, which are generally progressive.

The financing of the nation's two most popular programs for the elderly—social security and medicare part A[c]—do less well on the ability-to-pay equity test, although better than is often alleged.[4] Social security is financed through a flat payroll tax on wages up to a ceiling. This tax is technically regressive because nonwage income is excluded and because wages above the ceiling are not taxed. Social security taxes should not be considered separately from the benefits they provide, however, because the benefit formula redistributes funds to lower-income workers. That is, low earners receive higher benefits in relation to their contributions than do high earners, and high earners have a limit on how much they receive. When the overall program is consid-

a. Simple arithmetic suggests that the costs of a public long-term care insurance plan are too large to be shouldered solely by the elderly. For example, if the cost of home care and front-end nursing home coverage were paid entirely by the elderly, the per capita cost would be $2,840 in 1993. If only the elderly whose incomes were above 150 percent of poverty paid, then the per capita cost would be $4,122. Either way, it is too much to ask of most elderly. Estimates from the Brookings-ICF Long-Term Care Financing Model.

b. Progressive taxes place a proportionately heavier burden on those who have a greater ability to pay. In contrast, regressive taxes place a greater burden on lower-income groups with less ability to pay. Taxes that are proportional place an equal burden on all income groups.

c. Medicare part A is the hospital insurance program that everyone covered under social security is automatically entitled to at age 65. Part A also covers skilled nursing facility, home health, and hospice care.

ered, the strongly redistributive quality of the benefit formula offsets the regressivity of the payroll tax.

Although the flat payroll tax for medicare part A is also somewhat regressive, it is also true that upper-income people pay more than lower-income people for the same benefit package. For example, a worker making $120,000 pays six times as much as one who makes $20,000. In addition, the Omnibus Budget Reconciliation Act of 1993 totally removed the wage ceiling for medicare part A taxes, easing the regressivity of this revenue source. For beneficiaries, issues of equity are eclipsed by the fact that medicare is still a "good buy" for all income groups because payroll taxes and premiums cover less than a third of the average expected lifetime benefits.[5]

## ECONOMIC NEUTRALITY OR EFFICIENCY

Ideally, taxes should be neutral or interfere only minimally with economic decisions and behaviors in otherwise efficient or very price-sensitive markets.[6] In other words, taxes should not be so burdensome that they inhibit the consumer's behavior, impede freedom of choice, or distort the actual cost of the good being purchased.[d] For example, sales taxes raise the price of the item being purchased. Depending on the item and the level of taxation, the consumer may decide to buy less of the particular item than is desirable.

## SIMPLICITY

Finally, a tax structure should be simple and understandable to the taxpayer and free from arbitrary administration. The cost of administration and compliance, relative to the revenue generated, should be minimal. Despite other problems, payroll taxes are ideal from the administrative standpoint: they bring in large amounts of revenue, are simple to compute (a flat percentage with no exemptions), and are simple to administer because the employer withholds both the employer and employee contributions at the source.

## Principal Sources of Revenue

At least one or more of several large revenue-raising options—an income tax, a payroll tax, or a national consumption tax such as the

---

d. The exception is an excise tax imposed deliberately to discourage consumption, such as the excise taxes on liquor and tobacco.

value-added tax—will likely be needed to finance any of the major public long-term care financing options.[e] Payroll and individual income taxes already accounted for 82 percent of federal tax revenues in 1993.[7] Although the United States does not have a broad-based national consumption tax per se, it derived about $48 billion (or about 4 percent of total revenue) from miscellaneous excise taxes in 1993.[8] Payroll, income, and consumption taxes have the advantage of growing as the economy expands, something that will be critical for the future as the number of disabled elderly increases and their long-term care needs grow commensurately.

## PAYROLL TAXES

The country's principal social insurance programs—social security, medicare part A, and unemployment insurance—are all funded through payroll taxes. Employees and employers each contribute 6.2 percent of wages (subject to a taxable salary limit in 1993 of $57,600) to finance social security and 1.45 percent of wages (no taxable limits) to finance medicare. In 1988, 90 percent of American families (excluding families with zero or negative incomes) paid more in payroll taxes than in income taxes.[9]

Generally, payroll taxes encourage middle- and upper-income individuals to seek nonwage forms of income (such as paid vacation time, comprehensive medical insurance, and earnings on investments) that are not taxed. For low-income individuals, however, reduced take-home pay creates work disincentives. Businesses are usually opposed to payroll taxes because they increase the cost of labor. In contrast the public finds increases in payroll taxes to be fairer than increases in the income tax or property taxes—especially when the new taxes are used to fund a program the public finds desirable, such as long-term care, or when the increase makes the payroll tax less regressive.[10]

Because payroll taxes are broad based, increasing the tax rate raises revenue faster than increasing the taxable cap. Increasing the medicare payroll tax rate would be a more important potential source of revenue than was the recent removal of the cap on taxable income, which is expected to yield less than $6 billion a year.[11] By increasing the employee and employer contribution rates from 1.45 percent to 2.00 percent, for

e. Unless otherwise indicated, all years referred to in this chapter are fiscal years, and all estimates are in 1993 dollars. Where the revenue estimates have a phase-in period, the average annual figure is calculated for the period after the phase-in is complete and then adjusted back to 1993.

TABLE 9-1. *Total Expenditures for Public Long-Term Care as a Percentage of Payroll and Federal Personal Income Tax, Base Case and Public Insurance Options, Selected Periods*

| Option[a] | Payroll tax[b] | | | Income tax surcharge[c] | | |
|---|---|---|---|---|---|---|
| | 1993 | 2018 | 2048 | 1993 | 2018 | 2048 |
| Base case | | | | | | |
| Total costs | 2.37 | 3.61 | 6.85 | 14.58 | 21.41 | 40.21 |
| Public costs | 1.28 | 1.80 | 3.43 | 7.87 | 10.70 | 20.15 |
| Medicaid liberalization only | 1.48 | 1.93 | 3.83 | 9.03 | 11.47 | 21.48 |
| Expanded home care only | 1.89 | 2.42 | 4.58 | 11.57 | 14.34 | 25.72 |
| Front-end nursing home and expanded home care | 1.99 | 2.59 | 4.91 | 12.17 | 15.36 | 27.59 |
| Back-end nursing home and expanded home care | 2.28 | 3.15 | 6.08 | 13.96 | 18.67 | 34.14 |
| Comprehensive nursing home and expanded home care | 2.80 | 3.98 | 7.75 | 17.14 | 623.60 | 43.54 |

SOURCE: Brookings-ICF Long-Term Care Financing Model. The year 1993 represents the five-year average for the period 1991–95, 2018 the five-year average for the period 2016–20, and 2048 the five-year average for the period 2046–50.

a. All options except the base case include liberalization of medicaid eligibility rules.

b. Combined employee and employer contributions. No ceiling on taxable salaries.

c. An income tax surcharge is a flat percentage of the original tax liability. For example, if total long-term care costs in 1993 were paid using an income tax surcharge, someone in the 18 percent bracket would instead be in a 20.6 percent bracket.

example, the revenue gain for 1993 would have been three times that of removing the tax cap, or about $18.1 billion.[12]

Table 9-1 shows estimates of the payroll tax required to finance the medicaid liberalization policy modeled in chapter 6 and the four public long-term care insurance programs modeled in chapter 7. For comparison, the table also shows the level of taxation needed if only a payroll tax was used to finance the existing system. Estimates were developed by extrapolating long-term care expenditures of the elderly and wage information for the working population through the year 2050.[13] The payroll tax estimates represent employer and employee portions combined and assume there are no limits on the amount of wages that can be taxed.

In 1993 the various public options would require a payroll tax ranging from 1.48 to 2.80 percent.[14] Reflecting the growth in the number of elderly requiring long-term care, these rates grow substantially by 2048, ranging from 3.83 to 7.75 percent. For comparison, to finance the current public programs solely by a payroll tax, the tax rate would have to be 1.28 percent in 1993 and 3.43 percent in 2048. These are not trivial tax increases, especially since they would be in addition to existing social security and medicare taxes. Still, only the tax rates for the comprehensive social insurance program seem prohibitively high in absolute terms and then not until the baby boom generation starts to need long-term care.

## INCOME TAXES

Increasing income tax rates would be technically simple and progressive and offer great revenue-generating potential. For example, the new 36 percent income tax bracket created for filers with taxable incomes above $115,000 ($140,000 for couples), together with the 10 percent surcharge on those with incomes above $250,000, will yield more than $20 billion in 1993.[15] Despite the clear advantages to using an income tax mechanism to finance long-term care reform, President Clinton's 1993 economic package significantly raised rates for higher-income taxpayers, making the income tax a politically less desirable financing mechanism. Many policymakers are reluctant to rekindle the highly charged debate over income tax policy. Nonetheless, current tax rates are, arguably, still low enough that raising them slightly would not be punitive or harmful to economic incentives.[16]

Another strategy for raising revenue under the income tax structure is to broaden the tax base. In 1993, more than 120 separate tax preferences, representing $450 billion in lost tax revenues, remained in the tax code.[17] Critics of these tax preferences contend that they are frequently less efficient than direct expenditures at accomplishing the desired goals.[18] Ending some of these tax expenditures could raise large sums of money. For example, among these tax preferences, employer contributions to health insurance plans are the second largest tax expenditure (after the deductibility of mortgage interest on owner-occupied homes).[19] Not counting employer contributions to health insurance as income to employees cost the federal government $62.9 billion in lost federal income tax revenues in 1993,[20] or about three-fourths of the federal revenue spent on medicaid.[21]

Table 9-1 provides estimates of the income tax rates that would be necessary to finance the various options. These estimates assume that the income tax will continue to make up the same portion of federal revenues and gross domestic product through the year 2048 as it did in 1993.[22] The income tax surcharge assumes a pay-as-you-go structure.[f] In 2048 a 21.48 percent surcharge would be necessary to finance medicaid liberalization alone. For the most expensive public option—

f. A surcharge is a flat percentage of the original tax liability.

comprehensive coverage—the increase in 2048 would be 43.54 percent. For comparison, in 2048, if current public programs were financed solely by an income tax, the surcharge would have to be 20.15 percent.

## CONSUMPTION TAXES

Although income is considered the best indicator of a person's ability to pay, consumption offers an alternative measure of economic position.[23] Depending on how they are constructed, consumption taxes can generate significant amounts of revenue, need not be too regressive, and are predictable because consumption does not fluctuate as much as income.[24] In addition, consumption taxes seem less onerous because they are paid in small amounts spread throughout the year rather than all coming due on April 15th. Some suggest that a consumption tax might also provide an incentive to increase savings.[25]

The United States, primarily at the state and local levels, currently uses two kinds of consumption taxes—retail sales and excise—to raise revenues. Interest in a third kind, a national value-added tax, has grown considerably in recent years. Many of the same arguments can be made for and against each of these three different consumption taxes; in fact, the only major difference is the point at which each is collected. Retail sales taxes are collected at the point of sale to the ultimate consumer, while excise taxes are collected at the point of manufacture but passed on to the consumer through price increases. Value-added taxes are collected at each stage of production and fall on the increased value of output over the cost of goods and services purchased from others.

*Retail sales tax.* Retail sales taxes, the most widely used form of consumption tax, offer a direct, broad-based method of taxation. In 1990 forty-five states levied some form of general or selective retail sales taxes;[26] in 1989, 49 percent of states' total revenues were generated by those taxes.[27] A sales tax can be constructed to exclude basic items such as food, shelter, and medical care, and yet can still subject people who purchase luxury items to a heavier tax burden. Indeed, twenty-seven states attempt to make sales tax more equitable by excluding food, thirty-two exclude utility bills, and forty-three exempt prescription drugs.[28]

*Excise taxes.* Excise taxes are often levied so that they encourage socially desirable goals. These "offsetting virtues" may result in altered consumption patterns; for example, taxes on cigarettes and alcohol may discourage some use of those goods, while taxes on gasoline or diesel fuel may encourage conservation.[29] Frequently, these secondary benefits are considered as worthwhile as the revenue raised from the consumption tax itself. In fact, excise taxes made up only a small part—4 percent—of total federal receipts in 1993. In that year federal alcohol and tobacco taxes were estimated to bring in $13.5 billion; gasoline and diesel taxes were expected to generate only $15.4 billion that year.[30] President Clinton's health care reform plan would raise tobacco taxes substantially.[31] But it is highly unlikely that tobacco or alcohol taxes would increase fast enough to keep pace with the growing costs of long-term care.

*Value-added taxes (VAT)*. In recent years, interest in value-added taxes has increased not only in this country but worldwide. As of 1991 more than fifty countries had adopted a VAT, and another ten were seriously considering adopting one.[32] Among those countries utilizing a VAT, the tax rate ranged from 5 percent to 35 percent, depending on the relative importance of the VAT in the overall tax structure of the country.[33] Several reasons explain the VAT's popularity. In addition to the predictability and flexibility generally attributable to consumption taxes, the broad base of a VAT allows it to generate large amounts of revenue with low tax rates. For example, the Congressional Budget Office estimates that a 5 percent VAT would raise $50.8 billion annually for the least regressive formula, which excludes food, housing, and medical care, or $97.8 billion annually for a comprehensive VAT.[34]

Proponents believe that a VAT would be administratively and economically efficient. In addition, a VAT would extend the sales tax to the service industry, which is a growing portion of the economy.[35] The economic effects of the VAT are also favorable. It is considered pro-growth because, unlike the income tax, it does not tax return on savings and new investments and therefore does not inhibit the accumulation of capital.[36] By applying a uniform rate, a VAT is also neutral in two ways. It does not distort the allocation of capital among alternative uses,[37] and it creates no incentive for businesses to substitute capital for labor or vice versa.[38]

Based on the experiences of other countries, the cost of administering a VAT is also relatively low. Countries that are members of the Organization for Economic Cooperation and Development (OECD) and that have VATs lose as little as 0.33 to 1.0 percent of revenue to the administration of the tax.[39]

*Disadvantages of the consumption tax*. Those who oppose the use of consumption taxes to raise revenue for long-term care point out that all consumption taxes are regressive because lower-income individuals tend to use more of their income for consumption than do higher-income people. In 1985, for example, a 5 percent tax on all consumption, including food, would have amounted to 17.6 percent of income for the poorest 5 percent of families, while the richest 5 percent of families would allocate only 2.2 percent of their income for this tax.[40]

Finally, in the past, the federal government has made only limited use of consumption taxes, while state and local jurisdictions use them extensively. Consequently, any federal consumption tax would be considered an intrusion on state and local tax bases and would likely be opposed by these levels of government.

## Mechanisms to Ensure That the Elderly Pay Their Fair Share

Although taxes levied against the elderly alone (such as taxes on social security benefits or increases in medicare premiums), are unpopular with both the elderly and the broader nonelderly population, it is only fair for the elderly to help pay for a program that largely benefits them.[41] Therefore, all but low-income elderly should pay something in the form of insurance premiums or higher taxes toward the financing of a long-term care program, and the more well-to-do elderly should pay more. Indeed, the elderly have expressed a willingness to pay additional taxes for long-term care.[42]

### BENEFICIARY PREMIUMS

Most public long-term care insurance proposals would require the elderly to pay an insurance premium, both to address the issue of generational equity and to reduce the amount of new taxes needed. Politically, a premium paid by the beneficiaries would probably meet with less resistance than collecting the funds through the general tax system, because people receive a direct benefit in return for what they pay.

Although this premium should not be expected to pay the entire cost—public insurance programs are too expensive to spread over this number of people—a modest premium could offset a small but nontrivial portion of the costs. For example, a premium of $10 a month, assessed against all elderly whose incomes are more than 150 percent of the poverty level, would have raised about $2.9 billion in 1993.[43] A premium of 5 percent of income tax liability of the elderly, with no cap, would have raised $3.7 billion in 1993.[44] Policymakers must make sure that the premium is not overly burdensome when added to other health care expenditures that the elderly must make. To lessen the burden on

low-income elderly, medicaid could pay the premium for this population, as it does now for medicare part B.[g] Also, it is important to ensure
that any premium increases reflect the increased costs of the program
over time, so that the elderly pay a fair share of inflation and increases
in service use.

## TAXING SOCIAL SECURITY BENEFITS

Several revenue-raising proposals focus on increasing the portion of
social security benefits that are subject to the federal income tax. Up
until 1984, social security benefits were exempt from taxation altogether.
In that year, the law was changed to subject social security benefits to
tax if the recipient had total income above certain levels ($25,000 for
individuals; $32,000 for couples). The Omnibus Budget Reconciliation
Act of 1993 increased the proportion of social security benefits subject
to taxation and then offset that somewhat by also raising the level of
income subject to this increased taxation.[45] Starting in 1993 half of the
social security benefits of individuals with incomes between $25,000
and $34,000 (and couples with incomes between $32,000 and
$44,000) are subject to taxation, but 85 percent of the benefits are
considered taxable income for individuals with incomes greater than
$34,000 (and couples with incomes greater than $44,000).[46] This
change affects only beneficiaries with the highest incomes—about one-
eighth of all beneficiaries—and is expected to raise about $5 billion
annually starting in 1994.[47] If the income thresholds were removed
altogether and 85 percent of all social security income was taxed, the
revenue gain would be $21.8 billion annually.[48] Of all the options for
taxing the elderly to help pay for long-term care, this option would raise
by far the most revenue. A significant number of lower-income retirees
are highly dependent on their social security benefits, however, and have
very little in the way of private pensions.[49] Consequently, the mechanism
for generating the most revenue from the elderly is also the most harmful
to lower-income beneficiaries.

## TAXING THE ACTUARIAL VALUE OF MEDICARE

Currently, employers pay half of the payroll tax for medicare part A,
and general revenues finance three-quarters of the cost of part B. Neither

g. Medicare part B is the voluntary supplemental medical insurance program available
to all elderly that covers physician services, outpatient medical and health services, and
home health services not covered under part A. To participate the elderly must enroll and
pay a premium that approximates a quarter of the cost of the program.

benefit is treated as income to the beneficiary, and neither is subject to taxation. Some limitations could be placed on the tax exclusion of these benefits and revenues raised from taxing their actuarial value. If these benefits were treated as income and if the same income thresholds applied as applied to social security benefits in 1992 ($25,000 for individuals, $32,000 for couples), the revenue gain for 1994 would be $4.5 billion.[50] Taxing these benefits at their cash value would result in higher-income beneficiaries' receiving lower after-tax benefits than they do now and would increase the progressivity of the program.

## ESTATE TAXES

Because long-term care insurance would enable nursing home and home care patients to preserve more of their assets, increasing the estate tax or taxing capital gains at death are both logical sources of additional revenue.[51] These taxing mechanisms would reduce the intergenerational transfer of wealth and could increase the progressivity of the federal tax system.

The principal arguments against estate taxes are that they represent double taxation (the first being when the asset is acquired) and that any increase in the tax could negatively affect a person's spending and saving patterns. That is, a person would be less likely to save or to invest because the ultimate return would be reduced.[52] Estate taxes create an incentive for people to avoid taxation by transferring assets to children or other family members during their lifetime. A major drawback of estate taxes (and taxing capital gains at death) is that heirs may be forced to sell the assets in order to pay the tax. This could impose particular hardships on those who inherit small family businesses and family farms and who want to continue the enterprise.

Under current law, an estimated $12.9 billion was raised from taxation of estates in 1993.[53] A 1981 change in the laws governing estate taxes increased the amount of an estate exempt from taxation from $175,000 to $600,000, effectively reducing the number of estates subject to taxation to only one out of every one hundred.[54] As a result, in 1988 only $62.5 billion in assets was subject to taxation.[55] The legislation also gradually reduced the maximum tax rate from 65 percent to 50 percent and reduced the amount subject to the maximum rate of taxation from estates in excess of $4 million to estates in excess of $2.5 million. A modest increase in the tax rate or a reduction in the minimum estate subject to taxation would raise some, but not much, revenue. If the ceiling on exemptions were set at $300,000 rather than $600,000, less than $2.8 billion in new revenue would be gained annually. An additional 15 percent of estates would be subject to tax, but the vast majority of estates would still be exempt. If the top tax rate were increased to 55 percent, approximately $0.4 billion would be raised annually.[56]

An alternative way to tap this potential revenue source is to tax capital gains on the decedent's final income tax return or to require beneficiaries to pay capital gains based on the original purchase price. Currently, beneficiaries who sell an inherited asset pay taxes only on capital gains accumulated since the asset was inherited and only if the asset was included in an estate valued at $600,000 or more. Taxing capital gains at death would raise an additional $6.8 billion annually.[57] Economists prefer this avenue of raising revenue over a direct tax on estates because it may produce a "jolt to the economy" by removing the incentive for descendants to hold on to less profitable investments and to invest instead in more profitable and productive ventures.[58]

## MEDICARE AND SOCIAL SECURITY SAVINGS

An alternative to raising new revenues would be to reduce expenditures for other government programs. Indeed, President Clinton has proposed to finance both the expansion of long-term care services and the new prescription drug benefit for the elderly primarily by cutting in half the rate of increase in medicare spending for acute care.[h]

By not raising taxes, this approach sidesteps the most difficult political barrier to financing a major expansion in long-term care services. Moreover, because the medicare savings will be reinvested in services for the elderly, the spending reductions for acute care are not taking money away from the elderly. The key question is how much can be saved without seriously damaging access to and quality of acute care services for the elderly. On the one hand, every other country in the world provides universal health care to its population at far lower expense than does the United States. For example, per capita health care expenditures in the United States are already about 50 percent higher than they are in Canada and twice what they are for the average of the OECD countries.[59] Moreover, all other countries devote a

h. Baseline projections expect medicare to grow at more than 11 percent in 1994 and 1995 and then to decline to annual growth of 9.0 percent in 2000. Under the president's reform proposal, the rate of increase in medicare expenditures would decline from 7.4 percent in 1996 to 4.1 percent in 2000. See "Health Security Act" (Government Printing Office, 1993), pp. 734–86.

much smaller percentage of their economy to health care than does the United States.[60] Between 1985 and 1991 Germany and Sweden actually managed to reduce the percentage of their gross domestic product going to health care. Clearly, much lower expenditures for health care are technically possible.

On the other hand, the administration is proposing rates of increase in medicare (and health spending more generally) dramatically below the levels the program has ever experienced.[61] To achieve these savings, both the price and quantity of medicare services provided must be reduced. Historically, medicare has not been very effective in controlling usage. The presumption in the president's plan is that the nonelderly will eventually join health maintenance organizations (HMOs), which control their costs primarily by controlling the use of hospitals and specialist physicians. Only about 6 percent of the elderly are currently enrolled in HMOs, however, and there is some evidence that they are healthier than the average elderly person.[62] Most elderly, therefore, are likely to remain in the fee-for-service system. Additionally, some elderly enroll in HMOs simply to gain access to prescription drug benefits not included in fee-for-service medicare. Under the administration's reform plan, that incentive will be eliminated because the medicare benefit package will include prescription drugs. Thus, expenditures for the elderly will have to be controlled primarily by reducing payment rates, which have already been the focus of budget cuts throughout the last decade. Moreover, physicians and other providers are likely to offset fee reductions in part by increasing the volume or intensity of services. Achieving these projected savings in medicare will thus be difficult.

Closely related to medicare savings is the notion of reducing social security payments and using the savings to finance long-term care.[63] Indeed, public opinion polls suggest that many retirees are willing to accept reductions in either private pensions or social security in order to receive enhanced retiree health or medicare benefits; by analogy, they might be willing to accept a trade-off of cash benefits for long-term care coverage.[64] A 5 percent reduction in social security benefits would generate $13 billion in savings, before protections for low-income beneficiaries.[65] Politically, if the elderly are to help pay for the program, it is probably easier not to give them the money in the first place, rather than having to take the money back later as premium payments. "Tampering" with social security benefits is always politically explosive, however, even if the funds are used for other programs for the elderly.

## Prefunding versus Pay-as-You-Go

Starting in 2025, the aging of the baby boom generation will cause sharp increases in the need for long-term care services. As a result, a key issue is whether a public long-term care insurance program should be financed on a pay-as-you-go basis or on a prefunded basis, as social security is, so that a large reserve can be built up while the baby-boomers are still working.

Advocates of a prefunded system argue that the reserves can increase the national savings rate. That, in turn, would lead to increased investment, which would lead to a larger, stronger economy, out of which long-term care could be financed with less burden.[66] Unfortunately, a prerequisite to using public savings in a trust fund to increase national savings is for the rest of the federal budget to be balanced, something that, at least for the foreseeable future, seems unlikely. That means that any reserves for long-term care are likely to be used as the social security trust fund has been used—to finance the rest of the government rather than to increase national savings.[67]

Aside from the question of whether the reserves can actually function to increase national savings, pay-as-you-go advocates note that the trust fund does not operate like many people think it does. Many people envision it as a savings account in which the money is deposited and withdrawn as needed. Instead, the social security trust fund uses its reserves to buy federal government bonds, which will be redeemed for cash in the future. The problem is that, to obtain the cash necessary to redeem the bonds, the federal government will eventually have to raise additional tax revenues or sell new bonds. Thus, a surplus in a trust fund does not prevent the government from having to raise additional revenues at some later date.

## Conclusion

Because all public insurance options will require additional public spending, an important question is how to pay for it. One strategy is to raise additional revenue through increased taxes and premiums. The United States uses payroll taxes to finance social security and medicare. These taxes are simple to administer and require upper-income people to pay more than lower-income people. The principal arguments against payroll taxes are that they are technically regressive, they raise the cost of labor, and there is bound to be considerable political resistance to additional payroll taxes. An income tax is less regressive than a payroll tax, but it is probably the least popular of all taxes.

Consumption taxes have gained considerable attention in recent years because they can generate large sums of revenue even at low tax rates. Furthermore, given the lack of national savings the country faces, consumption taxes have the tangential benefit of encouraging savings rather than consumption. All twenty-four OECD countries, except the United States, have some form of consumption tax, either a VAT or a national sales tax.[68] The principal drawback to consumption taxes is that they are regressive because lower-income individuals tend to use more of their income for consumption than do higher-income people. However, proponents of a consumption tax argue that this regressivity can be mitigated by changing the lower end of the income tax rates or by exempting certain basic items such as food, shelter, and medical care from taxation.

Some financing should come from various other options, even though they will raise smaller amounts of revenue. For example, because any public insurance strategy will almost certainly provide some asset protection, raising the estate tax or taxing capital gains at death are attractive financing mechanisms. For reasons of generational equity and securing political support, an insurance premium paid by the elderly is likely to be included in any public long-term care insurance program.

The other basic strategy is to reduce expenditures or the rate of growth in expenditures for other government programs and use the savings for long-term care instead. President Clinton has proposed using large reductions in the rate of increase in medicare spending to finance an expansion of home care. The principal question is whether the proposed reductions are politically achievable and can be done without harming the medicare program. Although other countries have achieved much lower levels of per capita expenditures for health care than has the United States, the administration plan depends on low rates of increase that have never been seen in the program before and that have not been sustained in other industrialized countries.[69]

## Chapter Ten

# What Is to Be Done?
# Recommendations for Reforming
# Long-Term Care

Paying for long-term care, already a major problem for disabled people, their families, and society, will be an increasingly serious problem in the future. Because of greater longevity, many more people face a period of prolonged disability in older age. Most are cared for informally by relatives and friends, although often at great emotional and sometimes financial costs.

When the disabled and their families seek paid home care or nursing home services, they find that medicare and private insurance do not cover long-term care to any significant extent. Those who need paid care must use their own resources or, once those resources are gone, turn to medicaid, a severely means-tested program for the poor. Moreover, the service delivery system is highly tilted toward nursing home services rather than the home care services the elderly disabled prefer.

In developing recommendations for reform of the long-term care financing and delivery system, we were guided by five main goals. First, the need for long-term care should be treated as a normal risk of life and of growing old. In other words, there should be a financing system that people are confident will offer a way of paying for services if they need them.

Second, disabled individuals who use long-term care services should not have to bear the brunt of paying for them. The financial risk of long-term care should be pooled across a broad population. Moreover, the financing and delivery system should protect people against catastrophic out-of-pocket costs. From this it follows that people should not have to use an inordinately high proportion of their income and assets to purchase financial protection against these costs.

Third, because long-term care is a normal risk of living and growing old, it is a risk that should be insured against. As such, the current system's heavy dependence on welfare financing is inappropriate and should be limited to the extent possible.

Fourth, although disabled people of all ages want to live at home and to do so with some dignity, the current system does not provide them with much help in that regard. No proposal for long-term care reform should be accepted without some method for altering the institutional bias of the current system.

And, finally, political reality requires that new public expenditures and the taxes necessary to finance them be kept to some acceptable level. Americans tend to be more concerned with the level of government expenditures as opposed to how much society spends overall, and few would dispute that raising taxes in the United States is always difficult.

Our research findings, especially our simulation results, informed our evaluations of how close each of the various reform options would come to achieving these goals. Private long-term care insurance is likely to grow, but products geared toward purchase by the elderly face critical affordability barriers. The emerging employer-sponsored private long-term care insurance market offers the promise of solving much of the affordability problem, but that market is likely to remain small because of the difficulties in persuading employers to offer policies and employees to purchase them.

Because only a minority of the elderly and an even smaller percentage of the nonelderly are likely to have private long-term care insurance for the foreseeable future, public programs must be the primary vehicles for reforming the long-term care system. Modification of the medicaid program would reduce the level of catastrophic costs and would help shift the delivery system toward home care, but it would also increase the number of people dependent on welfare. Social insurance strategies do the best in reducing catastrophic out-of-pocket costs and in expanding home care, but they are by far the most costly in terms of increased public expenditures.

Our recommendations call for a mix of public and private initiatives and, within the public sector, a combination of social insurance and medicaid changes. Our reform strategy is similar to that proposed by the U.S. Commission on Comprehensive Health Care (the Pepper

Commission) in 1990.[1] It is also consistent with, albeit more far-reaching than, President Clinton's long-term care proposals.[2] We believe our recommendations will substantially reform the long-term care system at a price that policymakers and the public may be willing to pay.

## Private Insurance

In general, the market for private long-term care insurance has been small because demand is lacking and because the insurance industry has not marketed products to a broad population. It is not the result of major government barriers.

The government, however, should take some initiatives to encourage individuals with sufficient financial resources to help pay for their own long-term care needs. The government should work with the private sector to educate the public about the risks, costs, and financing options available for long-term care and about the current limitations of coverage under medicare, medicaid, and medigap insurance. To help solve the problems of affordability and adverse selection, government should encourage the development of employer-sponsored policies, especially for the population under age 65. In this regard, federal and state governments should set an example by making group long-term care insurance available to their own employees and retirees and sharing in the cost.

During the last five years, the quality of private long-term care insurance products has improved significantly, as has some state regulation of these policies. Unfortunately, many states have failed to upgrade their regulations to protect consumers, and the standards are not as strong as they should be. To correct this deficiency, new national standards for private long-term care insurance should be adopted. Federally imposed standards should exceed those outlined in the current Model Statute and Regulation developed by the National Association of Insurance Commissioners. Higher standards should be imposed in the areas of inflation protection, nonforfeiture benefits, standardization of benefit triggers, definitions of home care services, policy upgrades, financial standards for insurers, and marketing practices. Proper resolution of these regulatory issues is essential to ensuring that consumers actually get the benefits they think they are purchasing.

Many proposals have been made to provide tax incentives or to subsidize purchase of private insurance in other ways. As a rule, these proposals either primarily benefit upper-income people who can already afford to purchase insurance or provide too small a subsidy to make policies affordable for people of more modest means. Consequently, public subsidies are likely to have only small effects on long-term care financing in relation to the amount of federal revenue lost.

In particular, tax deductions or tax credits for the purchase of private long-term care insurance are ineffective ways to subsidize long-term care, at least in the range that has generally been discussed. Because only about half of the elderly pay any income tax at all, few low- or middle-income elderly would receive any benefit from a tax deduction or credit.[3] In addition, unless the tax credit is exceptionally large, it is unlikely to add greatly to the number of people with insurance. Moreover, our simulations suggest that the tax losses will far exceed the medicaid savings for more than twenty-five years. Advocates who contend that a tax deduction or credit would have a "sentinel" effect by indicating that private long-term care insurance is a worthwhile product have not offered convincing evidence that this would occur.

Some tax changes, however, should be made, so long as the tax loss is offset by other tax increases on the upper-income population who are most likely to benefit from these initiatives. Given the ambiguity of the current tax code, many of these provisions are arguably only clarifications of the tax code rather than actual changes. Indeed, in several instances, insurers and policyholders are already behaving as if the initiatives have already been adopted.

In essence, the tax code should make it clear that private long-term care insurance can build up reserves on a tax-free basis and that the product should otherwise be treated like health insurance. For the insured, that means that any benefits paid from long-term care policies or from riders on life insurance policies should not be considered taxable income. Moreover, employer contributions for long-term care insurance should be a tax-deductible expense and should not be counted as taxable income for employees. Rapidly rising health insurance costs, however, combined with the large unfunded liability for retiree acute care benefits, makes it unlikely that this tax change will result in many companies' deciding to contribute to the cost of long-term care insurance for their employees.

Providing easier access to medicaid for people who purchase private long-term care insurance has some things to recommend it, including a way to bring the public and private sectors together. Easier access to medicaid probably will not induce many more people to purchase insurance, however. Moreover, we are uncomfortable with an initiative that uses a means-tested welfare program to protect the assets of upper-middle- and upper-income individuals.[4]

Similarly, the difficulty of actually getting people to contribute to tax-favored savings accounts and to purchase insurance are very daunting, even though the simulation results for a combination of individual savings and insurance seem promising. The experience with individual retirement accounts leads us to put little faith in this approach.

## Public Sector Programs

The limitations in the role private long-term care insurance is apt to play make public programs central to reforming the long-term care financing and delivery system. Thus, the key question facing policy-makers is what kind of public financing system do Americans, as a society, want. We recommend moving away from using medicaid, a means-tested welfare program, as the principal way to finance long-term care toward a social insurance model, where services are provided to everyone who meets the disability eligibility criteria regardless of their financial status. Given the public costs of comprehensive social insurance, however, a hybrid system consisting of a combination of private insurance, medicaid, and social insurance is inevitable.

We propose to cover a wide variety of home care services for the severely disabled and the first six months of nursing home care through a non-means-tested, social insurance program. The rationale for this strategy is to concentrate new public spending on people who are at home or who have the greatest chance of returning home after a nursing home stay. These are the people with the greatest need for financial protection. Aggressively expanding home care would also bring more balance to the delivery system and provide the services that older people and their families want. Although this new program should be restricted to the severely disabled to limit expenditures, it should be available to all severely disabled persons regardless of age. To control utilization, all but the lowest-income beneficiaries should pay something out of pocket for both nursing home and home care services used.

Although these services should be provided on a non-means-tested basis, the program, especially the home care component, should operate on a very different basis from social security and medicare. First, although the program should be mostly federally funded, states should play a major role in its design and administration. It is essential that the people responsible for administering the long-term care program be close to the people receiving the services. Financing should be through a federal-state matching formula, with a federal contribution considerably higher than the existing medicaid match rate. Second, policymakers are unlikely to enact such a major initiative without some guarantee that its costs will not explode. To guarantee that expenditures will not run out of control, spending should be capped and adjusted annually for inflation in the costs of long-term care and the growth in the disabled population. Each state should be allocated a budget based on the estimated number of severely disabled persons and the cost of providing services in the state. Third, federal policymakers should recognize that quality of life and autonomy are important considerations in providing long-term care and thus should allow the states to cover a very broad range of services. This breadth of services is especially important to the nonelderly population. And, finally, the combination of capping expenditures and allowing coverage for a very wide range of services necessitates that services be provided on a funds-available rather than entitlement basis. Unfortunately, we can think of no way to ensure that expenditures will stay within the cap if people are entitled by law to these services. While this model of social insurance may seem strange to many Americans, it is the approach taken by many other countries that run heavily government-funded health programs.

In addition to the new social insurance programs, we recommend liberalizing the medicaid program by requiring the program to pay the home care cost sharing for low-income beneficiaries. In addition, the personal needs allowance for nursing home patients should be raised from $30 a month to $100 a month and the level of protected assets for individuals from $2,000 to $30,000. These increases would make daily life more comfortable for the elderly and significantly increase the level of financial protection against catastrophic costs, while still requiring individuals to contribute a substantial amount of their assets before obtaining help from the government. Few would contend that allowing nursing home patients to keep $30,000 in assets constitutes protection of the rich or seriously affects intergenerational transfer of wealth. These medicaid changes will primarily benefit persons with nursing home stays of more than six months, but they will also aid low-income persons

TABLE 10-1. *Revenue Raised under Recommended Options for Financing a Public Long-Term Care Program, Selected Periods*[a]
*Billions of 1993 dollars*

| Financing option | 1993 | 2018 |
|---|---|---|
| Current federal, state, and local spending[b] | 41.9 | 87.5 |
| Premiums[c] | 5.4 | 15.0 |
| Payroll tax[d] | 12.8 | 22.2 |
| Medicare savings[e] | 5.0 | 7.3 |
| PUBLIC COST | 65.1 | 132.0 |

SOURCE: Brookings-ICF Long-Term Care Financing Model. The year 1993 represents the five-year average for the period 1991–95; 2018 the five-year average for the period 2016–20.

　a. The recommended program would combine front-end nursing home coverage and expanded home care with liberalized eligibility criteria for medicaid.

　b. Medicaid and medicare for nursing home care; medicaid, medicare, and other payers for home care.

　c. Assessed against elderly with incomes greater than 150 percent of the poverty level. Assuming a premium increase 1.5 percent above inflation, monthly premiums start at $20 in 1993 and grow to $29 in 2018 in 1993 dollars.

　d. Combined employee and employer contributions and assuming a 0.39 percent tax rate in 1993 and 0.44 rate in 2018; no ceiling on taxable salaries.

　e. Assuming a 5.5 percent annual increase in savings.

who cannot afford the coinsurance for the nursing home or home care benefits under the social insurance program. They also will have the undesirable side effect of increasing the number of people on "welfare."

We recognize that combining front-end nursing home coverage with medicaid liberalization does not protect individuals from catastrophic costs as well as comprehensive nursing home coverage would. A comprehensive strategy has substantial intellectual appeal, but we do not believe that the public is willing to pay the taxes necessary to fund such a program.

## Financing

The cost of a public insurance program and medicaid liberalization will be high but not impossible to finance. Indeed, society will incur most of these long-term care costs whether the system is predominantly public or private.

Fully implemented, the new social insurance program and medicaid liberalization outlined above would have cost the government $23.2 billion in 1993 in addition to what it already spent. That would rise to $44.5 billion in 2018.[5] Note that this estimate does not include the cost of services for disabled people under age 65. Money to finance these public expenditures should come from four sources (table 10-1).

First, the bulk of the additional expenditures should be financed through an additional payroll tax, to be shared equally by employers and employees. For a fully phased-in program, we propose an initial payroll tax of 0.39 percent (employer and employee share combined), which would have raised $12.8 billion in 1993. The payroll tax rate would need to increase to 0.44 percent in 2018.

Second, although the required level of additional expenditures is too high to be financed solely by the elderly, it is fair that the elderly help finance this new program, for which they will be major beneficiaries. A $20 per month premium for elderly persons with incomes above 150 percent of the federal poverty level would have generated $5.4 billion in 1993.

Third, reductions in the rate of increase in medicare acute care expenditures should also help finance the new benefits, although reductions should be as large as those in President Clinton's proposal; the level of savings he is proposing will be very difficult to achieve. We propose to save $5 billion in medicare spending annually, most likely by reducing the reimbursement rates for physicians, hospitals, and other providers, and to redirect those savings to the long-term care program.

Finally, on an aggregate basis, states and the federal government should help finance the cost of long-term care, maintaining the level that they would have contributed under existing programs. It is probably easiest to ensure continued support from the states by requiring them to match federal funds. Because the average federal match rate would be high, states should find this program attractive even though some individual states might have to increase their long-term care expenditures slightly. Other states would find their long-term care expenses somewhat reduced.

## Final Thoughts

President Clinton's call for major health care reform has focused national attention on the problems of and possible cures for uncontrolled increases in health care costs and lack of adequate insurance. Although that focus has rightly been on acute care, long-term care should also be part of the reform package.

The Clinton administration has proposed significant reforms in long-term care, but their passage is uncertain. These initiatives will be costly, and not everyone agrees that public programs should take the lead in reforming the long-term care system.

If this round of long-term care reform falters, changing demographics are almost certain to bring it back to center stage. This will happen long before the baby boom generation starts needing large amounts of long-term care. Rather, by the end of this decade, virtually all of the parents of the baby boom generation will be elderly; many of them will be very elderly and starting to use long-term care. These elderly will turn to their adult children for care and, in some cases, financial assistance. Long-term care will no longer be an academic issue, but an intensely personal one from which baby boomers will not be able to escape. The question of "How are we going to take care of Mom?" will become a main concern for a substantial portion of a very large and influential generation. When that happens, long-term care will be an issue that neither Congress nor the president will be able to ignore.

# The Brookings-ICF Long-Term Care Financing Model

The Brookings-ICF Long-Term Care Financing Model simulates the use and financing of nursing home and home care by a nationally representative sample of elderly from 1986 through 2020.[a] A simplified method of extrapolating long-term care expenditures and possible sources of financing from 2020 through 2050 was also developed. The overall objective of the model is to simulate the effects of various financing and organizational reform options on future public and private expenditures for nursing home and home care. The model has been used by researchers not only at the Brookings Institution, but also by the Department of Health and Human Services, the General Accounting Office, the Pepper Commission, the American Association of Retired Persons, and Merrill Lynch. Originally developed in 1986 and 1987 as a joint project of the Brookings Institution and Lewin-VHI, a Washington-area consulting firm, the model was extensively refined and updated in 1988 and 1989 using newly available data. The second version of the model is substantially more sophisticated than the first.

Figure A-1 shows a flowchart of the model. The first part of the model, Lewin-VHI's Pension and Retirement Income Simulation Model (PRISM), simulates future demographic characteristics (age, gender, and marital status), income, and assets of the elderly (figure A-2). In general PRISM uses mortality and economic assumptions that

a. For a more detailed description of the model, see David L. Kennell, Lisa Marie B. Alexcih, Joshua M. Wiener, and Raymond J. Hanley, "Brookings-ICF Long-Term Care Financing Model: Model Assumptions" (Washington, D.C.: Lewin-ICF, May 1991). In 1992 Lewin-ICF became Lewin-VHI.

FIGURE A-1. **Brookings-ICF Long-Term Care Financing Model**

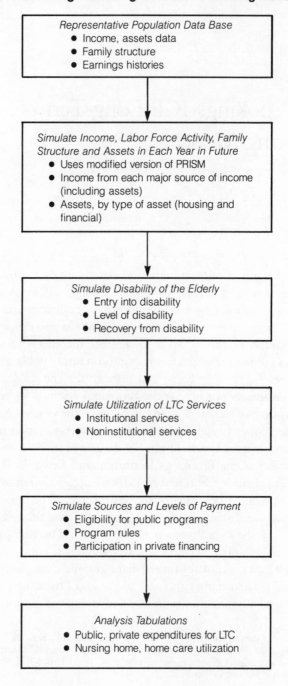

FIGURE A-2. **Pension and Retirement Income Simulation Model (PRISM) Flow Diagram**

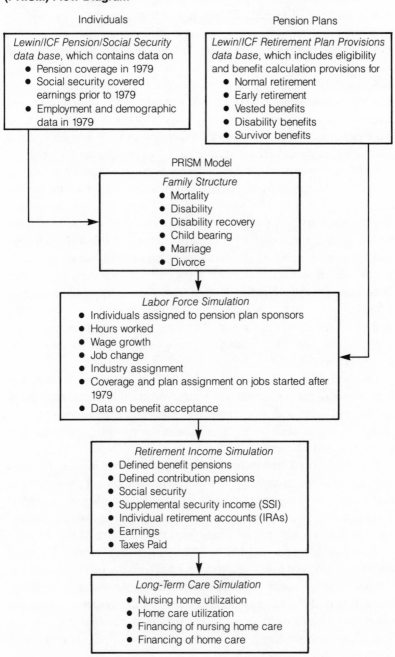

Individuals

*Lewin/ICF Pension/Social Security data base*, which contains data on
- Pension coverage in 1979
- Social security covered earnings prior to 1979
- Employment and demographic data in 1979

Pension Plans

*Lewin/ICF Retirement Plan Provisions data base*, which includes eligibility and benefit calculation provisions for
- Normal retirement
- Early retirement
- Vested benefits
- Disability benefits
- Survivor benefits

PRISM Model

*Family Structure*
- Mortality
- Disability
- Disability recovery
- Child bearing
- Marriage
- Divorce

*Labor Force Simulation*
- Individuals assigned to pension plan sponsors
- Hours worked
- Wage growth
- Job change
- Industry assignment
- Coverage and plan assignment on jobs started after 1979
- Data on benefit acceptance

*Retirement Income Simulation*
- Defined benefit pensions
- Defined contribution pensions
- Social security
- Supplemental security income (SSI)
- Individual retirement accounts (IRAs)
- Earnings
- Taxes Paid

*Long-Term Care Simulation*
- Nursing home utilization
- Home care utilization
- Financing of nursing home care
- Financing of home care

are consistent with the Social Security Administration's mid-range II-B assumptions. The second part of the model simulates disability, admission to and use of nursing homes, use of home care, and methods of financing long-term care services. It is based upon analyses of the 1982 and 1984 National Long-Term Care Surveys, the 1985 National Nursing Home Survey, the 1984 Survey of Income and Program Participation, and medicare and medicaid program data from the Health Care Financing Administration (HCFA). The model uses national data and does not take into account regional, state, or local variation. Model estimates of medicare and medicaid expenditures for nursing home and home care are benchmarked against HCFA program data for 1993.

The model operates on individual records from the May 1979 Current Population Survey Special Pension Supplement. The records include data on earnings histories provided by the Social Security Administration for the surveyed people. Thus, the model begins the simulation period with a nationally representative sample of 28,000 adults. To reduce random variation, the data base is run through the model twice. To smooth year-to-year variability of the estimates, results are presented as five-year averages. The final output from the model provides detailed information for each person aged 65 and older, for each year from 1986 to 2020, on age, marital status, disability, amount and sources of income, assets, and use of and payment source for nursing home and home care services.

The model uses a Monte Carlo simulation approach. For each person in each year of the projection period, it simulates changes in status based on the individual's demographic and economic characteristics. Each change in status, such as marriage, admission to a nursing home, and death, is called an event.

The model simulates events by drawing a random number between zero and one and comparing it with the predetermined probability of that event occurring for a person with particular sociodemographic characteristics. For example, the annual probability of death for an 85-year-old woman who requires help with two or more of the activities of daily living, or ADLs (that is, bathing, dressing, eating, getting in and out of bed, and toileting), and who does not live in a nursing home is 0.03. In other words, 3 out of every such 100 women are expected to die each year. If the random number drawn by the model is less than or equal to 0.03 for this 85-year-old woman, she is assumed to die in that year. If the number drawn lies between 0.03 and 1.0, she is assumed to continue to live during that year.

## Demographic Assumptions

For each year in the projection period, the model simulates individuals' marrying or divorcing, bearing children, becoming disabled or recovering from disability, and dying, based on a variety of assumptions. Changes in marital status are based on vital statistics data from the National Center for Health Statistics; aggregate marriage rates are kept consistent with the Social Security Administration's alternative II-B (mid-range) forecast in the 1988 Trustees' annual report.[1] Marriage rates vary by age, gender, education, and previous marital experience (that is, widowed, divorced, never married), and divorce rates vary by age. Marriage and divorce rates remain constant in the simulation period.

Childbearing rates are based on Census Bureau data for 1976–80, and aggregate fertility rates are constrained to the alternative II-B forecast. Childbearing varies by age, marital status, employment status, and number of children. The model does not follow children as they grow older.

Work disability rates for people under age 65 are based on the 1988 Trustees' annual report, and working age disability remission rates were developed by the social security actuary for 1979–80. Rates for becoming disabled vary by age and gender and remain constant over time. Recovery from disability also varies by years elapsed since becoming disabled. (For the disability assumptions for persons aged 65 and older, see the section on disability status.)

The overall mortality rates are based on alternative II-B projections, which assume substantial improvements in longevity over time. For persons under age 65, rates vary by age, gender, work disability status, and years since becoming disabled. After age 65, the model sets differential age-gender mortality rates for nursing home residents and, by functional disability, for persons living in the community. (For the mortality assumptions for persons aged 65 and older, see the section on mortality.)

## Labor Force and Economic Assumptions

The model simulates an employment history for each person from 1979 through his or her date of retirement (figure A-2). Each year the model calculates wage rates, hours worked, job change, and industry of employment. Average wage rates are based on alternative II-B projections from the 1989 Trustees' annual report, and aggregate work force

TABLE A-1. *Assumed Real Wage Growth*
*Percent*

| Year | Real wage growth | Year | Real wage growth |
|------|------------------|------|------------------|
| 1984 | 3.0 | 1993 | 1.6 |
| 1985 | 0.8 | 1994 | 1.6 |
| 1986 | 2.5 | 1995 | 1.5 |
| 1987 | 2.2 | 1996 | 1.5 |
| 1988 | 2.4 | 1997 | 1.6 |
| 1989 | 1.4 | 1998 | 1.4 |
| 1990 | 0.8 | 1999 | 1.4 |
| 1991 | 1.0 | 2000 | |
| 1992 | 1.2 | and after | 1.3 |

SOURCE: Alternative II-B assumptions from the *1989 Annual Report of the Board of Trustees of the Federal Old Age and Survivors Insurance and Disability Insurance Trust Funds* (Baltimore, Md.: Social Security Administration, April 1989).

and industry composition follow the 1987 Bureau of Labor Statistics forecast.[2] Inflation increases at the annual rate projected for the consumer price index specified under alternative II-B, about 4 percent a year in the long run.

Overall unemployment rates reflect actual data through 1986 and then follow the alternative II-B projections. Long-run unemployment is assumed to be 6 percent. Labor force participation rates follow the Bureau of Labor Statistics age-gender specific forecasts until the year 2000 and then remain constant, except for the group aged 62 to 67. Under these projections, labor force participation by women will grow substantially.

The Social Security Amendments of 1983, which will eventually raise the age at which full social security benefits are available, are assumed to increase the labor force participation of those aged 62 to 67 starting in the year 2000. When the normal retirement age increases from 65 to 66, retirement rates for persons aged 62 to 65 are assumed to decline 10 percent, and their labor force participation rates are assumed to increase 10 percent. The increase in retirement age from 66 to 67 scheduled to occur after 2017 is addressed the same way in the model.

Given the aggregate levels of labor force participation for different age-gender groups, the model simulates the number of hours each person will work during a year based on Census Bureau employment pattern data that vary by age, gender, marital status, presence of children, hours worked in the previous three years, and whether pension and social security benefits were received. Wage growth reflects actual rates until 1986 and then follows the aggregate macroeconomic projections shown in table A-1. Individual hourly wage rate adjustments are based

TABLE A-2. *Percent Distribution of Workers, by Industry of Employment Assumed in PRISM, Selected Years*
Percent

| Industry | 1980 | 1982 | 1984 | 1990 | 2000 and after |
|---|---|---|---|---|---|
| Mining | 0.89 | 0.95 | 1.30 | 0.88 | 0.78 |
| Construction | 4.53 | 4.20 | 4.44 | 4.81 | 4.62 |
| Manufacturing | 20.78 | 19.08 | 18.73 | 16.32 | 14.09 |
| Transportation | 5.02 | 5.03 | 5.32 | 4.96 | 4.74 |
| Trade | 18.71 | 19.24 | 19.28 | 19.86 | 20.58 |
| Finance | 5.09 | 5.32 | 5.38 | 6.09 | 6.06 |
| Service | 17.55 | 18.50 | 18.50 | 20.34 | 23.08 |
| State, local government | 12.96 | 12.96 | 12.61 | 12.29 | 11.73 |
| Federal government | 3.28 | 3.28 | 3.26 | 3.07 | 2.79 |
| Self-employed | 9.55 | 9.85 | 9.63 | 10.08 | 10.45 |
| Agriculture | 1.64 | 1.65 | 1.55 | 1.29 | 1.07 |

SOURCE: Lewin-VHI estimates based upon George T. Silverstri and John M. Lukasiewicz, "A Look at Occupational Employment Trends to the Year 2000," *Monthly Labor Review*, vol. 110 (September 1987), pp. 46–63.

on Census Bureau data. These rates vary by age, gender, and whether the person changed jobs during the year.

Job change rates are based on Census Bureau data on employment patterns for 1979 and vary by age, tenure, and part- or full-time status. These rates remain constant. People are assigned to an industry whenever they change jobs or enter or reenter the labor force. This assignment is based on Bureau of Labor Statistics projections of industry work force composition through 2000, which remains constant thereafter (table A-2). The projections assume an increasing proportion of employment in service industries and a falling proportion in manufacturing. The industry assigned to a person varies by age, part- or full-time status, and previous sector of employment.

## Pension Coverage and Retirement Assumptions

As a person changes jobs during the simulation period, the model determines whether he or she is covered by a pension plan and assigns covered workers to an actual plan. The model simulates early, normal, and late retirement. Retirement income sources simulated by the model include private defined-benefit and defined-contribution pension plans, Keoghs, individual retirement accounts (IRAs), social security, and supplemental security income. Social security rules, including the changes made by the 1983 amendments, are included. Interest rates for the

TABLE A-3. *Pension Coverage Assumptions, Selected Years*
*Percent*

| | Industry coverage rate | | |
|---|---|---|---|
| Industry | 1979 | 1983 | 1989 |
| Federal government | 93 | 93 | 93 |
| State, local government | 88 | 83 | 83 |
| Mining | 82 | 75 | 79 |
| Manufacturing | 76 | 70 | 73 |
| Transportation | 75 | 75 | 77 |
| Finance | 67 | 67 | 75 |
| Construction | 43 | 41 | 43 |
| Trade | 43 | 46 | 51 |
| Services | 43 | 47 | 52 |
| Agriculture | 19 | 22 | 22 |
| Self-employed | 14 | 14 | 14 |

SOURCE: Coverage rates for 1979 were derived from an ICF, Inc., analysis of the May 1979 Current Population Survey. Coverage rates for 1983 are based on a Lewin-VHI analysis of the May 1983 EBRI/HHS CPS Pension Supplement. Coverage rates for 1989 were estimated by Lewin-VHI, by adjusting the 1983 coverage rates to reflect the potential effect of the nondiscrimination rules in the Tax Reform Act of 1986.

defined-contribution plans and individual retirement accounts have an average annual rate of 7 percent, which is the alternative II-B forecast of interest rates for 1989 through 2005.

Pension coverage rates vary by industry of employment, part- or full-time status, age, and wage rate. Pension coverage rates are based on the May 1979 Current Population Survey Special Pension Supplement and the 1983 Employee Benefit Research Institute–Department of Health and Human Services Current Population Survey Pension Supplement (table A-3). Plan coverage on an industry basis is assumed not to change after 1989.

People are assigned to pension plans on the basis of industry of employment, firm size, social security coverage status, union coverage status, multi- or single-employer plan status, and hourly or salaried employee status. Pension plan assignment takes into account the number of people covered by specific plan sponsors. Thus, the model takes into account the reported participation and vesting status of the worker as well as plan contribution requirements and participation in a supplemental plan.

Using the actual provisions of the pension plans assigned, the model calculates each person's eligibility and benefit amount. In general, pension plan provisions are assumed to remain unchanged except in instances where plan rules must be changed to comply with the Retirement Equity Act of 1984. Starting in 1985 the Retirement Equity Act mandated that the minimum age requirement for pension participation be reduced from age 25 to age 21 and that service between the ages of 19 and 22 be considered for determining vesting.

Benefit formulas in defined-benefit pension plans and salary bend points are indexed to growth in wages throughout the simulation period. Private defined-benefit plans are indexed at half the rate of inflation annually, up to a maximum of 2 percent a year; early and normal retirement benefits for public sector retirement plans increase at the rate of inflation, up to a maximum of 4 percent a year. These cost-of-living adjustments for pension benefits are based on an analysis by Lewin-VHI of cost-of-living adjustments over a ten-year period for a representative sample of pension plans.

Acceptance of social security benefits is based on Social Security Administration data for 1980. Eligible persons aged 62 and older are automatically assumed to accept benefits when they become disabled or unemployed, or when they receive an employer pension. Acceptance also varies by age and gender. Social security survivors' benefits accrue to people in the first year they are eligible.

Pension benefit acceptance for employees meeting their assigned plan's eligibility provisions differs between defined-benefit and defined-contribution plans. Pension acceptance also varies by age, gender, and vesting status. In general, the rates are based on data from the Census Bureau's Current Poplation Survey Special Pension Supplement.

The model's treatment of IRAs is derived primarily from the May 1983 Employee Benefit Research Institute–Health and Human Services Current Population Supplement Survey, updated to reflect the effects of the 1986 Tax Reform Act. In the model, IRA adoption for each individual varies by family income, age, and whether the person is covered by a pension plan. Once an IRA is adopted for an individual, the annual probability of making a contribution varies by family income and the pension coverage status. The amount contributed, constrained to the tax-deductible maximum and indexed to growth in real wages after 1983, varies by a person's family income, age, gender, and marital status. The model assumes individuals will contribute to their IRA only if the contribution is tax deductible. Hence, beginning in 1987, the full contribution amount, up to the amount deductible under tax law in 1986 (typically $2,000), is considered tax deductible for persons with an adjusted gross income of less than $25,000 ($40,000 for joint filers). The deductibility is phased out over the next $10,000 of adjusted gross income. Also beginning in 1987, the maximum contribution amounts specified by law are indexed at 80 percent of the consumer price index over the projection period. At the time the individual accepts pension or social security benefits, but not before age 60, IRA funds are converted to an annuity.

## Levels of Assets

Because assets can be an important source of income for the elderly and also a source of financing for their long-term care, the model simulates both the level of housing equity and the value of nonhousing (financial) assets for individuals and couples aged 65 and older. The model assigns actual asset data records from the 1984 Survey of Income and Program Participation Wave 4, adjusted for inflation, to people in the model on the basis of age, marital status, and income level. Assigning the assets provides a distribution of assets rather than just an average amount for different demographic subgroups.

The asset assignment process in the model has two steps. Beginning in 1979 all family units aged 65 and older are assigned actual asset records that are deflated by the change in the consumer price index from 1979 to 1984. After 1979, as people reach age 65, the model assigns assets using data from records of people aged 63 to 67 in the 1984 Survey of Income and Program Participation Wave 4. The value of all assets is adjusted by the actual or expected rate of change in the consumer price index projected under alternative II-B.

After assets are assigned to people aged 65 and older in the model, the value of the assigned assets is adjusted over time. The value of housing equity increases 1 percentage point faster than the actual and projected rate of change in the consumer price index. Nonhousing assets are adjusted to reflect actual change observed longitudinally between waves 4 and 7 of the 1984 Survey of Income and Program Participation. The model assumes 35 percent of individuals increase their nonhousing assets annually by 2 percentage points above the consumer price index, 40 percent neither save nor dissave, and 25 percent decrease their nonhousing assets by 2 percent each year in real terms.

The assigned nonhousing assets are a source of income for the elderly in the model. Asset income is assumed to be 7 percent a year. All asset income produced during a year is assumed to be spent in that year. When a person dies, his or her spouse is assumed to receive all assets.

Disability Status

The likelihood of an elderly person using nursing home or home care services is affected by his or her disability status. For people aged 65 and older, disability rates are derived from the 1982 and 1984 National Long-Term Care Surveys and the Social Security Administration's 1982 New Beneficiary Survey. Disabled individuals are defined as persons who need help, for a health-related reason, with at least one instrumental activity of daily living, or IADL (that is, doing heavy work, doing light work, preparing meals, shopping for groceries or other personal items, getting around inside, walking outside, managing money, and using the telephone), or who need help with at least one of the five activities of daily living, which has lasted for at least ninety days. In the model, each person turning 65 is assigned one of four disability levels: no disability, requires help with an IADL only, requires help with only one ADL, or requires help with at least two ADLs.

After age 65, the model simulates a disability level for each individual in each simulated year. The model assumes the disability prevalence rates based on the 1984 National Long-Term Care Survey (table A-4). Disability rates remain constant over the projection period for each age-marital status group.

The model also assumes annual changes in disability levels based on a set of transition matrices constructed from the 1982 and 1984 National Long-Term Care Surveys. Annual changes in disability level happen at the beginning of the year and vary by age, marital status, and previous level of disability (table A-5). Changes in disability status include non-disabled persons becoming disabled and disabled persons becoming

TABLE A-4. *Disability Prevalence Rates for Elderly in the Community*
*Percentage needing help*

| Age group | Instrumental activity of daily living | | One activity of daily living | | Two or more activities of daily living | |
|---|---|---|---|---|---|---|
| | Married | Unmarried | Married | Unmarried | Married | Unmarried |
| 65–69 | 3.79 | 4.96 | 1.74 | 2.69 | 3.45 | 3.67 |
| 70–74 | 5.01 | 6.62 | 2.68 | 3.73 | 5.11 | 4.66 |
| 75–79 | 6.90 | 8.64 | 3.24 | 5.77 | 7.71 | 7.15 |
| 80–84 | 10.34 | 11.25 | 6.03 | 8.07 | 12.93 | 11.35 |
| 85–89 | 11.36 | 13.64 | 7.57 | 11.21 | 21.77 | 15.81 |
| 90 and older | 7.50 | 15.45 | 20.00 | 13.69 | 26.25 | 31.35 |

SOURCE: Brookings Institution and Lewin-VHI calculations using data from the 1982 and 1984 National Long-Term Care Surveys.

TABLE A-5. *Annual Disability Transition Probability Matrices for Community-Based Elderly*
*Percent*

| Disability level at time 1 | Disability level at time 2 | | | |
|---|---|---|---|---|
| | Non-disabled | IADL only | One ADL | Two or more ADLs |
| *Married* | | | | |
| *Age 65–74* | | | | |
| Nondisabled | 97.00 | 1.46 | 0.59 | 0.95 |
| IADL only | 11.86 | 70.10 | 9.79 | 8.25 |
| One ADL | 7.01 | 18.55 | 56.30 | 18.14 |
| Two or more ADLs | 2.52 | 7.36 | 10.31 | 79.80 |
| *Age 75–84* | | | | |
| Nondisabled | 93.50 | 3.57 | 1.08 | 1.85 |
| IADL only | 7.16 | 71.00 | 8.87 | 12.96 |
| One ADL | 4.36 | 19.20 | 48.50 | 27.93 |
| Two or more ADLs | 2.41 | 6.84 | 10.05 | 80.70 |
| *Age 85 and older* | | | | |
| Nondisabled | 82.60 | 7.51 | 3.75 | 6.14 |
| IADL only | 2.37 | 69.20 | 11.85 | 16.58 |
| One ADL | 3.96 | 7.92 | 48.50 | 39.62 |
| Two or more ADLs | 0.00 | 6.40 | 8.00 | 85.60 |
| *Unmarried* | | | | |
| *Age 65–74* | | | | |
| Nondisabled | 95.80 | 2.26 | 1.02 | 0.92 |
| IADL only | 9.58 | 71.90 | 12.20 | 6.32 |
| One ADL | 4.27 | 25.15 | 49.70 | 20.88 |
| Two or more ADLs | 2.48 | 8.87 | 13.84 | 74.80 |
| *Age 75–84* | | | | |
| Nondisabled | 90.80 | 4.71 | 2.67 | 1.82 |
| IADL only | 5.91 | 66.10 | 16.16 | 11.83 |
| One ADL | 3.13 | 19.10 | 59.60 | 18.16 |
| Two or more ADLs | 0.53 | 6.88 | 8.99 | 83.60 |
| *Age 85 and older* | | | | |
| Nondisabled | 25.30 | 28.51 | 24.50 | 21.69 |
| IADL only | 0.45 | 69.10 | 15.23 | 15.23 |
| One ADL | 0.62 | 11.13 | 56.70 | 31.55 |
| Two or more ADLs | 0.46 | 2.77 | 7.37 | 89.40 |

SOURCE: Lewin-VHI and Brookings Institution calculations using the 1982 and 1984 National Long-Term Care Surveys.

either more disabled, less disabled, or nondisabled. The model takes the outcome of annual disability transitions into account and then simulates additional persons' becoming disabled to meet the disability prevalence rates (table A-4). This allows the model to maintain a proportion of disabled in the community that matches the age-marital status disability rates after adjusting the total disabled count for death and remission from disability. Disability transition rates remain constant over the simulation period on an age-marital status basis.

Separate from the annual disability transitions, the model assumes that most individuals receiving social security disability insurance before age 65 will be chronically disabled in ADLs or IADLs at age 65. Reflecting the substantial difference between work disability and functional disability observed in the 1982 New Beneficiary Survey, the model assumes that 60 percent of individuals eligible for disability insurance at age 62 meet the more restrictive ADL or IADL definition of disability used upon reaching age 65.

## Mortality

The model uses alternative II-B mortality assumptions from the 1988 Social Security Trustees' annual report to estimate deaths for the projection period. As mentioned above, separate rates that vary by age and gender are applied to disabled and nondisabled persons under age 65. For those aged 65 and older, age-gender mortality rates are further disaggregated for elderly nursing home residents, disabled elderly in the community, and nondisabled elderly in the community. In addition, mortality rates for disabled elderly in the community vary by disability level.

For nursing home residents, the model assumes each individual survives for the entire assigned length of stay. As described more fully below, data from the 1985 National Nursing Home Survey are used to simulate whether individuals simulated to be admitted to a nursing home will be discharged alive or dead. The model then subtracts the age-gender specific mortality for persons who die in a nursing home from the overall alternative II-B mortality rate for each year in the projection period and distributes the residual mortality to each age-gender group in the community.

The relative mortality rates for each disability group in the community were based on information about the disability level of persons in 1982 who had died by 1984; the data were obtained from the 1982 and 1984 National Long-Term Care Surveys. The disability level adjustment for residual mortality rates (that is, net of deaths in nursing homes) is shown in table A-6. In general, for each age-gender group, mortality rates are highest for nursing home residents and then decrease with level of disability in the community so that nondisabled persons end up with the lowest mortality rate. This is not true for persons aged 85 and older in the community, probably because mortality rates are so high for this age group.

TABLE A-6. *Mortality Adjustments: Ratio of Disabled Mortality Rate to Nondisabled Mortality Rate*

| | Age | | |
|---|---|---|---|
| Disability level | 65–74 | 75–84 | 85 and older |
| IADL only | 1.9 | 1.2 | 1.0 |
| One ADL | 2.6 | 1.5 | 1.0 |
| Two or more ADLs | 3.8 | 2.1 | 1.0 |

SOURCE: Brookings Institution and Lewin-VHI calculations using the 1982 and 1984 National Long-Term Care Surveys.

## Nursing Home Use

For each year of the simulation, the model selects people to enter a nursing home. The model then determines the patient's length of stay and whether he or she is discharged dead or alive. The model uses nursing home admission probabilities estimated from longitudinal data in the 1982 and 1984 National Long-Term Care Surveys, adjusted by data from the 1985 National Nursing Home Discharge Survey. Nursing home length of stay probabilities were developed from the 1985 National Nursing Home Survey and then adjusted upward to reflect growth in nursing home residents by age.

The model simulates the entry of individuals into a nursing home using probabilities for the disabled that vary by age, marital status, disability level, and previous nursing home admission, and for the nondisabled that vary by age, gender, marital status, and previous nursing home admission (tables A-7 and A-8). Nursing home entry by nondisabled persons reflects admissions by persons who are nondisabled at the beginning of the year but become disabled at some time during the course of the year. Fully 46 percent of all elderly nursing home admissions in the twenty-four-month period between the 1982 and 1984 National Long-Term Care Surveys were people who were not chronically disabled in 1982.[3] Gender was not used to vary entry for disabled persons because it was found not to be a statistically significant determinant of nursing home admission in the regression model developed to estimate the entry probabilities.

The probabilities of nursing home entry in the model are estimated for individual years of age based on analyses of the 1982 and 1984 National Long-Term Care Surveys and the 1985 National Nursing Home Survey. To develop the probabilities, separate regression models of nursing home entry were estimated for disabled and nondisabled persons from the 1982 and 1984 National Long-Term Care Surveys.

TABLE A-7. *Annual Probability That Disabled Elderly Will Enter a Nursing Home, by Age, Marital Status, Level of Disability, and Previous Admission*[a]
Percent

| Age | Previous nursing home stay | | No previous nursing home stay | |
|---|---|---|---|---|
| | Unmarried | Married | Unmarried | Married |
| | *People who need help with two or more ADLs* | | | |
| 65 | 12.9 | 8.9 | 5.2 | 3.3 |
| 70 | 18.6 | 13.1 | 7.8 | 5.1 |
| 75 | 25.8 | 18.5 | 11.3 | 7.4 |
| 80 | 34.3 | 25.4 | 15.9 | 10.6 |
| 85 | 44.4 | 33.6 | 21.8 | 14.8 |
| 90 | 55.9 | 43.5 | 29.1 | 20.2 |
| 95 | 68.7 | 54.9 | 37.9 | 26.9 |
| 100 | 82.7 | 67.7 | 48.4 | 35.2 |
| | *People who need help with one ADL* | | | |
| 65 | 9.1 | 6.1 | 3.4 | 2.2 |
| 70 | 13.5 | 9.1 | 5.2 | 3.3 |
| 75 | 19.0 | 13.1 | 7.7 | 4.9 |
| 80 | 26.0 | 18.3 | 11.0 | 7.1 |
| 85 | 34.4 | 24.9 | 15.3 | 10.0 |
| 90 | 44.4 | 32.9 | 20.8 | 13.9 |
| 95 | 55.9 | 42.5 | 27.7 | 18.9 |
| 100 | 68.8 | 53.8 | 36.1 | 25.2 |
| | *People who need help with an IADL* | | | |
| 65 | 7.8 | 5.1 | 2.9 | 1.8 |
| 70 | 11.6 | 7.8 | 4.4 | 2.8 |
| 75 | 16.6 | 11.3 | 6.5 | 4.1 |
| 80 | 22.8 | 15.8 | 9.3 | 6.0 |
| 85 | 30.5 | 21.6 | 13.0 | 8.5 |
| 90 | 39.8 | 28.9 | 17.8 | 11.8 |
| 95 | 50.6 | 37.7 | 24.0 | 16.1 |
| 100 | 62.9 | 48.2 | 31.6 | 21.7 |

SOURCE: Lewin-VHI and Brookings Institution calculations using data from the 1982 and 1984 National Long-Term Care Surveys and the 1985 National Nursing Home Survey.
    a. Model actually uses probabilities that vary by individual year from age 65 to 100.

These twenty-four-month probabilities were then annualized and adjusted to correspond to totals in the 1985 National Nursing Home Survey. The model assumes that rates of nursing home entry remain constant over the simulation period unless some level of induced demand is specified in a simulation by the model's user. The model also assumes that individuals enter a nursing home only once during each simulated year.

Keeping nursing home admission rates constant throughout the projection period implicitly assumes that nursing home bed supply will increase throughout the simulation as necessary to accommodate admissions from an increasingly larger elderly population. Thus, the model

TABLE A-8. *Annual Probability That Nondisabled Elderly Will Enter a Nursing Home, by Age, Gender, Marital Status, and Previous Admission*[a]
Percent

| | Previous nursing home stay | | | | No previous nursing home stay | | | |
| | Male | | Female | | Male | | Female | |
| Age | Unmarried | Married | Unmarried | Married | Unmarried | Married | Unmarried | Married |
|---|---|---|---|---|---|---|---|---|
| 65 | 7.9 | 3.0 | 6.0 | 2.2 | 0.6 | 0.2 | 0.4 | 0.1 |
| 70 | 15.2 | 6.2 | 11.9 | 4.7 | 1.3 | 0.4 | 0.9 | 0.3 |
| 75 | 26.4 | 12.1 | 21.4 | 9.2 | 2.6 | 0.9 | 1.9 | 0.7 |
| 80 | 41.8 | 21.7 | 35.3 | 17.1 | 5.2 | 1.8 | 3.8 | 1.3 |
| 85 | 60.6 | 35.9 | 53.3 | 29.3 | 10.0 | 3.6 | 7.5 | 2.7 |
| 90 | 60.6 | 35.9 | 53.3 | 29.3 | 18.2 | 7.0 | 13.9 | 5.2 |
| 95 | 60.6 | 35.9 | 53.3 | 29.3 | 31.3 | 13.1 | 24.7 | 9.9 |
| 100 | 60.6 | 35.9 | 53.3 | 29.3 | 49.8 | 23.4 | 40.8 | 17.9 |

SOURCE: Lewin-VHI and Brookings Institution calculations using data from the 1982 and 1984 National Long-Term Care Surveys and the 1985 National Nursing Home Survey.
    a. Model actually uses probabilities that vary by individual year from age 65 to 100.

assumes that demand for nursing home care in the future will be no more constrained by the bed supply than it is now.

Both the length of stay assigned by the model to nursing home entrants and the mortality status of residents at the time of discharge are based on estimates from the 1985 National Nursing Home Survey and vary by age and marital status at admission (table A-9). To estimate the length of stay for individuals, the discharged resident survey had to be converted from a file of discharges to a file of individuals. This conversion was required because it is possible to be discharged from a nursing home more than once during the survey year, and a person could thus be counted more than once in the discharge file.[4] In converting discharges to individuals, only those persons for whom the survey discharge was the last nursing home stay in the survey year are included. This provided a completed length of stay for each patient.

Although the length of stay for the reference nursing home discharge is complete, it does not capture total length of stay for patients transferred from another nursing home or for those whose stay was interrupted by a period of hospitalization. To account for this underestimate, nursing home stays were aggregated if the previous discharge was within thirty days of the subsequent admission. As many as three of these types of previous stays were linked together with the reference discharge length of stay.

To finish the conversion of discharges to admissions, the unduplicated discharges with aggregated length of stays were adjusted to account for the cohort effect of growth in nursing home beds. That is, the discharge

TABLE A-9. *Probability of Nursing Home Length of Stay, by Age at Entry, Marital Status, and Mortality Status at Discharge*
Percent

| Length of stay (in days) | Age at entry | | | | | |
|---|---|---|---|---|---|---|
| | 65–74 | | 75–84 | | 85 and older | |
| | Discharged alive | Discharged dead | Discharged alive | Discharged dead | Discharged alive | Discharged dead |
| *Married* | | | | | | |
| 1–29 | 11.22 | 17.28 | 14.10 | 18.07 | 14.08 | 15.54 |
| 30–59 | 3.59 | 9.52 | 7.11 | 6.92 | 6.25 | 7.33 |
| 60–89 | 1.82 | 5.99 | 1.55 | 3.89 | 2.83 | 2.25 |
| 90–179 | 7.10 | 7.19 | 3.38 | 6.22 | 3.32 | 5.75 |
| 180–364 | 2.75 | 8.39 | 2.11 | 7.02 | 2.52 | 7.44 |
| 365–729 | 1.35 | 6.85 | 1.65 | 8.29 | 1.34 | 9.02 |
| 730–1,094 | 1.16 | 4.33 | 0.74 | 3.69 | 1.59 | 3.74 |
| 1,095–1,469 | 0.60 | 2.60 | 0.81 | 1.96 | 0.62 | 3.66 |
| 1,470–1,824 | 0.51 | 2.20 | 0.29 | 2.09 | 0.49 | 4.23 |
| 1,825–2,189 | 0.30 | 1.30 | 0.00 | 3.11 | 0.20 | 1.61 |
| More than 2,189 | 0.48 | 3.46 | 0.22 | 6.77 | 0.67 | 5.52 |
| TOTAL | 30.88 | 69.12 | 31.96 | 68.03 | 33.91 | 66.09 |
| *Unmarried* | | | | | | |
| 1–29 | 13.03 | 8.05 | 10.95 | 8.86 | 8.05 | 11.31 |
| 30–59 | 8.89 | 2.79 | 5.75 | 4.90 | 4.60 | 4.89 |
| 60–89 | 3.86 | 3.18 | 2.42 | 2.94 | 2.11 | 3.34 |
| 90–179 | 5.54 | 4.02 | 4.34 | 5.47 | 4.61 | 6.85 |
| 180–364 | 4.64 | 4.44 | 3.98 | 8.10 | 2.22 | 9.61 |
| 365–729 | 2.14 | 7.02 | 2.05 | 8.71 | 3.06 | 10.14 |
| 730–1,094 | 1.53 | 5.57 | 1.52 | 5.64 | 0.92 | 6.61 |
| 1,095–1,469 | 0.70 | 3.31 | 1.02 | 5.27 | 0.77 | 5.01 |
| 1,470–1,824 | 0.44 | 2.09 | 0.50 | 3.88 | 0.94 | 3.39 |
| 1,825–2,189 | 0.70 | 2.61 | 0.29 | 2.98 | 0.02 | 2.67 |
| More than 2,189 | 1.01 | 14.43 | 1.04 | 9.39 | 0.97 | 7.91 |
| TOTAL | 42.48 | 57.51 | 33.86 | 66.14 | 28.27 | 71.73 |

SOURCE: Brookings Institution and Lewin-VHI calculations using data from 1985 National Nursing Home Survey.

survey undercounted the number of people with long length of stays because there were fewer nursing home beds when people with long length of stays were admitted, and thus fewer people in the survey could have long length of stays. The number of people in each length-of-stay group was increased by a growth factor calculated from total growth in nursing home residents from 1977 to 1985 (1,402,000 to 1,624,000).

In the model, nursing home entrants are assigned a length of stay equal to the midpoint of the number of days within the range to which they are assigned (that is, a one-to-thirty-day length of stay becomes fifteen days). Individuals with a length of stay of more than 2,189 days are assumed to have a length of stay of nine years.

The model can simulate an increase in nursing home use as a result of changes in the way a nursing home stay is financed. The increase in use is often referred to as moral hazard, or induced demand. Induced demand is simulated by inflating the nursing home admission probabilities by the assumed level of induced demand specified by a user. For example, if a new public program is assumed to increase the demand for nursing home care by 20 percent, each of the entry probabilities shown in table A-5 is multiplied by 1.2. Individuals who enter a nursing home because of induced demand have the same length-of-stay distribution as other entrants but their mortality status at discharge is unchanged from the base case simulation. Mortality is unchanged; otherwise increased nursing home admissions would result in too many deaths.

## Home Care Use

Home care services in the model include home health services, chore and homemaker services, personal care, and meal preparation services. Using data from the 1982 and 1984 National Long-Term Care Surveys of noninstitutionalized, chronically disabled elderly and medicare program statistics, three separate groups are simulated to use paid home care services in each year: (1) individuals who are disabled at the beginning of the year; (2) individuals who are not chronically disabled at the beginning of the year but who become disabled during the course of the year; and (3) individuals who are not chronically disabled but who use medicare home health services as part of their recovery from acute illness. The likelihood of using home care is simulated separately for each of these groups.

Developing probabilities of annual use of paid home care services was difficult because, in contrast to nursing home use, longitudinal data from the 1982 and 1984 National Long-Term Care Surveys do not provide information on whether a person used home care in the period between the two surveys. The only information provided is whether a person is using home care at the time of each interview. Thus, the model incorporates estimates of the likelihood of a person using services in 1984 based on his or her characteristics in 1982. A problem with these data is that cross-sectional estimates undercount the number of people using services for a short time. To correct for the undercount, incidence rates (the number of new service users in a year) were computed by

TABLE A-10. *Annual Probability of Starting to Use Paid Home Care for Elderly Who Are Nondisabled at the Start of the Year*[a]
Percent

| Age | Male | | Female | |
|-----|------|------|--------|------|
|     | Unmarried | Married | Unmarried | Married |
| 65  | 1.56  | 0.92  | 2.14  | 1.26  |
| 70  | 2.29  | 1.35  | 3.14  | 1.86  |
| 75  | 3.36  | 1.99  | 4.59  | 2.73  |
| 80  | 4.91  | 2.92  | 6.67  | 4.00  |
| 85  | 7.12  | 4.28  | 9.61  | 5.82  |
| 90  | 10.25 | 6.22  | 13.70 | 8.42  |
| 95  | 14.57 | 8.98  | 19.23 | 12.05 |
| 100 | 20.39 | 12.83 | 26.46 | 17.02 |

SOURCE: Brookings Institution and Lewin-VHI estimates based on data from the 1982 and 1984 National Long-Term Care Surveys.
a. Model actually uses probabilities based on individual years of age from 65 to 100.

TABLE A-11. *Annual Probability of Starting to Use Paid Home Care Services for the Community-Based, Chronically Disabled Elderly*
Percent

| Disability level | Male | Female |
|------------------|------|--------|
| IADL only        | 12.9 | 22.0   |
| One ADL          | 15.9 | 26.6   |
| Two or more ADLs | 16.6 | 27.7   |

SOURCE: Brookings Institution and Lewin-VHI estimates based on analysis of the 1982 and 1984 National Long-Term Care Surveys.

dividing the prevalence rate of paid in-home service use by the duration of use reported in the survey.

The 1982 and 1984 National Long-Term Care Surveys were used to develop separate probabilities of using paid home care in 1984 for two groups of community-based elderly in 1982, the chronically disabled and the nondisabled. For the nondisabled group, probability of home care use varies by age, gender, and marital status (table A-10). For the two chronically disabled groups, home care varies by level of disability and gender; age and marital status were not significant predictors of home care use for this group (table A-11). Home care use is assumed to be independent of nursing home use.

Once a person from one of these groups is selected to receive paid home care, he or she is assigned a disability status estimated from users of paid home care in the 1984 National Long-Term Care Survey. The assigned disability level of home care users varies by age and marital status. As discussed below, this new disability status is used to vary the number of visits received by these home care users.

## MEDICARE COVERAGE

After the model simulates individuals to receive paid home care, it determines which ones will receive medicare reimbursement. Based on an analysis of the 1984 National Long-Term Care Survey, approximately half of the elderly receiving medicare-reimbursed home care are chronically disabled. For this half of medicare home care users, the model assigns a number of months to receive services; the assignment was based on data from the 1984 National Long-Term Care Survey adjusted to reflect a more complete episode of use (table A-12).

Once the number of months of any paid home care is determined, the model assigns the total number of visits based on a person's disability status (table A-13). The model then uses HCFA program data to apportion the number of total visits to be reimbursed by medicare. The actual number of visits covered by medicare in the model is the midpoint of each range shown in table A-14, and 150 visits for the 100-or-more visits category. If the total number of visits assigned is greater than the number of visits allocated for medicare reimbursement, the remainder are financed by another payment source, as described below.

For the half of all elderly medicare home care users that are not chronically disabled (and thus were not part of the National Long-Term

TABLE A-12. *Length of Use of Paid Home Care for Community-Based Elderly*

| Duration (months) | Percentage distribution | Assigned number of months |
|---|---|---|
| Less than 3 | 59.0 | 2.0 |
| 3–6 | 14.2 | 4.5 |
| 7–12 | 9.6 | 9.0 |
| 13–36 | 7.1 | 24.0 |
| 37–60 | 7.0 | 48.0 |
| 61 or more | 3.1 | 72.0 |

SOURCE: Brookings Institution estimates based on data from the 1984 National Long-Term Care Survey.

TABLE A-13. *Percentage Distribution of Monthly Formal Visits by Paid Home Care, by Disability Level*

| Monthly number of visits | Disability level | | |
|---|---|---|---|
| | IADL only | One ADL | Two or more ADLs |
| 1–10 | 69.9 | 59.1 | 38.7 |
| 11–20 | 8.4 | 8.0 | 11.8 |
| 21 or more | 21.7 | 32.9 | 49.5 |

SOURCE: Brookings Institution and Lewin-VHI calculations using data from the 1982 and 1984 National Long-Term Care Surveys.

TABLE A-14. *Percentage Distribution of Visits for Persons Receiving Medicare Home Health Visits*

| Number of reimbursed visits | Percentage distribution |
|---|---|
| 1–9 | 39.9 |
| 10–20 | 23.3 |
| 21–30 | 12.1 |
| 31–40 | 7.1 |
| 41–50 | 4.6 |
| 51–99 | 8.5 |
| 100 or more | 4.1 |

SOURCE: Brookings Institution and Lewin-VHI calculations using Health Care Financing Administration data from the medicare statistical system.

TABLE A-15. *Annual Medicare Home Health Admission Rate for Community-Based, Nonchronically Disabled Persons, by Age and Gender*
*Percent*

| Age | Male | Female |
|---|---|---|
| 65–74 | 3.06 | 3.32 |
| 75–84 | 4.77 | 4.75 |
| 85 and older | 9.35 | 16.41 |

SOURCE: Brookings Institution and Lewin-VHI calculations using the 1982 and 1984 National Long-Term Care Surveys data and 1984 medicare statistical system data.

TABLE A-16. *Distribution of Medicare Home Health Care for Nonchronically Disabled, by Length of Use*

| Length of use (months) | Percentage distribution | Length of use (months) | Percentage distribution |
|---|---|---|---|
| 1 | 58.6 | 7 | 0.6 |
| 2 | 19.6 | 8 | 0.7 |
| 3 | 9.2 | 9 | 0.7 |
| 4 | 3.0 | 10 | 0.7 |
| 5 | 3.0 | 11 | 0.7 |
| 6 | 2.6 | 12 | 0.6 |

SOURCE: Brookings Institution and Lewin-ICF calculations using HCFA medicare statistical system data.

Care Survey sample), the model uses a separate set of probabilities of use based on medicare program statistics that vary by age and gender (table A-15). When a member of this group is selected to receive medicare home visits, the person is assigned a length of use based on medicare program data (table A-16). This group of medicare home care beneficiaries receives seventeen visits a month, and all of their visits are paid for by medicare.

In 1989 a court case against the HCFA was settled in a way that substantially liberalized the conditions for medicare home health coverage.[5] To account for these rapidly increasing expenditures, the number of users and visits per user were substantially increased in the model to equal estimates of 1993 expenditures from HCFA.

## HOME CARE FINANCED BY OTHER PAYERS

After the model has simulated use of medicare-reimbursed home care, it determines which chronically disabled individuals pay out of pocket for home care and which receive reimbursement from medicaid or "other payers" (that is, state and local expenditures, social services block grant, Older Americans Act, Department of Veterans' Affairs services, charity, and out-of-pocket expenditures by someone other than the service recipient). The model assumes the same distribution of home care visits per month, which vary by disability level, as it did for the chronically disabled half of all medicare home care users (table A-13). Length of use for nonmedicare home care users is also identical to that used for disabled persons receiving medicare (see table A-12). The model can simulate an increase in home care use as a result of changes in the way home care is financed. Induced demand is simulated by inflating the home care use probabilities by the assumed level of induced demand specified by a user. For example, if a new public program is assumed to increase the demand for home care by 80 percent, each of the probabilities shown in tables A-10 and A-11 (or the subset of probabilities that reflect the new program's eligibility requirements) is multiplied by 1.8. Individuals who use home care because of induced demand have the same length-of-use distribution as other home care users (see table A-12).

## Financing Nursing Home Care

The model simulates expenditures and source of payment for nursing home care for all patients on a month-by-month basis. Expenditures are set equal to the person's simulated number of nursing home days multiplied by payments each day. In the base case nursing home patients pay for their care with reimbursements from medicare and medicaid, annual income, and assets. Medicaid's financial eligibility rules are modeled. Each person's payments are accumulated by source.

For nonmedicare admissions, and after medicare nursing home coverage ends, the model uses patient income and then assets to pay for care. If a person does not have sufficient income to pay the private charge, then the model covers the costs by subtracting the remaining

TABLE A-17. *Average Daily Rates for Nursing Home Care, by Source of Payment, 1988*
Dollars

| Payer | Average daily rate |
|-------|--------------------|
| Medicaid | 55.30 |
| Private payer | 75.90 |
| Medicare | 129.50 |

SOURCE: Brookings Institution and Lewin-VHI calculations using data from the 1985 National Nursing Home Facility file. Medicare estimates taken from HCFA cost estimates for the Medicare Catastrophic Coverage Act of 1988.

expenses from the person's nonhousing assets. Once these nonhousing assets are drawn down to the medicaid asset level, medicaid pays the difference between patient income and the medicaid payment rate, less a personal needs allowance ($30 a month in 1986). After 1986 the personal needs allowance increases at half the rate of change of the consumer price index.

Daily rates for nursing home care vary by source of payment (table A-17). The medicare rate is based on the average daily medicare rate for a skilled nursing facility for 1988; HCFA developed that rate to estimate coinsurance for skilled nursing facilities under the Medicare Catastrophic Coverage Act of 1988. To account for higher-than-expected inflation and retroactive adjustments of the rate ceiling, medicare payment levels for 1993 are benchmarked against estimates based on HCFA projections of 1993 medicare skilled nursing facility expenditures.

The medicaid nursing home rate is based on an average of the rates for skilled nursing and intermediate care facilities for 1985, weighted by the number of medicaid patients, estimated from the 1985 National Nursing Home Survey Facility file and inflated to 1988 using HCFA program data. The private pay rate, also estimated from the 1985 National Nursing Home Survey Facility file, is the average of the private charges for skilled nursing and intermediate care facilities in 1985, weighted by the total number of skilled nursing and intermediate care facility beds, inflated to 1988 by growth in daily nursing home revenue, taken from HCFA Office of National Cost Estimates data.

After 1988 all payment rates are assumed to increase 5.5 percent a year. This projected rate of growth is based on the 1989 Social Security Administration Office of the Actuary's long-run assumption that the consumer price index will increase at 4.0 percent a year, real wages at 1.3 percent a year, and fringe benefits at 0.2 percent a year.[6] This assumption presumes nursing home prices will continue to increase to keep pace with the projected wage growth; this assumption takes account of the heavy labor component in nursing home costs. In essence, providers will need to increase wages at a rate roughly comparable to the rest of the economy in order to obtain workers. Implicit in this assumption is the expectation that no significant productivity improvements will occur in nursing home care.

Nursing home patients generally incur other health care expenses affecting the amount of income and assets they have available to pay for nursing home care. To account for the additional expenses, each nursing home admission is assumed to have out-of-pocket acute care costs of $68 a month in 1989, which is indexed by the nursing home inflation rate. This includes medicare part B premiums, medicare deductibles and coinsurance, and other health care costs. This expense approximates the cost of a comprehensive medigap policy.

## MEDICAID COVERAGE

The model assumes that a portion of a patient's income and assets is available to pay the costs of nursing home care. The entire income of single persons is considered available to pay for health care expenditures. For married couples, the model assumes that one-half of the couple's combined social security and asset income is available to the institutionalized spouse. Pension and individual retirement account income is assigned to the spouse who earned or owns the benefit.

The model also simulates transfers of income from one spouse to another in accordance with the Medicare Catastrophic Coverage Act spousal impoverishment provisions. When the spouse remaining at home has individual income below 122 percent of the poverty level for a couple in 1989 (133 percent in 1990, 150 percent in 1992), the model assumes an income transfer from the nursing home patient to raise his or her spouse's income to the amount specified above. The federal monthly poverty level income for elderly couples in 1988 was $597 and is assumed to rise annually by the rate of increase in the consumer price index.

Through 1988 all of a person's nonhousing assets, less the supplemental security income level of protected assets, are assumed to be available for nursing home costs. As mandated by the Deficit Reduction Act of 1984, beginning in 1984 the asset limit for single individuals increased by $100, and the limit for married couples increased by $150, each year until 1989 when they equaled $2,000 and $3,000, respectively. After 1989, the asset limits for individuals are assumed to increase at one-half the annual rate of increase in the consumer price index. The Omnibus Budget Reconciliation Act of 1993 provision requiring states to recover medicaid expenditures for nursing home stays from the estates of deceased patients is not modeled.

Starting in 1989, as a result of the Medicare Catastrophic Coverage Act spousal impoverishment provisions, the community spouse of a married couple may keep $12,000 or half of the couple's nonhousing assets up to $60,000, whichever is higher. The remainder less $2,000 is available to pay for nursing home care. After 1989, the asset limit for married couples is assumed to increase annually by the rate of increase in the consumer price index. When both spouses are in a nursing home during the year, assets are divided equally between the couple, each retaining $2,000.

In an effort to replicate more closely other recent estimates of the proportion of nursing home patients who spend down their assets to medicaid eligibility levels, the model adjusts the financial resources of certain nursing home patients to make simulated results consistent with national data. Several recent studies have found that the proportion of elderly nursing home patients who spend down to medicaid eligibility is smaller than commonly thought—in the range of 15 to 25 percent.[7] Conversely, the proportion of elderly nursing home patients who are medicaid eligible at admission is higher than previously assumed.

To make the model results more closely conform to these recent estimates, three adjustments were made. First, the model assumes that some unmarried nursing home residents sell their homes to pay for care. Although the "homestead" is generally an excluded asset when determining medicaid eligibility, it is hard to see how many people could avoid spend-down without using this asset to help pay for their care. Thus, to increase available resources and thereby reduce the level of medicaid spend-down, the model assumes a certain proportion of single nursing home patients sell their homes upon entry. Among unmarried medicaid patients, 5 percent with three- to six-month stays liquidate their housing equity to pay for care. The proportion increases to 10 percent for persons with six- to twelve-month stays, and 15 percent for those staying longer than twelve months. For unmarried nonmedicaid patients, 25 percent with three- to six-month stays sell their homes, as do 50 percent of those with six- to twelve-month stays, and 75 percent who stay longer than twelve months.

The second adjustment also increases the resources available to nursing home residents. Based on an analysis of the 1984 Survey of Income and Program Participation, the model assumes 10 percent of single nursing home residents who are paying privately for their care receive an additional $200 a month of income from their relatives.

Third, by reducing their level of financial assets, the model increases the proportion of nursing home patients who are eligible for medicaid at admission. This adjustment is intended to proxy asset transfers, major medical expenses in the community, legally allowable deductions (such as a burial plot), and repayment of debts. In general, the model assumes that persons with a lower level of assets and a longer length of stay are more likely to reduce their assets. The proportion of entrants assigned a stay shorter than six months who reduce assets at admission to the $2,000 medicaid eligibility level are 90 percent of those with nonhousing assets between $2,000 and $5,000, 20 percent with nonhousing assets between $5,000 and $10,000, and 10 percent with nonhousing assets valued at more than $10,000. For persons assigned a stay longer than six months, those percentages are 90 percent for people with nonhousing assets between $2,000 and $5,000, 50 percent for those with assets between $5,000 and $10,000, and 25 percent for those with more than $10,000 in nonhousing assets.

## MEDICARE COVERAGE

Except for 1989, the only year in which Medicare Catastrophic Coverage Act provisions were in effect, the model assumes that a predetermined proportion of all nursing home admissions receives full medicare coverage in a skilled nursing facility for the first twenty days. The model further assumes that, after the twentieth day, medicare pays only the residual daily costs after the patient pays the required coinsurance (set at one-eighth of the deductible under medicare part A, or $74 in 1990) for the remainder of the medicare-covered stay. The medicare coinsurance requirement is assumed to increase at 5.5 percent a year.

The predetermined proportion of nursing home admissions assumed to receive medicare coverage varies by the assigned length of stay. The model assumes that before 1989 medicare covers 33 percent of those patients who stay less than three months, 21 percent of those who stay from three to six months, 14 percent of those who stay from six to twelve months, and 10 percent of those who stay longer than twelve months. All of these patients receive thirty days of medicare coverage.

The model assumes that in 1989 medicare benefits for skilled nursing facilities follow the provisions of the Medicare Catastrophic Coverage Act. After 1989 and the repeal of the Medicare Catastrophic Coverage

Act, this medicare benefit returns to its pre-1989 structure. In 1988, however, just before the implementation of the Medicare Catastrophic Coverage Act, certain administrative changes were made in medicare benefits that liberalized coverage guidelines for skilled nursing facilities. Thus, after 1989, the model assumes medicare covers substantially more admissions than it did before 1989. Medicare benefits are assigned to 61 percent of those who stay less than three months, 38 percent of those who stay three to six months, 27 percent of those who stay six to twelve months, and 20 percent of those who stay longer than a year. All of these patients receive forty-five days of medicare coverage.

## Financing Home Care Services

The model simulates expenditures and sources of payment for home care. Expenditures are set equal to the number of visits multiplied by the price per visit. Sources of payment are out-of-pocket, medicare, medicaid, and other payers. The other payer category includes funding from state and local programs, the Older Americans Act, social services block grants, Department of Veterans' Affairs programs, and charity.

The out-of-pocket price per visit is based on data from the 1984 National Long-Term Care Survey and the 1987 National Medical Expenditure Survey. Medicare and medicaid visit rates are based on HCFA program data, and the other payer rate is a weighted average of the medicare and out-of-pocket rates (one-third medicare, two-thirds out-of-pocket). The payment rates for 1988 are shown in table A-18. The model assumes that prices increase 5.5 percent a year. Before 1988, prices are assumed to increase annually by 2 percentage points more than the consumer price index.

When the model selects a person to start receiving nonmedicare home care services or when an individual receiving medicare-reimbursed home care exceeds the maximum number of visits covered by medicare, the model assigns him or her to the medicaid, out-of-pocket, or other payers payment category based on data from the 1982 and 1984 National Long-Term Care Surveys, the 1984 Survey of Income and Program Participation, and medicare and medicaid program data.

The model first assigns home care users to medicaid reimbursement and then to the out-of-pocket and other payers categories. The percentage of people receiving home care reimbursed by medicaid was estimated from the 1982 National Long-Term Care Survey. Because that survey does not have detailed asset information, however, the 1984

TABLE A-18. *Average Price per Visit for Home Care,*
*by Source of Payment, 1988*
Dollars

| Payer | Charge per visit |
|---|---|
| Medicaid | 48.70 |
| Medicare | 51.10 |
| Out-of-pocket | 12.50 |
| Other payers[a] | 25.20 |

SOURCE: Brookings Institution and Lewin-VHI calculations using data from the 1982 and 1984 National Long-Term Care Surveys and the 1987 National Medical Expenditure Survey.
    a. Other payers include state and local expenditures, social service block grants, Older Americans Act and Department of Veterans' Affairs home care funds, charity, and out-of-pocket expenditures by people other than the service recipient.

Survey of Income and Program Participation was used to adjust the final probabilities by determining the proportion of persons in each income category with nonhousing assets sufficiently low to qualify for medicaid coverage (that is, below the supplemental security income level of $2,000 for single individuals and $3,000 for couples in 1989). These probabilities vary by income and marital status. These assumptions did not account for more widespread coverage of home care by state medicaid programs between 1984 and 1993. Therefore, the results were benchmarked against estimates based on HCFA projections of 1993 medicaid home care expenditures.

The model assumes that out-of-pocket and other payer financing of home care by persons not selected for medicaid coverage also varies by income. People selected to pay out of pocket for home care are assumed to use up to 30 percent of their income before drawing on their nonhousing assets. If nonhousing assets are depleted, the model assumes individuals return to their income to pay for home care.

## Extrapolating Long-Term Care Expenditures and Financing through 2050

Although the full model projects nursing home and home care use and expenditures from 1986 through 2020, the baby boom cohort and the demand for long-term care will peak well after 2020. One reason for not extending the full model past 2020 is that nearly all of the model's 1979 starting population of working-age adults will have reached age 65 or died by 2020, leaving too few people to turn age 65 after 2020 for detailed modeling. In addition, behavioral and economic assumptions beyond 2020 become highly questionable. Thus, to estimate long-term care expenditures for the baby boom cohort, a simplified method for extrapolating long-term care expenditures to 2050 was developed.

Estimation of expenditures began by calculating the per capita long-term care expenditures for seven age groups for each year between 1989 and 2020. Then, the assumed rate of growth in long-term care expenditures between 2021 and 2050 (1.5 percent over real) was applied to the average per capita expenditures for the average of the period 2016 to 2020 and projected forward to 2050. Using population projections from the Social Security Administration, the age-specific level of expenditures was then multiplied by the expected number of elderly in each year between 2021 and 2050.[8] Summing across all age groups produced the estimated annual total long-term care costs.

Alternative options for financing public long-term care expenditures through 2050 include a payroll tax. The method for calculating the overall proportion of payroll needed to finance public long-term care expenditures was similar to that employed for extrapolating expenditures through 2050. The annual total public long-term care expenditures were simply calculated as a percentage of all wages and salaries estimated by the Social Security Administration between 1991 and 2050.

# Pricing Methodology for Prototype Private Long-Term Care Insurance Policies

This study's analysis of private long-term care insurance relies on premiums for prototype private long-term care insurance policies developed using the Brookings-ICF Long-Term Care Financing Model.[a] Insurance premiums have a benefit portion (known to economists as the "actuarially fair premium" and to actuaries as the "net premium") and an administrative and profit portion. Using output from the model, the basic pricing methodology is to make the present value of the benefit stream equal to the present value of the benefit portion of the premium and then to apply a factor to account for administrative and profit costs. In brief, the methodology has four main steps.

First, to calculate the present value of benefits, it is assumed that different age cohorts (for example, 65–69, 70–74) purchase an insurance policy with a specific set of benefits. The stream of benefit expenditures is simulated in the model for each year between 1986 and 2020. The expenditures are then discounted to find the present value of the benefit payment stream in 1986. The benefit stream implicitly discounts for mortality.

Second, to calculate the present value of premiums, it is assumed that each policyholder pays an arbitrary annual premium of $120 a year. The

a. This description of pricing prototype premiums draws from Joshua M. Wiener, Katherine A. Harris, and Raymond J. Hanley, *Premium Pricing of Prototype Private Long-Term Care Insurance Policies,* report prepared for the Office of the Assistant Secretary for Planning and Evaluation, U.S. Department of Health and Human Services (Brookings, 1990).

aggregate stream of premium payments for each cohort is simulated in the model for each year between 1986 and 2020, and the premium stream is then discounted back to 1986. The premium stream also implicitly discounts for mortality.

Third, to estimate the benefit portion of the premium, the ratio of the present value of aggregate benefit payments to the present value of aggregate premiums is calculated. This establishes the ratio of benefits to premiums actually paid. Multiplying the ratio by the annual premium paid—$120—yields the actuarially fair premium per year.

Fourth, to calculate the final premiums, the actuarially fair premium is divided by the loss ratio. A loss ratio of 70 percent is used for individual policies and 80 percent for group products.

## Calculation of the Actuarially Fair Premium

Numerous issues must be addressed in calculating the actuarially fair premium, including benefit structure, payment rates, inflation adjustments, type of premium, medical underwriting, lapse rates, induced demand, and discount rates.

### BENEFITS

Policies modeled cover two or four years each of nursing and home care after a deductible (sixty days for nursing home care and thirty visits for home care). The benefit stream excludes any nursing home and home care services reimbursed by medicare. Home care benefits are available only to individuals who have problems with two or more of the five activities of daily living or who are cognitively impaired. These policies have a lifetime maximum equal to the length of covered stay for each service (for example, the two-year policy would have a lifetime maximum of two years of nursing home care and two years of home care).

The deductible is applied on a spell-of-illness basis. Thus, nursing home stays interrupted by a hospital stay or a short discharge are subject to a single deductible. There is a "waiver of premium" for people receiving nursing home care under the policy. People receiving home care continue to pay premiums.

### PAYMENT RATES AND INFLATION ADJUSTMENTS

Initial payment rates for all policies are $60 a day for nursing home care and $30 a visit for home care. Indemnity levels are adjusted for inflation on a compound basis, increasing by 5.5 percent a year, the assumed rate of increase in long-term care prices in the Brookings-ICF Long-Term Care Financing Model.

## LEVEL OR INDEXED PREMIUMS

Virtually all current long-term care insurance policies have level premiums. That is, unless premiums are raised for all policyholders in a class, the premiums remain the same throughout the life of the policy. From an affordability standpoint, this clearly makes sense for the elderly, who tend to have fixed or declining real incomes. Level premiums make less sense for the nonelderly, whose incomes over time will be rising in real or at least in nominal terms. In our premium estimates, policies for the elderly are calculated assuming level premium payments. Premiums for the nonelderly increase at 5.5 percent a year until age 65 and then are level. Indexed premiums are estimated by adjusting the stream of $120 premium payments by the indexing factor.

## MEDICAL UNDERWRITING

Private insurers do not sell policies to people they think have a good chance of using covered services in the near future. This medical underwriting is approximated in the Brookings-ICF Long-Term Care Financing Model by allowing only nondisabled persons to buy policies. Nondisabled individuals include persons with no problems with the activities or instrumental activities of daily living.

Most insurance companies are more restrictive than this and also exclude people with certain medical diagnoses, which may not manifest themselves in functional problems. These additional restrictions were not simulated because data on medical conditions are not in the model, and randomly dropping some percentage of individuals to account for these restrictions seemed too arbitrary.

The practical effect of not simulating medical restrictions may be minimal. A standard actuarial assumption is that the effects of medical underwriting wear off after five to fifteen years, after which service use approximates that of the general population. Our own comparisons of simulations where only the nondisabled may buy policies with those where the total population may buy produced a stream of benefits that is consistent with this actuarial assumption.

## LAPSE RATES

For a variety of reasons, not all people who initially purchase a policy make premium payments until death. Any voluntary termination or lapse reduces premiums for other policyholders because fewer benefit payments must be paid. In addition, because insurers will receive premium payments for a period of time without having to pay claims, policyholders who lapse "subsidize" the premiums of policyholders who continue to be insured.

Lapses are calculated as a percent of existing policies for that year. Our lapse rates assume 5 percent of the policies terminate each year for the first two years, then 3 percent each year for the next six years. We assume that no policyholders terminate after eight years. Although not much is known about actual lapse rates, this rate is lower than those assumed in some other efforts to price prototype private long-term care insurance policies.[1]

The effect of lapse rates was calculated outside of the model by multiplying the aggregate benefit and premium streams by the lapse rate. For example, assuming an annual lapse rate of 5 percent for the first two years and then 3 percent thereafter, the premium streams are adjusted by multiplying the first year's aggregate premiums by 0.95, the second year's aggregate premiums by 0.90 (that is, $0.95 \times 0.95$), the third year's premiums by 0.88 (that is, $0.95 \times 0.95 \times 0.97$), and so forth. A similar procedure is applied to the benefit stream.

This procedure implicitly assumes that the people likely to drop the policy are no different from those who are likely to retain the policy (that is, there is no adverse or favorable selection). Two competing scenarios make this assumption valid in the aggregate. On the one hand, healthier people might be more likely to drop their policies. On the other hand, people developing cognitive problems such as Alzheimer's disease are less likely to keep their policies in force through timely payment of premiums.

Most insurers, however, suppose some adverse selection in their lapse assumptions. That is, the healthier population is more likely to drop the policies. Thus, within the range of lapses examined, our estimates probably reflect an upper-bound estimate of the effect of lapse rates.

### INDUCED DEMAND

Private insurance will almost certainly increase use of nursing homes and home care services, largely because the out-of-pocket cost of services will decline. Conventional economics argues that people buy more of a good or service when it costs less. How much use will increase is uncertain, and the empirical evidence on which to base the assumptions is weak.[2] In estimating these premiums, it was assumed that the insured would increase their nursing home use by 20 percent and their home care use by 80 percent. Based on judgments of how quickly the supply of nursing home and home care services could change, the increase in nursing home use was phased in over ten years but the increase in home care use was immediate. This change in use represents a combination of increases in the number of users, length of nursing home stays, and number of home care visits, as well as disability "creep" (that is, people with lower levels of disability who claim to have a higher level of disability to qualify for benefits). To calculate this increase, the present value of the benefits was multiplied by the applicable increase in use.

## DISCOUNT RATES

Virtually all private long-term insurance policies are designed to build up substantial reserves in the early years for payout in the later years. Thus, the rate of return earned on the reserves is a critical factor in calculating premiums. Obviously, there is no way to know how well the economy will function thirty to sixty years into the future. The Technical Panel to the 1991 Advisory Panel on Social Security urged that the real interest rate assumption used by the social security actuaries for their mid-range, alternative II-B projection be raised from 2.0 percent to 2.8 percent.[3] We used a nominal rate of 7.5 percent, 3.5 percent real interest, as our parameter to estimate our premiums.

## COMPLETING THE BENEFIT AND PREMIUM STREAMS FOR THE YOUNG ELDERLY

A few people aged 65 through 69 in 1986 will not have completed their long-term care use or premium payments by 2020, when the Brookings-ICF Long-Term Care Financing Model simulations end. We base their subsequent experience on the rate of decline in the premium and benefit streams at very old ages by using model data on the older cohorts (75–79 and 80–84) who have finished their experience.

### Calculating Premiums for the under-65 Population

The Brookings-ICF Long-Term Care Financing Model simulates long-term care use and premium payments for people aged 65 and older from 1986 through 2020. This means that the premium and benefit streams of the under-65 population must be calculated outside the model. These calculations require a complicated methodology that adjusts the experience of the 65–69-year-old cohort to proxy the long-term care use of the under-65 cohorts.

*Estimating the Complete Experience of the 65–69 Cohort*

The methodology requires completing the experience of the 65–69 cohort by extending premium and benefit streams beyond the simulated time period—both back to when the cohort was aged 40–44 and forward through death. On the premium side, adjustment is made because within a given cohort, there are more people alive at younger ages to pay premiums. Using the Social Security Administration II-B life table unique to the 65–69 cohort, the premium stream for each age between 42 and 66 is calculated by computing the ratio of people alive at younger ages relative to the number alive at age 67 (the midpoint between age 65 and 69).[4] For example, if the life table estimates that 18 percent more people are alive at age 55 than at age 67, then we would multiply the premium payments at age 67 by 1.18 to estimate the premium payment at age 55.

On the benefit side, the use of long-term care services by the non-elderly population must be estimated. Although use is extremely low at younger ages, there is some utilization for which insurance benefits would be paid. Data from the Health Care Financing Administration were used to estimate aggregate nursing home expenditures for each age between age 42 and 66.[5] These estimates were then used to compute the ratio of nursing home expenditures at each age relative to expenditure at age 67. A benefit stream was calculated for both nursing home and home care for each age between 42 and 66 using the age-specific ratios. For example, the nursing home expenditure at age 42 is 41 percent of the expenditure at age 67. We estimate the expenditure at age 42 by multiplying the age 67 expenditure by 0.41. To simulate underwriting at earlier ages, we reduce this newly estimated expenditure by one-third to account for persons with congenital or early onset disability (such as mental retardation, multiple sclerosis, and spinal cord injury) who would not be able to purchase private insurance.

*Constructing the Experience of the Rest of the under-65 Population*

The experience of the 65–69 cohort from the time that its members were age 40–44 through death is used as a "blueprint" from which to construct the experience of younger cohorts, taking into account that younger cohorts will live longer and presumably use more long-term care than will the 65–69 cohort. Age-specific changes in mortality are calculated using Social Security Administration II-B life tables unique to each of these younger cohorts.[6] Premium and benefit streams were adjusted from our "blueprint" to account for improvements in mortality between the younger cohorts and the 65–69 cohort. For example, the life table projections indicate that there will be 28 percent more people alive at age 85 in the 40–44 cohort than in the 65–69 cohort. The 40–44 cohort's expenditures at age 85 were estimated by multiplying the 65–69 expenditure at age 85 by 1.28.

*Insuring Only the Nondisabled*

Even though we can construct the experience of people purchasing insurance under the age of 65 from the medically underwritten 65–69 cohort, we have not yet accounted for the effects of medical underwriting at different ages. Because disability is strongly related to age, fewer people will be able to purchase insurance at ages 65–69 than at younger ages. Only a very small percentage of people under the age of 65 are disabled. Therefore, the future long-term care use of the population buying insurance under age 65 is best approximated by the long-term care use of the 65 and older population as a whole, rather than by the use of a medically underwritten population. To account for this, we adjust the benefit streams of the cohorts under age 65 by a factor that accounts for their additional long-term care use. This factor is the ratio of the premium for a policy where the entire population is allowed to purchase long-term care insurance to the premium for a policy where only the nondisabled may buy. Starting with the 40–44 cohort, there is a gradual transition from a set of benefits with no medical underwriting to a set of benefits that is medically underwritten by age 65–69.

*Inflation*

Because benefits are indexed for inflation in the model, the experience of the 65–69 cohort cannot be used as a proxy for the under-65 population until it is adjusted for the fact that younger cohorts will be using long-term care farther into the future and, thus, will be subject to a longer period of inflation. By the time the 40–44 cohort is in its eighties and at highest risk of needing long-term care, that care will be reimbursed at a higher rate than the long-term care used by the 65–69 cohort. For example, because the 40–44 cohort will use long-term care most intensively twenty-five years after the 65–69 cohort, an additional twenty-five years of inflation adjustment must be added to the benefit stream of the 65–69 cohort.

## Administrative and Other Load Factors

In addition to paying benefits, the insurance premium charged consumers must cover administrative and marketing costs, profits, and taxes. The percentage of the total premium that goes to pay benefits is known as the "loss ratio." The model regulation developed by the National Association of Insurance Commissioners suggests a minimum loss ratio of 60 percent for individual products, and there has been discussion of a 70 percent loss ratio for group products.[7] Because the goal of this analysis is to estimate premiums for policies that are better than those offered in the current market, a higher loss ratio was assumed—70 percent for individual policies and 80 percent for group products. To derive the final premium to be paid by consumers, the estimated actuarially fair premium was divided by 0.7 and 0.8, respectively.

# Social Insurance without Medicaid Liberalization: Simulation Assumptions and Results

To assess public insurance options without the effects of medicaid liberalization, we simulated four prototype social insurance programs using the Brookings-ICF Long-Term Care Financing Model. Table C-1 summarizes the simulation assumptions for these four programs. Home care benefits are modeled identically for all social insurance strategies. All options are modeled as if they were fully implemented immediately, with no phase-in period. All four options impose a moderate 20 percent copayment on home care and nursing home care, when covered. In all cases, medicaid pays the coinsurance for low-income people who are eligible for the program. Varying assumptions are made to account for the increased demand for services that typically follows the availability of additional monies for services.

Because all but the most comprehensive public insurance program leaves at least part of the nursing home stay uncovered, private long-term care insurance is included as a complement to the public benefits. Medicaid, medicare, and other public programs for nursing home and home care remain unchanged.

Table C-2 presents public and private nursing home and home care expenditures under the four options for 1993 and 2018. Figure C-1 estimates what public expenditures on long-term care would be for the various reform strategies.

The HOME CARE ONLY strategy would increase public expenditures by $15 billion over the BASE CASE in 1993. The FRONT-END

FIGURE C-1. **Annual Public Expenditures for Long-Term Care, Public Insurance Options without Medicaid Liberalization, Selected Periods[a]**

Billions of 1993 dollars

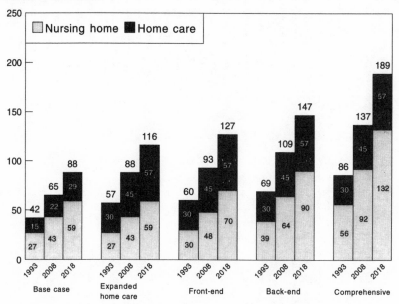

SOURCE:: Brookings-ICF Long-Term Care Financing Model.
a. Here and in figure C-3, 2008 represents the five-year average for the period 2006–10.

and BACK-END options would increase public expenditures by $18 billion and $27 billion, respectively. As expected, the COMPREHENSIVE strategy is substantially more expensive than other options. For 1993 public costs under this option would increase by $44 billion dollars. By 2018, the incremental public costs of all of the options would more than double in constant dollars. By comparison, public insurance strategies that include liberalization of medicaid are all approximately $5 billion more expensive in 1993 and $7 billion more expensive in 2018 (see chapter 7).

Tables C-3 and C-4 and figure C-2 suggest that the overwhelming majority of total and incremental public spending for nursing home and home care in 1993 and 2018 would go to persons with incomes under $40,000.[a] In 2018 only 27 percent of new spending for home care under all the social insurance strategies would go to people with incomes above

a. The Home Care Only option is not included on tables C-2 or C-3 because under this strategy, no new social insurance expenditures go toward nursing home care.

TABLE C-1. *Eligibility Criteria, Benefits, and Program Characteristics of Public Long-Term Care Insurance Options without Medicaid Liberalization*

| Option | Nursing home benefits | Home care benefits | Medicaid and medicare benefits | Private insurance[a] |
|---|---|---|---|---|
| Expanded home care only | Current medicaid and medicare benefits only. | For severely disabled,[b] broad home care coverage of unlimited duration; 20 percent coinsurance; for less disabled, current medicaid and medicare benefits. | Medicaid and medicare benefits unchanged. | People buy what they can afford; two- or four-year nursing home policies after sixty-day deductible period; no home care benefits; age-based affordability criteria include premiums as a percentage of income and minimum financial assets; annual premiums range from $1,145 to $4,021;[c] people with ADL or IADL problems cannot buy; policies lapse if premium exceeds 20 percent of income. |
| Front-end | First six months of nursing home stay covered for everyone. | For severely disabled,[b] broad home care coverage of unlimited duration; 20 percent coinsurance; for less disabled, current medicaid and medicare benefits. | Medicaid and medicare benefits unchanged. | People buy what they can afford; two- or four-year nursing home policies after six-month deductible period; no home care benefits; age-based affordability criteria include premiums as a percentage of income and minimum financial assets; annual premiums range from $1,064 to $3,738;[c] people with ADL or IADL problems cannot buy; policies lapse if premium exceeds 20 percent of income. |

| | | | | |
|---|---|---|---|---|
| Back-end | Nursing home stay covered after two-year deductible period for everyone. | For severely disabled,[b] broad home care coverage of unlimited duration; 20 percent coinsurance; for less disabled, current medicaid and medicare benefits. | Medicaid and medicare benefits unchanged. | People buy what they can afford; two-year nursing home policy after sixty-day deductible period; no home care benefits; age-based affordability criteria include premiums as a percentage of income and minimum financial assets; annual premiums range from $1,145 to $2,525;[c] people with ADL or IADL problems cannot buy; policies lapse if premium exceeds 20 percent of income. |
| Comprehensive | First day unlimited nursing home coverage for everyone. | For severely disabled,[b] broad home care coverage of unlimited duration; 20 percent coinsurance; for less disabled, current medicaid and medicare benefits. | Medicaid and medicare benefits unchanged. | No private insurance. |

a. People do not purchase private long-term care insurance until age 67.
b. Severely disabled defined as two or more problems with the activities of daily living or cognitive impairment.
c. Premiums depend on initial age at purchase and length (two or four years) of nursing home coverage.

TABLE C-2. *Total Expenditures for Nursing Home and Home Care, by Source of Payment, Base Case and Public Insurance Options without Medicaid Liberalization, Selected Periods*[a]
*Billions of 1993 dollars*

| Payment source | Base case | Expanded home care only | Front-end nursing home and expanded home care | Back-end nursing home and expanded home care | Comprehensive nursing home and expanded home care |
|---|---|---|---|---|---|
| | | | *1993* | | |
| Total long-term care expenditures | 75.5 | 94.8 | 94.9 | 99.9 | 107.3 |
| **Nursing home** | | | | | |
| Medicaid | 22.4 | 22.5 | 18.3 | 9.9 | 2.2 |
| Medicare | 4.3 | 4.3 | 4.3 | 4.3 | 4.3 |
| Public insurance | 0.0 | 0.0 | 7.5 | 25.2 | 49.9 |
| Private insurance | 0.0 | 0.0 | 1.8 | 1.5 | 0.0 |
| Family cash | 17.0 | 17.0 | 14.5 | 12.3 | 10.6 |
| Family assets | 11.0 | 11.1 | 8.6 | 6.7 | 0.5 |
| TOTAL | 54.7 | 54.8 | 54.9 | 59.9 | 67.4 |
| **Home care** | | | | | |
| Medicaid | 3.6 | 1.5 | 1.5 | 1.5 | 1.5 |
| Medicare | 9.4 | 9.4 | 9.4 | 9.4 | 9.4 |
| Other payers[b] | 2.2 | 1.0 | 1.0 | 1.0 | 1.0 |
| Public insurance | 0.0 | 18.1 | 18.1 | 18.1 | 18.1 |
| Private insurance | 0.0 | 0.0 | 0.0 | 0.0 | 0.0 |
| Out-of-pocket | 5.5 | 9.9 | 9.9 | 9.9 | 9.9 |
| TOTAL | 20.7 | 39.9 | 39.9 | 39.9 | 39.9 |
| | | | *2018* | | |
| Total long-term care expenditures | 168.3 | 205.1 | 211.7 | 219.5 | 234.8 |
| **Nursing home** | | | | | |
| Medicaid | 49.0 | 49.0 | 39.2 | 20.5 | 4.8 |
| Medicare | 10.0 | 9.9 | 9.9 | 9.9 | 9.9 |
| Public insurance | 0.0 | 0.0 | 20.8 | 59.5 | 117.3 |
| Private insurance | 0.0 | 0.0 | 14.7 | 12.7 | 0.0 |
| Family cash | 42.6 | 42.6 | 33.0 | 26.6 | 24.2 |
| Family assets | 26.6 | 26.6 | 17.2 | 13.4 | 1.8 |
| TOTAL | 128.2 | 128.1 | 134.8 | 142.6 | 158.0 |
| **Home care** | | | | | |
| Medicaid | 5.2 | 2.5 | 2.5 | 2.5 | 2.5 |
| Medicare | 19.0 | 18.8 | 18.8 | 18.8 | 18.8 |
| Other payers[b] | 4.3 | 1.9 | 1.9 | 1.9 | 1.9 |
| Public insurance | 0.0 | 33.7 | 33.7 | 33.7 | 33.7 |
| Private insurance | 0.0 | 0.0 | 0.0 | 0.0 | 0.0 |
| Out-of-pocket | 11.6 | 20.0 | 20.0 | 20.0 | 20.0 |
| TOTAL | 40.1 | 76.9 | 76.9 | 76.9 | 76.9 |

SOURCE: Brookings-ICF Long-Term Care Financing Model.

a. In this and other tables and figures in this appendix, 1993 represents the five-year average for the period 1991–95; and 2018 represents the five-year average for 2016–20.

b. Other payers include state and local expenditures, social service block grants, Older Americans Act and Department of Veterans' Affairs home care funds, charity, and out-of-pocket expenditures by people other than the service recipient.

TABLE C-3. *Public Expenditures for Nursing Home Care, by Demographic and Income Groups, Base Case and Public Insurance Options without Medicaid Liberalization, Selected Periods*[a]
Percent unless otherwise noted

| Patient characteristics | Base case | Front-end nursing home | Back-end nursing home | Comprehensive nursing home |
|---|---|---|---|---|
| | | *1993* | | |
| Public nursing home expenditures (billions of 1993 dollars) | 33.6 | 36.4 | 48.1 | 67.1 |
| Age | | | | |
| 65–74 | 20 | 19 | 20 | 19 |
| 75–84 | 34 | 35 | 34 | 35 |
| 85 and older | 46 | 46 | 46 | 46 |
| Marital status | | | | |
| Married | 33 | 33 | 34 | 32 |
| Unmarried | 67 | 67 | 66 | 68 |
| Gender | | | | |
| Men | 29 | 29 | 30 | 30 |
| Women | 71 | 71 | 70 | 70 |
| Family income (1993 dollars) | | | | |
| Less than 7,500 | 31 | 29 | 26 | 25 |
| 7,500–15,000 | 40 | 39 | 37 | 36 |
| 15,000–20,000 | 11 | 11 | 12 | 12 |
| 20,000–30,000 | 13 | 13 | 15 | 15 |
| 30,000–40,000 | 3 | 3 | 4 | 5 |
| 40,000–50,000 | 1 | 1 | 1 | 1 |
| More than 50,000 | 2 | 3 | 5 | 6 |
| | | *2018* | | |
| Public nursing home expenditures (billions of 1993 dollars) | 64.2 | 75.1 | 100.7 | 145.3 |
| Age | | | | |
| 65–74 | 15 | 16 | 16 | 17 |
| 75–84 | 32 | 33 | 30 | 31 |
| 85 and older | 52 | 52 | 54 | 51 |
| Marital status | | | | |
| Married | 30 | 29 | 30 | 29 |
| Unmarried | 70 | 71 | 70 | 71 |
| Gender | | | | |
| Men | 30 | 30 | 31 | 32 |
| Women | 70 | 70 | 69 | 68 |
| Family income (1993 dollars) | | | | |
| Less than 7,500 | 19 | 17 | 15 | 13 |
| 7,500–15,000 | 33 | 32 | 29 | 27 |
| 15,000–20,000 | 14 | 14 | 12 | 12 |
| 20,000–30,000 | 20 | 20 | 20 | 19 |
| 30,000–40,000 | 7 | 8 | 9 | 10 |
| 40,000–50,000 | 3 | 4 | 5 | 6 |
| More than 50,000 | 4 | 6 | 11 | 12 |

SOURCE: Brookings-ICF Long-Term Care Financing Model.
a. These data are based on the public expenditures for an admission cohort over the entire length of the nursing home stay.

TABLE C-4. *Incremental Public Expenditures for Nursing Home Care, by Demographic and Income Groups, Base Case and Public Insurance Options without Medicaid Liberalization, Selected Periods*[a]
*Percent unless otherwise noted*

| Patient characteristics | Front-end nursing home | Back-end nursing home | Comprehensive nursing home |
|---|---|---|---|
| | | *1993* | |
| Public nursing home expenditures (billions of 1993 dollars) | 36.4 | 48.1 | 67.1 |
| Incremental public nursing home expenditures (billions of 1993 dollars) | 2.8 | 14.5 | 33.5 |
| Age | | | |
| 65–74 | 14 | 21 | 19 |
| 75–84 | 38 | 32 | 35 |
| 85 and older | 48 | 47 | 46 |
| Marital status | | | |
| Married | 24 | 36 | 31 |
| Unmarried | 76 | 64 | 69 |
| Gender | | | |
| Men | 31 | 32 | 30 |
| Women | 69 | 68 | 70 |
| Family income (1993 dollars) | | | |
| Less than 7,500 | 12 | 16 | 19 |
| 7,500–15,000 | 34 | 31 | 31 |
| 15,000–20,000 | 14 | 13 | 13 |
| 20,000–30,000 | 13 | 19 | 17 |
| 30,000–40,000 | 11 | 7 | 8 |
| 40,000–50,000 | 3 | 2 | 2 |
| More than 50,000 | 12 | 12 | 10 |
| | | *2018* | |
| Public nursing home expenditures (billions of 1993 dollars) | 75.1 | 100.7 | 145.3 |
| Incremental public nursing home expenditures (billions of 1993 dollars) | 10.9 | 36.5 | 81.1 |
| Age | | | |
| 65–74 | 18 | 18 | 18 |
| 75–84 | 35 | 27 | 31 |
| 85 and older | 48 | 56 | 51 |
| Marital status | | | |
| Married | 20 | 29 | 28 |
| Unmarried | 80 | 71 | 72 |
| Gender | | | |
| Men | 29 | 32 | 33 |
| Women | 71 | 67 | 67 |
| Family income (1993 dollars) | | | |
| Less than 7,500 | 7 | 8 | 8 |
| 7,500–15,000 | 25 | 20 | 23 |
| 15,000–20,000 | 12 | 10 | 11 |
| 20,000–30,000 | 18 | 19 | 19 |
| 30,000–40,000 | 12 | 13 | 13 |
| 40,000–50,000 | 6 | 8 | 8 |
| More than 50,000 | 20 | 22 | 19 |

SOURCE: Brookings-ICF Long-Term Care Financing Model.
a. These data are based on the public expenditures for an admission cohort over the entire length of the nursing home stay.

FIGURE C-2. **Income Distribution of Annual Public Expenditures for Expanded Home Care without Medicaid Liberalization, Selected Periods**

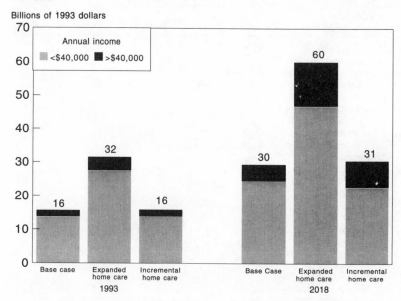

Billions of 1993 dollars

SOURCE: Brookings-ICF Long-Term Care Financing Model.

$40,000. For nursing home care, the percentage of new public spending for people with incomes above $40,000 ranges from 26 percent to 30 percent. The results are roughly the same when medicaid liberalization is included with the various options.

Table C-5 shows the impact that the various social insurance options would have on catastrophic costs in 2018. Absolute out-of-pocket spending under the BASE CASE would average $44,000 in 2018, and approximately 33 percent of all nursing home patients would spend more than $20,000 out of pocket. As expected, the COMPREHENSIVE option without medicaid liberalization has the most dramatic impact, although even under this option almost one-quarter of nursing home admissions would pay more than $20,000 out of pocket, and average out-of-pocket spending in 2018 would be $16,000. In contrast, the COMPREHENSIVE option with medicaid liberalization shows 22 percent of nursing home admissions spending more than $20,000 out of pocket, with average out-of-pocket spending at $14,000.

Table C-5 also provides projections for the percentage of people who, under various public options, incur catastrophic costs relative to their

TABLE C-5. *Effect of Public Insurance Options without Medicaid Liberalization on Catastrophic Out-of-Pocket Expenditures for Nursing Home Care, 2018*

| Measure | Base case | Expanded home care only | Front-end | Back-end | Comprehensive |
|---|---|---|---|---|---|
| Absolute expenditure[a] | | | | | |
| Average out-of-pocket spending (thousands of 1993 dollars) | 44 | 37 | 33 | 24 | 16 |
| Percentage of admissions spending more than $20,000 out of pocket | 33 | 28 | 26 | 28 | 24 |
| Relative expenditure[b] | | | | | |
| Percentage of admissions spending more than 40 percent of income, assets on care | 39 | 36 | 31 | 32 | 21 |
| Target efficiency[c] | | | | | |
| Percentage of incremental spending for people who would otherwise have incurred catastrophic out-of-pocket costs | ... | ... | 49 | 76 | 72 |

SOURCE: Brookings-ICF Long-Term Care Financing Model.
a. These data are based on the total out-of-pocket payments for an admissions cohort over the entire length of the nursing home stay.
b. The numerator is equal to the out-of-pocket contribution to nursing home care for the entire length of stay; the denominator is equal to income during the stay plus nonhousing assets.
c. These data are based on incremental public expenditures for an admission cohort for the entire length of stay. In 2018 incremental spending for front-end care was $10.9 billion, for back-end care $36.5 billion, and for comprehensive care $81.1 billion.

income and assets. Under the BASE CASE in 2018, 39 percent of nursing home admissions spend more than 40 percent of their income and assets on their care. The various public options reduce this proportion to between 21 and 36 percent. By comparison, with liberalized medicaid benefits, these proportions range from 18 to 30 percent.

In 2018 roughly three-quarters of the marginal public spending for nursing home care in the BACK-END and COMPREHENSIVE strategies is projected to go for people who currently spend more than 40 percent of their income and nonhousing assets on nursing home care (table C-5). Because the catastrophic costs of nursing home care generally result from longer stays, the FRONT-END strategy does not fare as well in this test of target efficiency, with only about one-half of incremental expenditures benefiting this group. Adding medicaid liberalization improves the target efficiency of the FRONT-END option

FIGURE C-3.  **Reductions in Number of Medicaid Nursing Home Patients from Base Case Public Insurance Options without Medicaid Liberalization, Selected Periods**

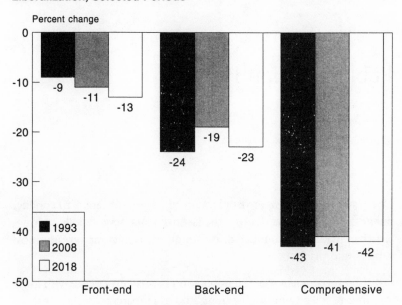

SOURCE: Brookings-ICF Long-Term Care Financing Model.

but does not affect the target efficiency of either the BACK-END or COMPREHENSIVE option.

One reason for creating a social insurance program is to reduce the number of nursing home patients dependent on welfare. Figure C-3 suggests that large reductions in the number of medicaid nursing home patients through social insurance coverage can be realized when no medicaid liberalization is included. Indeed, the number of medicaid nursing home patients would decrease at least 40 percent under a COM-PREHENSIVE strategy in each of the three time periods. Combining medicaid liberalization with the public insurance options often offsets a large part of that reduction. Not liberalizing medicaid, of course, means that people must severely impoverish themselves before receiving government aid.

# Public Opinion Polls

One way to find out what people want in long-term care is to conduct public opinion surveys. During the last five years, several polls on long-term care have been conducted. Although the results vary greatly, most surveys find that:

- A substantial portion of the population has had experience with long-term care, mostly through parents and grandparents.
- The vast majority of people do not think that they have enough financial resources to pay for long-term care.
- Americans strongly support an increased government role in financing long-term care.
- A majority of Americans favor a strategy that would finance long-term care on a non-means-tested basis and that would cover people of all ages, with the federal government playing a major role.
- The public does not have a good idea about what such a program would cost. Although people are generally willing to pay some amount to help finance a new government program, it is usually not enough to cover a comprehensive social insurance program.
- The public voices very strong support for additional home care services but is also concerned about coverage of nursing home care.

Although useful, these surveys are limited in several ways. First, many of them were done before 1990, and so it is uncertain how accurately they reflect current sentiment. Second, almost all of the polls were commissioned by interest groups with a point of view to promote. Thus, questions may be subtly or not so subtly slanted to generate the desired response. Third, in many instances the questions are poorly worded, making it difficult to evaluate the responses. Finally, respondents were rarely asked to make difficult trade-offs among options.

## Experience with Long-Term Care

Many Americans have had experience with long-term care through their relatives.

- In a 1989 survey by the Daniel Yankelovich Group for the American Association of Retired Persons (AARP), 47 percent of respondents said a member of their family (grandparent, parent, child, or other family member) had needed long-term care.
- In a 1993 survey by the ICR Survey Research Group of AUS Consultants for the AARP, 43 percent of those interviewed had experienced need for long-term care in their immediate family.
- In a 1993 survey by the Gallup Organization for the Employee Benefit Research Institute (EBRI), 21 percent of respondents said that a member of their family (grandparent, parent, or other family member) received long-term care within the previous five years.

## Inability to Pay for Long-Term Care

Most people cannot afford long-term care.

- In a 1988 survey by Louis Harris and Associates, 82 percent of respondents said that they "could not afford" the cost of nursing home care.
- In the 1989 survey by the Daniel Yankelovich Group, 73 percent of persons polled were "not very confident" or "not at all confident" about being able to "deal with the cost of long-term care."

## Support for Government Programs for Long-Term Care

Support for additional government financing of long-term care is very strong. Most surveys find a majority of people in favor of social insurance programs rather than means-tested programs. These questions are often poorly phrased, however, and do not make clear that medicaid will provide financing for nursing home care to those who impoverish themselves, not just to those who are already poor.

- A 1987 survey by RL Associates for the AARP and the Villers Foundation found that 61 percent of persons polled wanted a long-term care program "available to everyone regardless of how rich or poor they are."

- A 1989 survey by the Daniel Yankelovich Group for the AARP found that 68 percent of respondents would "strongly support" a federal long-term care program.
- In the 1989 poll by the Daniel Yankelovich Group, 67 percent of persons surveyed stated that they "strongly supported" a "federal program similar to social security or medicare to help pay for long-term care for the elderly and disabled." Using conjoint analysis, the group found that universal eligibility for a long-term care program is favored by most Americans.
- In addition, a 1989 survey by the Gallup Organization for EBRI found that 64 percent of persons surveyed supported "government helping people to purchase private long-term care insurance, even if it meant raising . . . taxes."
- In a 1993 survey by the ICR Survey Research Group, 69 percent of those interviewed preferred a "government program of long-term care similar to medicare or social security that would provide coverage for all and be financed by everyone" and 25 percent preferred "leaving it up to individuals to pay for private insurance, with the government providing coverage only for the very poor."
- The 1993 Gallup poll for EBRI found that 69 percent of persons interviewed supported federal assistance for long-term care for the elderly, even if it meant increasing income taxes. The poll also found that 53 percent of respondents said that government (federal government, state government, government-non-specific, medicare/medicaid, and taxpayers) should play the priority role in providing financial assistance for long-term care.
- On the other hand, a 1993 survey by the Gallup Organization for the American Health Care Association found that 76 percent of persons polled believed that "the government should pay only for nursing home care for those who can't afford it."
- In a 1993 survey by the Gallup Organization for EBRI, 65 percent of respondents said that they would be willing to purchase long-term care insurance from an insurance company or through an employer.

## Willingness to Pay

Most surveys find that respondents say they are willing to pay additional taxes to support a public long-term care program. Talking to a pollster is easier than actually paying taxes, so it is difficult to know how seriously to take these results.

- In a 1987 survey by Hamilton, Frederick & Schneiders for the AARP, from 59 to 65 percent of persons polled said that they would be willing to pay $20 to $58 a month in additional taxes to finance a federal long-term care program for the elderly and disabled.
- In a 1988 survey by Peter D. Hart Associates, Inc., 65 percent of respondents said that a program that would provide long-term health care for the elderly and disabled would be "an important investment (for which they would be) willing to see taxes raised."
- In a 1989 survey by the Gallup Organization for EBRI, 43 percent said that they would be willing to pay $10 a week for private or public long-term care insurance.
- In a 1991 survey by the Gallup Organization for EBRI, 42 percent of respondents did not know how much they would be willing to pay for a program that provided long-term care to the elderly. Fully 40 percent would be willing to pay nothing or less than $100 a year.
- In a 1993 survey by the ICR Survey Research Group, respondents were told that some taxes would be needed to pay for health care reform. They were asked whether they would rather pay $30 a month in additional taxes for a health reform plan that guaranteed everyone hospital and doctor care only, or $50 a month in additional taxes to guarantee hospital, doctor, and long-term care. Nearly half (47 percent) opted for the broader coverage, whereas 37 percent preferred the less expensive plan without long-term care.
- In the 1993 survey by the Gallup Organization for EBRI, 69 percent of respondents supported "the federal government providing long-term care assistance for the elderly, (even) if it meant an increase in your taxes." Fully 28 percent of those who said yes did not know how much they would be willing to pay in additional income taxes. Almost four families in ten (38 percent) said that they would be willing to pay more than $100 annually.

## Relative Importance of Home Care and Nursing Home Care

The surveys clearly show that Americans prefer home care to nursing home care and want to see those services expanded. They also recognize that nursing home care is expensive, however, and want protection against the catastrophic costs associated with institutionalization.

- In a 1988 Louis Harris and Associates poll, 78 percent of respondents said that they would "prefer to receive care . . . in (their) own home."
- A 1992–93 survey conducted by LH Research for HealthRight found that 83 to 86 percent of respondents supported a new federal home care program for persons of all ages.
- Even when round-the-clock care is needed, a 1991 survey Straw of AARP found that half of respondents still preferred home care over nursing home care.
- In a 1993 survey by the Kaiser Family Foundation and Harris and Associates, 33 percent chose home care as a new benefit for the elderly, 18 percent chose nursing home care, and 36 percent chose prescription drugs.
- In a 1993 poll by ICR Survey Research Group for AARP, respondents were asked to choose between coverage for home and community-based care and nursing home care. Fully 62 percent chose home care, compared to 30 percent who chose nursing home care.
- On the other hand, the 1989 survey by the Daniel Yankelovich Group for the AARP using conjoint analysis found that "the extent of nursing home coverage (in years) is the most important factor in evaluating the desirability of long-term care packages."

## Impact on Support for Health Care Reform

Inclusion of long-term care services increases general support for health reform.

- In a 1993 survey by the ICR Survey Research Group for the AARP, 58 percent of respondents said that it was "very important" for President Clinton to include nursing home care and home care in his health care reform package.
- That same survey asked respondents the extent to which they favored health care reform plans that do and do not include coverage of long-term care. Only 46 percent of those interviewed said they would "somewhat favor" or "strongly favor" a plan that covered hospital and doctor care only. When asked about a health care reform plan that included coverage of long-term care, as well as hospital and doctor care, those in favor increased to 83 percent.
- A 1993 survey by the ICR Survey Research Group also asked respon-

dents how inclusion of home and community-based care for severely disabled persons of all ages would affect their view of President Clinton's health care reform proposal. Fifty-seven percent of respondents stated that it would make them more likely to support the proposal; only 7 percent said that it would make them less likely to support it.

## References

Daniel Yankelovich Group, Inc. *Long Term Care in America: Public Attitudes and Possible Solutions, Executive Summary.* Washington, D.C.: American Association of Retired Persons (AARP), January 1990.

Gallup Organization. *Public Attitudes on Long-Term Care, 1989.* Survey prepared for the Employee Benefit Research Institute (EBRI). Washington, D.C., 1989.

———. *Public Attitudes on Long-Term Care, 1991.* Survey prepared for EBRI. Washington, D.C., 1991.

———. *Public Attitudes on Long-Term Care, 1993.* Survey prepared for EBRI. Washington, D.C., 1993.

———. *Issues Related to the Financing of Nursing Home Care in America.* Survey prepared for the American Health Care Association. Princeton, N.J., 1993.

Hamilton, Frederick & Schneiders. "Attitudes of Americans Over 45 Years of Age on Long-Term Care." Survey prepared for the American Association of Retired Persons. Washington, D.C., February 1988.

ICR Survey Research Group of AUS Consultants. "Long Term Care Survey." Prepared for the AARP. Media, Pa., 1993.

———. "AARP Poll Finds Americans Want Long-Term Care as Part of Health Care Reform." *AARP News* (Washington, D.C.), November 11, 1993.

Kaiser Family Foundation/Harris National Health Care Survey, 1993. Letter from Dennis F. Beatrice, Vice President, The Henry J. Kaiser Family Foundation, Menlo Park, Calif., May 7, 1993.

LH Research. *The Public Mandate for Health Care Reform in America.* Washington, D.C.: HealthRight, 1993.

Louis Harris and Associates. "A Telephone Survey of 1,500 Adults Nationwide Conducted between February 18–23, 1988." Cited in Rosita M. Thomas, "Public Opinion on Long-Term Health Care Needs, Costs, and Financing." CRS 90-151-GOV. Washington, D.C.: Congressional Research Service, March 19, 1990.

Peter D. Hart Research Associates, Inc. "A Post-Election Survey among Voters Conducted for AFSCME." Washington, D.C., 1988.

RL Associates. "The American Public Views Long Term Care." Survey conducted for the AARP and the Villers Foundation. Princeton, N.J., October 1987.

Straw, Margret K. "Home Care: Attitudes and Knowledge of Middle-Aged and Older Americans." American Association of Retired Persons, Washington, D.C., 1991.

# Notes

## Chapter 1

1. Authors' estimates based on data from the Office of National Health Statistics, Office of the Actuary, Health Care Financing Administration, Baltimore, Md., 1992.

2. Teresa A. Coughlin, Korbin Liu, and Timothy D. McBride, "Severely Disabled Elderly Persons with Financially Catastrophic Health Expenses: Sources and Determinants," *Gerontologist,* vol. 32 (June 1992), pp. 391–403. See also Korbin Liu, Maria Perozek, and Kenneth Manton, "Catastrophic Acute and Long-Term Care Costs: Risks Faced by Disabled Elderly Persons," *Gerontologist,* vol. 33 (June 1993), pp. 299–307.

3. American Association of Retired Persons (AARP), "AARP Poll Finds Americans Want Long-Term Care as Part of Health Reform," *AARP News,* Washington, November 11, 1993; ICR Survey Research Group of AUS Consultants, "Long-Term Care Survey," prepared for AARP (Media, Pa., 1993); and Gallup Organization, "Executive Summary," poll prepared for Consumers Union (Princeton, N.J., 1993).

4. AARP, "AARP Poll Finds Americans Want Long-Term Care as Part of Health Reform."

5. Authors' calculations based on Tamra J. Lair and Doris Cadigan Lefkowitz, *Mental Health and Functional Status of Residents of Nursing and Personal Care Homes,* National Medical Expenditure Survey, Research Findings 7, Agency for Health Care Policy and Research (Rockville, Md.: U.S. Department of Health and Human Services [DHHS], Public Health Service, 1990), table 1, p. 5.

6. This section draws from Alice M. Rivlin and Joshua M. Wiener, with Raymond J. Hanley and Denise A. Spence, *Caring for the Disabled Elderly: Who Will Pay?* (Brookings, 1988), pp. 5–8.

7. Authors' calculations using data from Joel Leon and Tamra Lair, *Functional Status of the Noninstitutionalized Elderly: Estimates of ADL and IADL Difficulties,* National Medical Expenditures Survey, Research Findings 4, Agency for Health Care Policy and Research (Rockville, Md.: DHHS, Public Health Service,

1990), table 2, figure 2, pp. 7–8; and Lair and Lefkowitz, *Mental Health and Functional Status of Residents of Nursing and Personal Care Homes*, table 1, p. 5.

8. Authors' calculations based on Leon and Lair, *Functional Status of the Noninstitutionalized Elderly*, table 3, p. 9; and Lair and Lefkowitz, *Mental Health and Functional Status of Residents of Nursing and Personal Care Homes*, table 1, p. 5.

9. The population aged 85 and older is projected to increase from 3.3 million in 1990 to 15.3 million in 2050 and from 10 percent to 22 percent of the elderly population over the same time period. U.S. Senate Special Committee on Aging, AARP, the Federal Council on the Aging, and the U.S. Administration on Aging, *Aging America: Trends and Projections, 1991 Edition* (DHHS, 1991), table 1-2, p. 7.

10. Brookings-ICF Long-Term Care Financing Model. As chapter 6 describes, the asset test for married nursing home residents is less straightforward.

11. Bureau of the Census, "The Need for Personal Assistance with Everyday Activities: Recipients and Caregivers," *Current Population Reports, Household Economic Studies*, Series P-70, No. 19 (U.S. Department of Commerce, 1990), table A, p. 3.

12. Authors' calculations based on Lair and Lefkowitz, *Mental Health and Functional Status of Residents of Nursing and Personal Care Homes*, table 1, p. 5.

13. Authors' calculations based on ibid.; and Leon and Lair, *Functional Status of the Noninstitutionalized Elderly*, table 2, p. 7.

14. Margaret K. Straw, "Home Care: Attitudes and Knowledge of Middle-Aged and Older Americans," AARP, Washington, 1991.

15. Raymond J. Hanley and others, "Predicting Elderly Nursing Home Admissions: Results from the 1982–1984 National Long-Term Care Survey," *Research on Aging*, vol. 12 (June 1990), p. 213.

16. Robyn Stone, Gail Lee Cafferata, and Judith Sangl, "Caregivers of the Frail Elderly: A National Profile," *Gerontologist*, vol. 27 (October 1987), p. 620.

17. Korbin Liu and Kenneth G. Manton, "Disability and Long-Term Care," paper presented at the Methodologies of Forecasting Life and Active Life Expectancy Workshop, sponsored by the National Institute on Aging, the American Council of Life Insurance, and the Health Insurance Association of America (HIAA), Bethesda, Md., June 25–26, 1985, p. 14.

18. See, for example, Leonard I. Pearlin and others, "Caregiving and the Stress Process: An Overview of Concepts and Their Measures," *Gerontologist*, vol. 30 (October 1990), pp. 583–94; Bob G. Knight, Stephen M. Lutzky, and Felice Macofsky-Urban, "A Meta-analytic Review of Interventions for Caregiver Distress: Recommendations for Further Research," *Gerontologist*, vol. 33 (April 1993), pp. 240–48; Ada C. Mui, "Caregiver Strain Among Black and White Daughter Caregivers: A Role Theory Perspective," *Gerontologist*, vol. 32 (April 1992), pp. 203–12; Shirley J. Semple, "Conflict in Alzheimer's Caregiving Families: Its Dimensions and Consequences," *Gerontologist*, vol 32 (October 1992), pp. 648–55; and Marilyn M. Skaff and Leonard I. Pearlin, "Caregiving: Role Engulfment and the Loss of Self," *Gerontologist*, vol. 32 (October 1992), pp. 656–64.

19. Elaine M. Brody, "Parent Care as a Normative Family Stress," *Gerontologist*, vol. 25 (February 1985), p. 20; and Joshua M. Wiener and Katherine M. Harris, "Myths and Realities: Why Most of What Everybody Knows About Long-Term Care Is Wrong," *Brookings Review*, vol. 8 (Fall 1990), pp. 29–34.

20. National Center for Health Statistics, *Health, United States, 1991* (Hyattsville, Md.: DHHS, Public Health Service, 1992), tables 105, 111, pp. 255, 264.

21. Brookings-ICF Long-Term Care Financing Model.

22. Suzanne W. Letsch and others, "National Health Expenditures, 1991," *Health Care Financing Review,* vol. 14 (Winter 1992), table 19, p. 25.

23. Brookings-ICF Long-Term Care Financing Model.

24. Pamela Farley Short and others, "Public and Private Responsibility for Financing Nursing-Home Care: The Effect of Medicaid Asset Spend-Down," *Milbank Quarterly,* vol. 70, no. 2 (1992), table 1, p. 284.

25. Denise A. Spence and Joshua M. Wiener, "Estimating the Extent of Medicaid Spend-Down in Nursing Homes," *Journal of Health Politics, Policy and Law,* vol. 15 (Fall 1990), pp. 607–26. For a good review of the extensive literature estimating the extent of medicaid spend-down, see E. Kathleen Adams, Mark R. Meiners, and Brian O. Burwell, "Asset Spend-Down in Nursing Homes: Methods and Insights," *Medical Care,* vol. 31 (January 1993), pp. 1–23.

26. Raymond J. Hanley, Joshua M. Wiener, and Katherine M. Harris, "The Economic Status of Nursing Home Users," Brookings, 1994, p. 21.

27. Because some of the costs of nursing home care reflect ordinary living expenses, such as room and board, not all of the higher levels of out-of-pocket expenses should be of concern.

28. Brian O. Burwell, E. Kathleen Adams, and Mark R. Meiners, "Spend-Down of Assets Before Medicaid Eligibility Among Elderly Nursing-Home Recipients in Michigan," *Medical Care,* vol. 28 (April 1990), pp. 349–62.

29. In a similar analysis in Connecticut, Gruenberg and others found that only 25 percent of the nursing home patients in 1978–79 were eligible for medicaid on the day of admission to the nursing home. Leonard Gruenberg and others, "An Analysis of the Spend-Down Patterns of Individuals Admitted to Nursing Homes in the State of Connecticut," Connecticut Partnership for Long Term Care Research Institute, Discussion Paper DP1-89 (Hartford, September 1989).

30. Beth Jackson, "Patterns of Formal and Informal Service Use," tables prepared for The Changing Face of Informal Caregiving, a conference sponsored by the Office of the Assistant Secretary for Planning and Evaluation, DHHS, Berkeley Springs, W. Va., October 15, 1992.

31. Estimates from the Brookings-ICF Long-Term Care Financing Model.

32. LH Research, *The Public Mandate for Health Care Reform in America* (Washington: HealthRight, 1993), p. v.

33. *Overview of Entitlement Programs: Background Material and Data on Programs Within the Jurisdiction of the Committee on Ways and Means,* Committee Print, prepared for the House Committee on Ways and Means, 102 Cong. 2 sess. (Government Printing Office, 1992), table 11, p. 262.

34. Letter to authors from Susan Coronel, HIAA, November 1, 1993.

35. Rivlin and others, *Caring for the Disabled Elderly,* pp. 76–77; Robert Friedland, *Facing the Costs of Long-Term Care* (Washington: Employee Benefit Research Institute [EBRI], 1990); Sheila R. Zedlewski and others, *The Needs of the Elderly in the 21st Century* (Washington: Urban Institute Press, 1990); and William H. Crown, John Capitman, and Walter N. Leutz, "Economic Rationality, the Affordability of Private Long-Term Care Insurance, and the Role for Public Policy," *Gerontologist,* vol. 32 (August 1992), pp. 478–85.

36. American Council on Life Insurance, *1992 Life Insurance Fact Book Update* (Washington, 1993), pp. 13, 16.

37. HIAA, *Long-Term Care Insurance in 1991* (Washington, 1993), p. 4.

38. Ibid., p. 32.

39. LifePlans, Inc., *Who Buys Long-Term Care Insurance?* (Washington: HIAA, 1992), figure 1:7, p. 26.

40. Daniel Yankelovich Group, Inc., *Long Term Care in America: Public Attitudes and Possible Solutions, Executive Summary* (Washington: AARP, January 1990), p. B-6; Research USA, Inc., "National Committee to Preserve Social Security and Medicare: Membership Survey," Washington, December 1988, p. 13; RL Associates, "The American Public Views Long Term Care," survey conducted for the American Association of Retired Persons and the Villers Foundation (Princeton, N.J., October 1987), p. 5; and Hugh Heclo, "The Political Foundations of Antipoverty Policy," in Sheldon H. Danziger and Daniel H. Weinberg, eds., *Fighting Poverty* (Harvard University Press, 1986), pp. 312–40.

41. Daniel Yankelovich Group, Inc., *Long Term Care in America: Public Attitudes and Possible Solutions;* Hamilton, Frederick & Schneiders, "Attitudes of Americans Over 45 Years of Age on Long Term Care," survey prepared for AARP, Washington, February 1988; and RL Associates, "The American Public Views Long Term Care."

42. Wiener, Hanley, and Harris, "The Economic Status of Elderly Nursing Home Users."

43. Rivlin and others, *Caring for the Disabled Elderly,* p. 199; Pearlin and others, "Caregiving and the Stress Process," pp. 583–93.

44. Using data from the national Channeling demonstration, Coughlin and colleagues observed that prescription drugs and long-term nursing home care were the major sources of catastrophic costs among the frail elderly. On the one hand, prescription drugs were a more certain cause of extreme out-of-pocket costs, and they were more likely to be burdensome to the poor than to the well-off. On the other hand, long-term nursing home care, when needed, made individuals, regardless of income, extremely vulnerable to catastrophic costs. Coughlin, Liu, and McBride, "Severely Disabled Elderly Persons with Financially Catastrophic Health Care Expenses," pp. 391–403.

45. Denise A. Spence and Joshua M. Wiener, "Nursing Home Length of Stay Patterns: Results from the 1985 National Nursing Home Survey," *Gerontologist,* vol. 30 (February 1990), table 2, p. 18.

46. "Long-Term Care Assistance Act of 1988," S. 2305, 100 Cong. 2 sess., introduced by Senator George Mitchell of Maine (April 21, 1988). See also Senator Edward M. Kennedy of Massachusetts, introducing "LifeCare Long-Term Care Protection Act" (S. 2163), *Congressional Record,* February 22, 1990, pp. S1510–20.

47. Spence and Wiener, "Nursing Home Length of Stay Patterns," p. 18.

48. "Elder-Care Long-Term Care Protection Act of 1988," H.R. 5320, 100 Cong. 2 sess., introduced by Representative Henry Waxman (September 16, 1988); and "Chronic-Care Medicare Long-Term Care Coverage Act of 1988" H.R. 5393, 100 Cong. 2 sess., introduced by Representative Fortney "Pete" Stark (September 27, 1988).

49. Our proposals differ from the president's in five respects. First, we propose coverage of the first six months of nursing home care under social insur-

ance, while the president does not. Second, our liberalization of medicaid would allow individuals to keep $30,000 in assets; the administration would allow the states to increase the limit only to $12,000. Third, we would increase the personal needs allowance to $100 a month; the president would raise it to $50. Fourth, our home care program would cover people with somewhat lower levels of disability than the president's proposal. Finally, we rely less than the president does on medicare savings to finance the plan.

## Chapter Two

1. This chapter draws from Alice M. Rivlin and Joshua M. Wiener, with Raymond J. Hanley and Denise A. Spence, *Caring for the Disabled Elderly: Who Will Pay?* (Brookings, 1988), pp. 30–50.

2. *1988 Annual Report of the Board of Trustees of the Federal Old-Age and Survivors Insurance and Disability Insurance Trust Funds.*

3. Although some substitution is to be expected, the amount is likely to be small. For a review of the literature on this topic, see Joshua M. Wiener and Raymond J. Hanley, "Caring for the Disabled Elderly: There's No Place Like Home," in Stephen M. Shortell and Uwe E. Reinhardt, eds., *Improving Health Policy and Management: Nine Critical Research Issues for the 1990s* (Ann Arbor, Mich.: Health Administration Press, 1992), pp. 90–93.

4. "Other payers" include state and local expenditures, the social services block grants, home care programs under the Older Americans Act and Department of Veterans' Affairs, and out-of-pocket expenditures by people other than the recipient of the services.

5. *1992 Annual Report of the Board of Trustees of the Federal Old-Age and Survivors Insurance and Disability Insurance Trust Funds.*

6. In calculating the out-of-pocket experience for each individual, the numerator is the out-of-pocket contributions to nursing home care during the entire length of stay. The denominator is the income that the individual would have received during the nursing home stay had he or she not entered the nursing home (that is, to correct for asset income used to pay for nursing home care) plus the individual's nonhousing assets at admission. Thus, for a patient with a three-year stay who paid $90,000 out of pocket and had $20,000 in income and $90,000 in nonhousing assets, the out-of-pocket catastrophic costs ratio would be 0.60 (that is, $90,000/($20,000 x 3 + $90,000).

7. Medicare home health expenditures more than tripled, from $2.5 billion in 1989 to $8.2 billion in 1992. Prospective Payment Assessment Commission, *Medicare and the American Health Care System: Report to the Congress* (Washington, June 1993), table 4-4, p. 112.

8. Nancy N. Eustis, Rosalie A. Kane, and Lucy Rose Fischer, "Home Care Quality and the Home Care Worker: Beyond Quality Assurance as Usual," *Gerontologist,* vol. 33 (February 1993), pp. 64–73; Penny Hollander Feldman, "Work Life Improvement for Home Care Workers: Impact and Feasibility," *Gerontologist,* vol. 33 (February 1993), pp. 47–54; Margaret MacAdam, "Home Care Reimbursement and Effects on Personnel," *Gerontologist,* vol. 33 (February 1993), pp. 55–63; Patricia A. Riley, "Quality Assurance in Home Care," American Association of Retired Persons, Washington, February 1989; and Institute of Medicine, *Improving the Quality of Care in Nursing Homes* (Washington: National Academy Press, 1986), pp. 89–91.

9. For example, the proportion of elderly discharged from nursing homes who needed assistance with mobility and toileting increased from 36 to 47 percent between 1976 and 1984. Edward S. Sekscenski, "Discharges from Nursing Homes: 1985 National Nursing Home Survey," *Vital and Health Statistics,* series 13, no. 103 (Hyattsville, Md.: U.S. Department of Health and Human Services [DHHS], National Center for Health Statistics, March 1990), pp. 9–10. See also Peter W. Schaughnessy and Andrew M. Kramer, "The Increased Needs of Patients in Nursing Homes and Patients Receiving Home Health Care," *New England Journal of Medicine,* vol. 332 (January 4, 1990), pp. 21–27.

10. See, for example, Kenneth G. Manton, Larry S. Corder, and Eric Stallard, "Estimates of Change in Chronic Disability and Institutional Incidence and Prevalence Rates in the U.S. Elderly Population from the 1982, 1984, and 1989 National Long Term Care Survey," *Journal of Gerontology: Social Sciences,* vol. 48 (July 1993), pp. S153—S166.

11. This methodology and the premiums are drawn from Joshua M. Wiener, Katherine M. Harris, and Raymond J. Hanley, "Premium Pricing of Prototype Private Long-Term Care Insurance Policies," Final Report to the Office of the Assistant Secretary for Planning and Evaluation, DHHS (Brookings, December 1990).

12. Ibid., appendix 3.

13. According to the Health Insurance Association of America (HIAA), the average premium for a policy, offered by the leading insurers, that covers four years of nursing home and home care, with an $80-a-day nursing home benefit, a $40-a-day home care benefit, a lifetime inflation protection feature of 5 percent compounded annually, and a nonforfeiture benefit (typically, return of premium) costs $2,525 at age 65. HIAA, *Long-Term Care Insurance in 1991* (Washington, 1993), table 6, p. 19. A policy that pays only $60 a day for nursing home care and $30 a visit for home care should cost 75 percent of that premium, or $1,894.

## Chapter Three

1. The number of companies selling policies declined by eight between 1990 and 1991. Health Insurance Association of America (HIAA), *Long-Term Care Insurance in 1991* (Washington, February 1993), figure 4, p. 6; and letter from Susan A. Coronel, HIAA, November 1, 1993.

2. Daniel B. Radner, "An Assessment of the Economic Status of the Aged," Social Security Administration, Office of Research and Statistics, Washington, April, 1992.

3. Bureau of the Census, "Poverty in the United States: 1988 and 1989," *Current Population Reports,* series P-60, no. 171 (U.S. Department of Commerce, 1991), pp. 19, 25.

4. These premiums are for policies with an $80-a-day nursing home benefit, a $40-a-day home health benefit, a twenty-day deductible, a four-year benefit period for nursing home care, a lifetime inflation protection feature of 5 percent compounded annually, and a nonforfeiture benefit (typically, return of premium). Premiums for policies with only inflation protection or nonforfeiture benefits averaged about $1,700 at age 65 and about $5,700 at age 79. HIAA, *Long-Term Care Insurance in 1991,* p. 19.

5. In 1990, 29 percent of the individuals who purchased private long-term

care insurance at age 55 or older had total household income of $20,000 or less, compared with 64 percent of the general population. Similarly, 42 percent of insurance purchasers had more than $100,000 in liquid assets, compared with 7 percent of the general population. Marc A. Cohen, Nanda Kumar, and Stanley S. Wallack, "Who Buys Long-Term Care Insurance?" *Health Affairs*, vol. 11 (Spring 1992), p. 210.

6. Alice M. Rivlin and Joshua M. Wiener, with Raymond J. Hanley and Denise A. Spence, *Caring for the Disabled Elderly: Who Will Pay?* (Brookings, 1988), p. 77; Robert B. Friedland, *Facing the Costs of Long-Term Care* (Washington: Employee Benefits Research Institute [EBRI], 1990), pp. 278–93; Families USA Foundation, "Nursing Home Insurance: Who Can Afford It?" Washington, February 1993; Sheila Rafferty Zedlewski and Timothy D. McBride, "The Changing Profile of the Elderly: Effects on Future Long-Term Care Needs and Financing," *Milbank Quarterly*, vol. 70, no. 2 (1992), pp. 247–75; and William H. Crown, John Capitman, and Walter N. Leutz, "Economic Rationality, the Affordability of Private Long-Term Care Insurance, and the Role for Public Policy," *Gerontologist*, vol. 32 (August 1992), pp. 478–85. Similarly, a study in the United Kingdom using prototype premiums found that the market for private long-term care insurance was also limited in that country. In that study Wittenberg assumed that 65-year-olds who were not dependent on state pensions were willing to spend up to 5 to 10 percent of their disposable income for private long-term care insurance. On that basis Wittenberg estimated that between 10 and 15 percent of married couples could afford the insurance. Raphael Wittenberg, "Prototype Insurance Policy for Long Term Care," Government Economic Service Working Paper 105 (London: Department of Health, April 1989).

7. Rivlin and others, *Caring for the Disabled Elderly*, p. 77; and Zedlewski and McBride, "The Changing Profile of the Elderly."

8. Marc A. Cohen and others, "The Financial Capacity of the Elderly to Insure for Long-Term Care," *Gerontologist*, vol. 27 (August 1987), pp. 494–502; Marc A. Cohen and others, "Financing Long-Term Care: A Practical Mix of Public and Private," *Journal of Health Politics, Policy and Law*, vol. 17 (Fall 1992) pp. 403–23; and "Testimony of Ronald D. Hagen," *Long-Term Care Insurance*, Hearings before the Subcommittee on Oversight and Investigations of the House Committee on Energy and Commerce, 101 Cong. 2 sess. (Government Printing Office, May 2, 1990), pp. 180–207.

9. Mark A. Cohen, Nanda Kumar, and Stanley S. Wallack, "New Perspectives on the Affordability of Long-Term Care Insurance and Potential Market Size," *Gerontologist*, vol. 33 (February 1993), p. 105–13.

10. Rivlin and others, *Caring for the Disabled Elderly*, pp. 63, 75.

11. In a survey of purchasers of private long-term care insurance in 1990, 39 percent spent less than 3 percent of their income, 24 percent spent between 3 and 5 percent of their income, and 37 percent spent more than 5 percent of their income. Cohen, Kumar, and Wallack, "New Perspectives on the Affordability of Long-Term Care Insurance and Potential Market Size," p. 111.

12. Ibid., pp. 105–13.

13. Peter Kemper and Christopher M. Murtaugh, "Lifetime Use of Nursing Home Care," *New England Journal of Medicine*, vol. 324 (February 28, 1991), pp. 595–600; and Christopher M. Murtaugh, Peter Kemper, and Brenda C. Spillman, "The Risk of Needing Nursing Home Use in Later Life," *Medical Care*, vol. 28 (October 1990), pp. 952–62.

14. In a recent public opinion survey, only 51 percent of adults knew that medicare does not pay for long-term care for the elderly. EBRI, "Public Attitudes on Long-Term Care, 1993: Summary Report," Washington, 1993, p. 17.

15. For a review of the literature on induced demand in long-term care, see Teresa Fama and David L. Kennell, "Should We Worry About Induced Demand for Long-Term-Care Services?" *Generations,* vol. 14 (Spring 1990), pp. 37–41.

16. A large body of literature deals with determinants of use for both nursing home care and home care. See, for example, Raymond J. Hanley and Joshua M. Wiener, "Use of Paid Home Care by the Chronically Disabled Elderly," *Research on Aging,* vol. 13 (September 1991), pp. 310–32.

17. For example, only about 29 percent of the disabled elderly living at home reported use of any paid in-home services in 1989. Beth Jackson, "Patterns of Formal and Informal Use," tables prepared for The Changing Face of Informal Caregiving, a conference sponsored by the Office of the Assistant Secretary for Planning and Evaluation, Department of Health and Human Services, Berkeley Springs, W. Va., October 15, 1992.

18. National Center for Health Statistics, *Health, United States, 1991* (Hyattsville, Md.: U.S. Department of Health and Human Services [DHHS], Public Health Service, 1992), table 111, pp. 264–65. Utilization in Europe also varies substantially. Pamela Doty, "Long-Term Care in International Perspective," *Health Care Financing Review,* Annual Supplement (1988), pp. 145–55.

19. Coronel letter. The group association market should be viewed as part of the individual market. The only difference is that policies are often marketed by mail and with an association endorsement to members of groups such as the American Association of Retired Persons.

20. In 1987 only 25 percent of men and 14 percent of women aged 67 were still in the labor force. Rivlin and others, *Caring for the Disabled Elderly,* p. 75. In 1990, 26 percent of men and 17 percent of women aged 65 to 69 were still in the labor force. Murray Gendell and Jacob S. Siegel, "Trends in Retirement Age by Sex, 1950–2005," *Monthly Labor Review,* vol. 115 (July 1992), p. 24.

21. For an earlier analysis of the potential effect of a variety of private long-term care initiatives on medicaid spending and the number of medicaid nursing home patients, see Joshua M. Wiener and Rose M. Rubin, "The Potential Impact of Private Long-Term Care Financing Options on Medicaid: The Next Thirty Years," *Journal of Health Politics, Policy and Law,* vol. 14 (Summer 1989), pp. 327–40.

22. This section draws from HIAA, *Long-Term Care Insurance in 1991,* pp. 4–6, 27–33; and Coronel letter.

23. Joshua M. Wiener, Katherine M. Harris, and Raymond J. Hanley, "Premium Pricing of Prototype Private Long-Term Care Insurance Policies," Final Report to the Office of the Assistant Secretary for Planning and Evaluation, DHHS (Brookings, December 1990), table 1.

24. Data from the Survey of Income and Program Participation suggest that only 0.9 percent of adults under 65 years of age need assistance with personal care, compared with 6.6 percent of those 65 or older. Bureau of the Census, "The Need for Personal Assistance with Everyday Activities: Recipients and Caregivers," *Current Population Reports, Household Economic Studies,* series P-70, no. 19 (U.S. Department of Commerce, 1990), table B, p. 4.

25. In an effort to keep premiums as low as possible, however, General Mills requires even active employees to undergo underwriting. Personal communication with Alan Ritchie, Vice President, Director of Compensation and Benefits,

General Mills, August 24, 1990. At Bell Atlantic, employees hired before January 1981 are "grandfathered" into guaranteed issue of insurance. All employees hired after that date are medically underwritten. Bell Atlantic, "Protect Your Financial Security," circa 1990.

26. Of persons aged 21 to 64 who need personal assistance with the activities or instrumental activities of daily living, only 21 percent were employed in 1990. Jack McNeill, "Census Bureau Data on Persons with Disabilities: New Results and Old Questions About Validity and Reliability," paper presented at the annual meeting of the Society for Disability Studies, Seattle, Wash., June 17–19, 1993, table 21.

27. Robert C. Levin, "Employer Views on Group Long Term Care Insurance," Washington Business Group on Health, Washington, October 1991.

28. Friedland, *Facing the Costs of Long-Term Care*, pp. 257–58.

29. Of these, approximately 53 percent are active employees, 19 percent are their spouses, 2 percent are their parents, grandparents, parents-in-law, or grandparents-in-law, and 17 percent are retirees or their spouses. HIAA, *Long-Term Care Insurance in 1991*, p. 32.

30. The HIAA estimates that the average premium per person actually paid for an unindexed policy was $183 at age 40 and $341 at age 50. Ibid., p. 30.

31. Wiener, Harris, and Hanley, "Premium Pricing of Prototype Private Long-Term Care Insurance Policies," table 1.

32. LifePlans, Inc., *Who Buys Long-Term Care Insurance?* (Washington: HIAA, 1992), table 2-7, p. 71.

33. Similarly, 89 percent stated that they would be more willing to purchase a policy if the government provided a tax break. Ibid., table 2-8, p. 75.

34. Ibid., table 2-7, p. 71.

35. Bruce Boyd, "LTC: It's Your Choice," *Generations*, vol. 14 (Spring 1990), pp. 23–27.

36. American Council of Life Insurance (ACLI), *1992 Life Insurance Fact Book* (Washington, 1992), p. 37.

37. Nearly two-thirds of all elderly admitted to nursing homes terminate their stay because of death, and most die within a year of admission. Denise A. Spence and Joshua M. Wiener, "Nursing Home Length of Stay Patterns: Results from the 1985 National Nursing Home Survey," *Gerontologist*, vol. 30 (February 1990), p. 18.

38. ACLI, *1992 Life Insurance Fact Book*, p. 41.

39. This description of the different types of accelerated death benefits is taken from "Accelerated Death Benefits/Living Benefit Riders," *Tillinghast Update* (New York: Tillinghast, August 1990).

40. Almost half of this amount is attributable to one company that added long-term care coverage to all its existing life insurance policies. HIAA, *Long-Term Care Insurance in 1991*, figure 3, p. 5.

41. ACLI, *1992 Life Insurance Fact Book*, p. 27.

42. Authors' calculations using data from ACLI, *1992 Life Insurance Fact Book Update* (Washington, 1992), pp. 13, 16. The average face value of a life insurance policy with a long-term care rider was $60,000 in 1991. HIAA, *Long-Term Care Insurance in 1991*, p. 6.

43. ACLI, *1992 Life Insurance Fact Book*, p. 38.

44. "Life Insurance Part 3: Should You Buy a Whole-Life Policy?" *Consumer Reports*, vol. 58 (September 1993), pp. 600–02.

45. In a study of elderly admitted to nursing homes between 1982 and 1984, Hanley and others found that 24 percent of patients were married. Hanley and others, "Predicting Elderly Nursing Home Admissions," *Research on Aging*, vol. 12 (June 1990), p. 209.

46. "Life Insurance Part 2: Choosing a Universal-Life Policy," *Consumer Reports*, vol. 58 (August 1993), p. 527.

## Chapter Four

1. For a discussion of the tax issues concerning private long-term care insurance see U.S. General Accounting Office (GAO), *Long-Term Care Insurance: Tax Preferences Reduce Costs More for Those in Higher Tax Brackets*, GAO/GGD-93-110 (June 1993); and U.S. Department of the Treasury, *Financing Health and Long-Term Care: Report to the President and to the Congress* (March 1990).

2. Treasury, *Financing Health and Long-Term Care*, pp. 44–45.

3. In a survey of employees who were offered employer-sponsored, but not employer-paid, private long-term care insurance in 1990, 90 percent of non-purchasing employees said they would be more likely to buy a policy "if my employer would pay for part of the insurance premium." Among purchasers, only 43 percent stated that it was important or very important to them that "my employer was behind the program, so I knew it must be worthwhile." LifePlans, Inc., *Who Buys Long-Term Care Insurance?* (Washington, Health Insurance Association of America, 1992), pp. 68, 75. Many economists contend that employer contributions to the cost of the long-term care insurance would ultimately be paid by the employees in the form of reduced wages. U.S. Congressional Budget Office, *Economic Implications of Rising Health Care Costs* (October 1992), pp. 34–41.

4. GAO, *Retiree Health Plans: Health Benefits Not Secure Under Employer-Based System*, GAO/HRD-93-125 (July 1993), and GAO, *Employee Benefits: Companies' Retiree Health Liabilities Large, Advance Funding Costly*, GAO/HRD-89-51 (June 1989), pp. 4–5, 34. The Employee Benefit Research Institute (EBRI) estimated that the 1988 liability for retiree health insurance, assuming no changes in medicare coverage, totaled $247 billion for private sector employers. EBRI, "Issues and Trends in Retiree Health Insurance Benefits," *EBRI Issue Brief*, no. 84 (November 1988), p. 8. Warshawsky estimated that liability of companies for retiree health benefits in 1989 at $345 billion. Mark J. Warshawsky, *The Uncertain Promise of Retiree Health Benefits: An Evaluation of Corporate Obligations* (Washington: AEI Press, 1992), table 9-2, p. 112.

5. Bureau of Labor Statistics, "Employee Benefits in Medium and Large Private Establishments, 1991," Bulletin 2422 (Department of Labor, May 1993), table 63, p. 65; and EBRI, "Features of Employer-Sponsored Health Plans," *EBRI Issue Brief*, no. 128 (August 1992), table 14, p. 26.

6. Executive Office of the President, *Health Security Act* (1993).

7. Marc A. Cohen and others, "Financing Long-Term Care: A Practical Mix of Public and Private," *Journal of Health Politics, Policy and Law*, vol. 17 (Fall 1992), pp. 403–24.

8. Fiscal Associates, Inc., "Tax Policies to Promote Long-Term Care," in *Report to Congress and the Secretary by the Task Force on Long-Term Health Care Policies* (Department of Health and Human Services, September 21, 1987), pp. 189–90. In 1991 filers of tax returns with adjusted gross income of less than

$30,000, which accounts for about two-thirds of all returns, paid less than 9 percent of their income in federal income tax. Laura Y. Prizzi and Jeffrey B. Curry, "Individual Income Tax Returns, 1991: Taxpayer Usage Study," *Statistics of Income Bulletin*, vol. 12 (Fall 1992), figure B, p. 9.

9. Prizzi and Curry, "Individual Income Tax Returns, 1991," table 5, p. 18.

10. Ibid. In 1991, 46 percent of tax returns with itemized deductions had adjusted gross incomes of $50,000 or more. Conversely, only 4 percent of tax returns with the standard deductions had adjusted gross incomes of $50,000 or more.

11. John R. Gist, "Did Tax Reform Hurt the Elderly?" *Gerontologist*, vol. 32 (August 1992), table 2, p. 474.

12. Charles L. Schultze, "The Federal Budget and the Nation's Economic Health," in Henry J. Aaron, ed., *Setting National Priorities: Policy for the Nineties* (Brookings, 1990), pp. 19–64; and Alice M. Rivlin, *Reviving the American Dream: The Economy, the States, and the Federal Government* (Brookings, 1992).

13. For an earlier analysis of tax-advantaged savings for long-term care, see Alice M. Rivlin and Joshua M. Wiener, with Raymond J. Hanley and Denise A. Spence, *Caring for the Disabled Elderly: Who Will Pay?* (Brookings, 1988), pp. 109–22.

14. In 1984 only 15 percent of tax returns claimed an individual retirement account deduction. Rivlin and others, *Caring for the Disabled Elderly*, p. 111.

15. Prizzi and Curry, "Individual Income Tax Returns, 1991," table 5, p. 15.

16. Rivlin and others, *Caring For the Disabled Elderly*, pp. 111–12.

17. These calculations assume that individuals are saving enough to have money at age 80 to pay for their care during the deductible period. Individuals are assumed to earn 7.5 percent after tax on their savings accounts.

18. Peter Kemper and Christopher M. Murtaugh, "Lifetime Use of Nursing Home Care," *New England Journal of Medicine*, vol. 324 (February 28, 1991), p. 597.

19. In an analysis of the 1985 National Nursing Home Survey, Spence and Wiener estimated that only 19.1 percent of all nursing home days occur between the 1st and 180th day, whereas 36.7 percent of all days occur after the second year of stay. Denise A. Spence and Joshua M. Wiener, "Nursing Home Length of Stay Patterns: Results from the 1985 National Nursing Home Survey," *Gerontologist*, vol. 30 (February 1990), table 4, p. 19.

20. For descriptions of these initiatives, see Nelda McCall, James Knickman, and Ellen Jones Bauer, "Public/Private Partnerships: A New Approach to Long-term Care," *Health Affairs*, vol. 10 (Spring 1991), pp. 164–76; Mark R. Meiners, "An Improved Insurance Alteration to Medical Gaming," paper presented at the National Academy of Elder Law Attorneys Public Policy Forum, Alterations to Medicaid: Funding Long-term Care, Arlington, Va., October 26, 1992; Center on Aging, "Partnership for Long Term Care: Program Description," University of Maryland, College Park, Md., circa 1993; Kevin J. Mahoney and Terrie Wetle, "Public-Private Partnerships: The Connecticut Model for Financing Long-Term Care," *Journal of the American Geriatrics Society*, vol. 40 (October 1992), pp. 1026–30; and GAO, *Long-term Care Insurance: Proposals to Link Private Insurance and Medicaid Need Close Scrutiny*, GAO/HRD-90-154 (September 10, 1990).

21. In theory, the level of protected assets has no limit. A policy that will pay up to $1,000,000 in benefits will allow the insured to keep up to $1,000,000

in assets and still be eligible for medicaid. As a practical matter, however, the level of protected assets is limited by the cost and duration of nursing home and home care.

22. Medicaid finances more than 80 percent of the patient days in New York State's nursing homes. New York State Department of Social Services, "A Public-Private Partnership for Financing Long Term Care," internal planning memorandum, circa 1988.

23. LifePlans, Inc., *Who Buys Long-Term Care Insurance?* p. 26. In the same survey, however, 72 percent of purchasers said that asset protection was a "very important" reason they bought insurance, and 26 percent of purchasers said it was an "important" reason.

24. Excluding home equity, the median net worth of elderly households was only $23,856 in 1988; for elderly aged 75 and older, it was only $18,819. Daniel B. Radner, "An Assessment of the Economic Status of the Aged," *Studies in Income Distribution,* no. 16 (Washington: Social Security Administration, May 1993), table 4, p. 35.

25. LifePlans, Inc., *Who Buys Long-Term Care Insurance?* p. 68.

26. John A. Nyman, "The Effects of Competition on Nursing Home Expenditures Under Prospective Reimbursement," *Health Services Research,* vol. 23 (October 1988), pp. 555–74; William J. Scanlon, "A Theory of the Nursing Home Market," *Inquiry,* vol. 17 (Spring 1980), pp. 25–41; and Institute of Medicine, *Improving the Quality of Care in Nursing Homes* (Washington: National Academy Press, 1986), pp. 17–19, 91–95.

27. Greg Arling, Shelley Hagan, and Harald Buhaug, "The Feasibility of a Public-Private Long-Term Care Financing Plan," *Medical Care,* vol. 30 (August 1992), pp. 699–717.

28. "Medicaid: Asset Transfers," *Long-Term Care Management,* vol. 22 (August 11, 1993), p. 5.


## Chapter Five

1. This chapter draws from Joshua M. Wiener and Katherine M. Harris, "High Quality Private Long-Term Care Insurance: Can We Get There from Here?" *Journal of Aging and Social Policy,* vol. 3, no. 3 (1991), pp. 17–32. For an excellent discussion of the regulatory and consumer issues relating to private long-term care insurance, see Susan E. Polniaszek and James P. Firman, "Long-Term Care Insurance: A Professional's Guide to Selecting Policies," United Seniors Health Cooperative, Washington, February 1991; and James P. Firman and Susan Polniaszek, "Eight Recommendations for Improving Private Long-Term Care Insurance," United Seniors Health Cooperative, June 1991.

2. Catherine E. Wilson and William G. Weissert, "Private Long-term Care Insurance: After Coverage Restrictions Is There Anything Left?" *Inquiry,* vol. 26 (Winter 1989), pp. 493–507.

3. For example, Consumers Union, United Seniors Health Cooperative, American Association of Retired Persons (AARP), and the authors have all voiced concern over the quality of early products. *Standards for Private Long-term Care Insurance,* Hearings before the Subcommittee on Health of the House Committee on Ways and Means, 101 Cong. 1 sess. (Government Printing Office, 1989); *Long-term Care Insurance,* Hearings before the Subcommittee on Over-

sight and Investigations of the House Committee on Energy and Commerce, 101 Cong. 2 sess. (GPO, 1990).

4. Robyn I. Stone and others, *State Variation in the Regulation of Long-term Care Insurance Products* (Washington: AARP, 1992).

5. Kenneth J. Meier, *The Political Economy of Regulation: The Case of Insurance* (State University of New York Press, 1988).

6. Health Care Financing Administration, "Unpublished Estimates from the Office of National Cost Estimates, Office of the Actuary," U.S. Department of Health and Human Services (DHHS), Baltimore, Md., 1992.

7. As important as inflation adjustments are to the elderly, they are critical for policies sold to active workers, where thirty to forty years could easily elapse between the initial purchase and use of long-term care services. Assuming that nursing home and home care costs rise at 5.5 percent a year, a consumer who purchases an unindexed policy today at age 50 with a nursing home benefit of $60 a day and uses it at age 85 would have the same purchasing power as a person who bought a long-term care policy today with a $12-a-day benefit.

8. LifePlans, Inc., *Who Buys Long-Term Care Insurance?* (Washington: Health Insurance Association of America [HIAA], 1992), pp. 38–39.

9. HIAA, *Long-Term Care Insurance in 1991* (Washington, 1993), pp. 42–43.

10. Ibid., figure 8, p. 23.

11. For active workers, this approach requires the insured to monitor nursing home and home care prices and consciously decide every few years to buy additional coverage.

12. Joshua M. Wiener, Katherine M. Harris, and Raymond J. Hanley, "Premium Pricing of Prototype Private Long-Term Care Insurance Policies," Final Report to the Office of the Assistant Secretary for Planning and Evaluation, DHHS (Brookings, December 1990), table 1.

13. Stanley S. Wallack and others, "Consumer Protection and Long-Term Care Insurance," LifePlans, Inc., Waltham, Mass., October 1991, pp. xi–xiii.

14. William M. Mercer, Inc., "Inflation Protection and Nonforfeiture Benefits in Long-Term Care Insurance Policies: New Data for Decision Making," AARP, Washington, June 1992, p. 7. See, for example, National Association of Insurance Commissioners (NAIC) Long-Term Care Actuarial Task Force, "Inflation Protection and Nonforfeiture Benefits in Long-Term Care Insurance Policies: Final Report," Kansas City, Mo., April 10, 1991, p. 6. In an analysis of five insurance companies accounting for 50 percent of the individual private long-term care insurance market, the U.S. General Accounting Office (GAO) found an assumption, on average, that 50 percent of policyholders would allow their policies to lapse within five years of purchase and about 65 percent within ten years. Limited data available to GAO suggest that the actual lapse rate is a bit lower than commonly assumed, at least for the first two years. GAO, *Long-Term Care Insurance: High Percentage of Policyholders Drop Policies,* GAO/HRD-93-129 (August 1993), pp. 5–7.

15. "Testimony of Gordon R. Trapnell," *Long-term Care Insurance,* Hearings, pp. 123–46.

16. Marc A. Cohen, Nanda Kumar, and Stanley S. Wallack, "Who Buys Long-Term Care Insurance?" *Health Affairs,* vol. 11 (Spring 1992), p. 210.

17. GAO, *Long-term Care Insurance: Better Controls Needed in Sales to People with Limited Financial Resources,* GAO/HRD-92-66 (1992).

18. "NAIC Mandates LTC Nonforfeiture," *Medicine and Health*, vol. 47 (June 28, 1993), p. 2.

19. "Statement of Paul S. Rapo, on Behalf of the Health Insurance Association of America," *Standards for Private Long-Term Care Insurance Policies*, Hearing before the Subcommittee on Health and the Environment of the House Committee on Energy and Commerce, 102 Cong. 2 sess. (GPO, 1992), p. 394.

20. Wiener, Harris, and Hanley, "Premium Pricing of Prototype Private Long-Term Care Insurance Policies."

21. David Kennell and others, *Estimated Costs of a Proposed Home Care Program* (Washington: Lewin-ICF, Inc., 1989).

22. Joshua M. Wiener and Raymond J. Hanley, "Measuring the Activities of Daily Living Across the Elderly: A Guide to National Surveys," Final Report to the Interagency Forum on Aging-Related Statistics, Committee on Estimates of Activities of Daily Living in National Surveys (Brookings, October 1989), p. 6.

23. Chairman of the Subcommittee on Health and Long-Term Care, *Private Long-Term Care Insurance: Unfit for Sale?* House Select Committee on Aging, 101 Cong. 1 sess. (GPO, 1989); Chairmen of the Subcommittee on Health and Long-Term Care of the House Select Committee on Aging and the Subcommittee on Regulation, Business Opportunities, and Energy of the House Committee on Small Business, *Abuses in the Sale of Long-Term Care Insurance to the Elderly*, 102 Cong. 1 sess. (GPO, 1991); "Agents' Secrets: How They Mislead and Confuse," *Consumer Reports*, vol. 56 (June 1991), pp. 427–28; and "Testimony of Ronald F. Pollack," *Long-term Care Insurance*, Hearings, pp. 14–19.

24. See, for example, "Statement of Robert W. DeCoursey, President, Association of Health Insurance Agents, Philadelphia, Pa.," *Long-Term Care Insurance Standards*, Hearing before the Subcommittee on Medicare and Long-Term Care of the Senate Committee on Finance, 102 Cong. 2 sess. (GPO, 1993), pp. 33–35, 49–53; and "Statement of Ronald D. Hagen, Vice President, Product Development and Government Relations, Amex Life Assurance Co., San Rafael, Calif," ibid., pp. 35–37, 54–73.

25. NAIC, "Long-Term Care Insurance Model Regulation," Kansas City, Mo., 1993.

26. In an analysis of nine provisions of the NAIC Model Act and Regulation, most of which focused on consumer protection issues, the HIAA found that forty-four states were less than 60 percent compliant with these provisions as of July 1992. Part of the slowness may reflect that NAIC had adopted eight of the nine provisions only in 1990 or 1991. Arguably, some of these provisions may also repeat more general state health insurance laws and regulations. HIAA, *Long-Term Care Insurance in 1991*, figure 12, p. 26.

27. DeCoursey testimony, pp. 33–37; and Hagen testimony, pp. 54–73.

28. See also Chairmen, *Abuses in the Sale of Long-Term Care Insurance to the Elderly*, p. 7; and GAO, *Long-Term Care Insurance: High Percentage of Policyholders Drop Policies*, pp. 11–12.

29. Prepared statement of Gail Shearer, *Long-Term Care Insurance Standards*, Hearings, p. 129.

30. Hagen testimony, pp. 72–73.

31. HIAA, *Long-Term Care Insurance in 1991*, pp. 7–8.

32. Of the fifty states and the District of Columbia, twenty-nine were more than 80 percent in compliance, twelve were 60 to 79 percent in compliance,

and ten were less than 60 percent in compliance. HIAA, *Long-Term Care Insurance in 1991*, p. 23. This does, however, represent a substantial increase in compliance from April 1991. Stone and others, *State Variation in the Regulation of Long-term Care Insurance Products*, pp. 14–16.

33. This is especially true of the leading sellers of long-term care insurance policies. HIAA, *Long-Term Care Insurance in 1991*, pp. 25–26.

## Chapter Six

1. Of the total $54.7 billion spent in 1993 for nursing home care for the elderly, $22.4 (41 percent) came from medicaid. Of the $20.8 billion spent on home and community-based care, $3.6 billion (17 percent) was covered by medicaid. Estimates from the Brookings-ICF Financing Model.

2. Of the $114 billion spent on medicaid in fiscal year 1992, $33 billion went to institutional long-term care (both nursing facilities and intermediate care facilities for the mentally retarded) and $6 billion to home and community-based services. These figures include spending for the elderly and nonelderly both. Health Care Financing Administration (HCFA) 64 data, Office of State Agency Financial Management, cited in Brian Burwell, "Medicaid Long-Term Care Expenditures for FY 1992 (Amended)," memorandum, SysteMetrics, Lexington, Mass., March 23, 1993, table 1. In 1993, 86 percent of medicaid spending for long-term care for the elderly was on nursing homes (estimates from the Brookings-ICF Financing Model). Pamela Farley Short and others, "Public and Private Responsibility for Financing Nursing-Home Care: The Effect of Medicaid Asset Spend-down," *Milbank Quarterly*, vol. 70, no. 2 (1992), pp. 277–98.

3. U.S. Bipartisan Commission on Comprehensive Health Care (Pepper Commission), *A Call for Action: Final Report* (Government Printing Office, 1990), pp. 119–32.

4. Robert Stevens and Rosemary Stevens, *Welfare Medicine in America: A Case Study of Medicaid* (Free Press, 1974), pp. 23–24, 28–32.

5. *Social Security Amendments of 1965*, Committee Print, House Committee on Ways and Means, 89 Cong. 1 sess. (GPO, March 29, 1965), p. 73.

6. Stevens and Stevens, *Welfare Medicine in America*, pp. 57–69.

7. In 1993 the Federal Medical Assistance Percentage (FMAP), or federal share, ranged from the statutory minimum of 50 percent (in twelve states and the District of Columbia) to 79 percent in Mississippi, with the remaining portion covered by state and, occasionally, local monies. Federal Funds Information for States (FFIS), "Federal Medical Assistance Percentages: 1980–1995," Washington, 1992. Because the federal match rate is based on the average per capita income of a state and does not take into account other characteristics that influence the demand for long-term care (such as the number of people aged 85 and older) and because each state has its own budget priorities, the amount spent on long-term care varies greatly from state to state.

8. *Overview of Entitlement Programs: Background Material and Data on Programs Within the Jurisdiction of the Committee on Ways and Means*, Committee Print, prepared for the House Committee on Ways and Means, 102 Cong. 2 sess. (GPO, 1992), p. 1652.

9. Kaiser Commission on the Future of Medicaid, *Medicaid at the Crossroads* (Baltimore: Henry J. Kaiser Foundation, November 1992), table 2-3, p. 21.

10. In general states must provide coverage to individuals and families who

receive cash assistance from the supplemental security income (SSI) program or the aid to families with dependent children (AFDC) program; to certain low-income pregnant women, infants, and children; and to low-income elderly and disabled medicare beneficiaries. The mandatory services all states must cover include inpatient and outpatient hospital care; physician services; prenatal care; family planning; nurse-midwife services; early and periodic screening, diagnosis and treatment for children; laboratory and x-ray services; and services provided in rural health clinics and other federally qualified health centers. Kaiser Commission, *Medicaid at the Crossroads,* tables 2-1, 2-2, pp. 16, 19.

11. For example, forty states provide social and rehabilitative long-term care services in the home and in other community-based settings through so-called 2176 waivers, but the types of services offered and numbers of people served vary considerably. Richard Price, *Medicaid Home and Community-Based Care Programs* (Washington: Congressional Research Service [CRS], November 25, 1992).

12. Almost all easily liquidated assets, such as bank accounts, stocks, and certificates of deposit, must be used before medicaid helps pay for care. Other less-liquid assets are exempt from these limits. For example, a person's home, regardless of value, is not counted as an asset as long as the recipient, spouse, or dependent child lives there or the recipient is expected to return after a nursing home stay. Within reasonable limits, personal property, an automobile, life insurance, burial space, and funds for burial are also exempt. CRS, *Medicaid Source Book: Background Data and Analysis (A 1993 Update),* prepared for the Subcommittee on Health and the Environment of the House Committee on Energy and Commerce, Comitttee Print, 103 Cong. 1 sess. (January 1993), p. 203.

13. Under these spousal impoverishment rules, in 1993 a spouse who remains in the community is allowed to keep income from either spouse of at least $1,179 (150 percent of the federal poverty level) but no more than $1,769 a month (depending on whether the spouse has "excess shelter expenses" for housing and utilities). States must also allow the noninstitutionalized spouse to keep half of the combined assets totaling not less than $14,148 up to a maximum of $70,740. All of these figures are adjusted annually by the consumer price index. *Conference Report to Accompany H.R. 2470,* H. Rept. 100-661, 100 Cong. 2 sess. (GPO, May 31, 1988), pp. 80–83; "Annual Update of the HHS Poverty Guidelines," *Federal Register,* vol. 58 (February 12, 1993), p. 8287; and personal communication with Joe Davis, Health Care Financing Administration, Department of Health and Human Services (DHHS), June 25, 1993.

14. In general states use income limits, a definition of medically needy, or a combination of both to determine eligibility for medicaid. In 1991 thirty-five states used either the 300 percent rule or some lower special income level to determine eligibility for medicaid coverage of institutional care. In the seventeen states that exclusively use an income rule, individuals with incomes in excess of this amount are ineligible for medicaid, regardless of how high their medical expenses might be. In states where medical need is included in the criteria for eligibility, persons who demonstrate that their medical expenses are greater than their income may be considered eligible for medicaid. CRS, *Medicaid Source Book,* p. 218.

15. States are required to provide coverage to this "categorically needy" group. In 1993 the monthly SSI payment level was set at $434 for individuals and $652 for couples. Those whose earnings were less than this amount and

who also had liquid assets, excluding the value of their home and personal effects, totaling no more than $2,000 ($3,000 for couples), qualified for SSI and consequently medicaid. Because the monthly SSI payment represents less than 75 percent of the federal poverty level, some states choose to supplement it with state-only funds and to set more generous standards for medicaid eligibility. Twelve "209(b)" states are allowed to retain more stringent medicaid eligibility criteria that were in place before January 1, 1972. *Overview of Entitlement Programs,* Committee Print, pp. 790, 798, 1642.

16. States must use the same income standard for both the elderly and families with dependent children. By law, income under this standard cannot exceed 133 percent of the AFDC payment limit. Because AFDC payment levels are so low, these limits are often below the SSI benefit level. For example, 133 percent of the median AFDC payment level for a family of two in 1993 was $388, compared with an SSI payment level of $652. Social Security Administration (SSA), "Social Security Update 1993," SSA Publication 05-10003 (DHHS, January 1993); and Administration on Children, Youth and Families, "Need and Payment Amounts," DHHS, May 25, 1993. To qualify for medically needy coverage, individuals must have low levels of financial assets (usually the same as the categorically needy).

17. Letty Carpenter, "Medicaid Eligibility for Persons in Nursing Homes," *Health Care Financing Review,* vol. 10 (Winter 1988), p. 69.

18. Tocqueville, Marmor and colleagues, and Morris all discuss the various conflicts between individual freedom to seek solutions in the marketplace and government intervention for the purpose of achieving societal goals. Alexis de Tocqueville, *Democracy in America* (Harper and Row, 1969); Theodore R. Marmor, Jerry L. Mashaw, and Philip L. Harvey, *America's Misunderstood Welfare State: Persistent Myths, Enduring Realities* (Basic Books, 1990); and Robert Morris, *Social Policy of the American Welfare State: An Introduction to Policy Analysis* (Harper and Row, 1979).

19. Jack A. Meyer and Marion Ein Lewin, "Poverty and Social Welfare: An Agenda for Change," *Inquiry,* vol. 23 (Summer 1986), pp. 122–33.

20. Marc A. Cohen and others, "Financing Long-Term Care: A Practical Mix of Public and Private," *Journal of Health Politics, Policy and Law,* vol. 17 (Fall 1992), p. 417; and Health Insurance Association of America (HIAA), "HIAA Proposal for Financing Long-Term Care," Washington, 1990, p. 4.

21. Only 37 percent of all nursing home patients are discharged alive. Denise A. Spence and Joshua M. Wiener, "Nursing Home Length of Stay Patterns: Results from the 1985 National Nursing Home Survey," *Gerontologist,* vol. 30 (February 1990), p. 18.

22. Peter J. Ferrara, "Long-Term Care: Why a New Entitlement Program Would Be Wrong" *Policy Analysis,* no. 144 (Cato Institute, Washington, December 13, 1990), p. 4.

23. Robert J. Myers, "The Future of Medicare and Its Implications for the Private Insurance Industry," paper presented as part of the Drake University Insurance Center Distinguished Lecture Series, Des Moines, November 30, 1988.

24. For a detailed description of the budget process, see Congressional Budget Office (CBO), *The Economic and Budget Outlook, Fiscal Years 1993–1997* (January 1992), pp. 27–45.

25. Sheldon Danziger, Robert Haveman, and Robert Plotnick, "How Income Transfer Programs Affect Work, Savings, and the Income Distribution: A

Critical Review," *Journal of Economic Literature,* vol. 19 (September 1981), pp. 975–1028.

26. Hyneman, for example, urges governments to "forgo revolutionary change in favor of gradual adaptation," because "even when we are caught flat-footed by the deficiencies of existing arrangements, [a quick installation of fundamental changes] is likely to defeat the very purposes which cause it to be advocated." Charles Hyneman, *Bureaucracy in a Democracy* (New York: Harper and Brothers, 1950), p. 563.

27. Robert M. Ball, with Thomas N. Bethell, *Because We're All in This To-gether: The Case for a Long Term Care Insurance Policy* (Washington: Families USA Foundation, 1989), pp. 92–99; Pepper Commission, *A Call for Action.*

28. HIAA, "HIAA Proposal for Financing Long-Term Care," pp. 4–5.

29. Korbin Liu, Maria Perozek, and Kenneth Manton, "Catastrophic Acute and Long-Term Care Costs: Risks Faced by Disabled Elderly Persons," *Geron-tologist,* vol. 33 (June 1993), pp. 299–307; Teresa A. Coughlin, Korbin Liu, and Timothy D. McBride, "Severely Disabled Elderly Persons with Financially Catastrophic Health Care Expenses: Sources and Determinants," *Gerontologist,* vol. 32 (June 1992), pp. 391–403; Thomas Rice, "The Use, Cost, and Eco-nomic Burden of Nursing-Home Care in 1985," *Medical Care,* vol. 27 (Decem-ber 1989), pp. 1133–47; and Thomas Rice and Jon Gabel, "Protecting the Elderly against High Health Care Costs," *Health Affairs,* vol. 5 (Fall 1986), pp. 5–21.

30. Coughlin, Liu, and McBride, "Severely Disabled Elderly Persons with Financially Catastrophic Health Care Expenses."

31. *Overview of Entitlement Programs,* Committee Print, p. 805.

32. Beginning in 1991 medicaid was required to pay medicare part B pre-miums and coinsurance and deductibles for medicare services for "qualified medicare beneficiaries" (QMBs). To be a QMB, an individual must be eligible for medicare, have an income of less than 100 percent of the federal poverty level, and have limited financial resources—up to two times that allowable under SSI. As of October 1992, medicaid paid the part B medicare premiums for fewer than 4 million people. Medicaid also pays the part A premiums for the small number of elderly—fewer than 200,000—who do not qualify for medi-care. CRS, *Medicaid Source Book,* pp. 239–43.

33. Short and others, "Public and Private Responsibility for Financing Nurs-ing Home Care," p. 283.

34. Raymond J. Hanley, Joshua M. Wiener, and Katherine M. Harris, "The Economic Status of Elderly Nursing Home Users," Brookings, January 1994.

35. Despite the high cost of nursing home care, several recent studies have found that only a modest number of nursing home patients who are private pay at admission "spend down" to medicaid eligibility levels as a result of their nursing home stay. For example, see Leonard Gruenberg, Hillel Alpert, and Brian Burwell, *An Analysis of the Impact of Spend-Down on Medicaid Expenditures* (DHHS, Office of the Assistant Secretary for Planning and Evaluation, January 1992); Denise A. Spence and Joshua M. Wiener, "Estimating the Extent of Medicaid Spend-Down in Nursing Homes," *Journal of Health Politics, Policy and Law,* vol. 15 (Fall 1990), pp. 607–26; Brian O. Burwell, E. Kathleen Adams, and Mark R. Meiners, "Spend-Down of Assets Before Medicaid Eligibility among Elderly Nursing Home Recipients in Michigan," *Medical Care,* vol. 28 (April 1990), pp. 349–62; Korbin Liu, Pamela Doty, and Kenneth Manton, "Medicaid Spenddown in Nursing Homes," *Gerontologist,* vol. 30 (February

1990), pp. 7–15; and Leonard Gruenberg and others, *Analysis of the Spend-Down Patterns of Individuals Admitted to Nursing Homes in the State of Connecticut* (Waltham, Mass.: Long-Term Care Data Institute, 1989).

36. Tom W. Smith, "That Which We Call Welfare by Any Other Name Would Smell Sweeter," *Public Opinion Quarterly*, vol. 51 (Spring 1987), pp. 75–83; Lee Rainwater, "Stigma in Income-Tested Programs," in Irwin Garfinkel, ed., *Income-Tested Transfer Programs: The Case For and Against* (Academic Press, 1982), pp. 19–46; Robert Moffitt, "An Economic Model of Welfare Stigma," *American Economic Review*, vol. 73 (December 1983), pp. 1023–35; and Patricia M. Horan and Patricia Lee Austin, "The Social Bases of Welfare Stigma," *Social Problems*, vol. 21 (June 1974), pp. 648–57.

37. Low enrollment rates have been cited as evidence that some welfare stigma is attached to federal programs that benefit the elderly. It is estimated that 40 to 50 percent of those eligible for SSI have not applied for it. Martin Tolchin, "Federal Aid for Destitute Reaching Just Half of Those Eligible," *New York Times*, May 19, 1988, p. A21. In a study of this issue, 65 percent of the people who were eligible but did not apply said a "major reason" was that they "don't like the idea of accepting what some people might call welfare." It is unclear whether this factor alone kept people from applying. More than half (55 percent) of those questioned said they had never heard of the SSI program, 43 percent thought the benefits were too low to bother seeking, 62 percent did not know where to apply or could not get there, and 43 percent "do not like to be involved with anything connected with government." Louis Harris and Associates, "Follow-up Study of Poor Elderly Persons: Strategies to Increase Participation in SSI," survey prepared for the American Association of Retired Persons, Washington, February 1988. See also Vernon L. Allen, "Stigma in Income-Tested Programs: Discussion," in Garfinkel, *Income-Tested Transfer Programs*, p. 49; and Bernard Beck, "Welfare as a Moral Category," *Social Problems*, vol. 14 (Fall 1966), pp. 258–77.

38. Richard M. Coughlin, "Welfare Myths and Stereotypes," in Richard M. Coughlin, ed., *Reforming Welfare, Lessons, Limits, and Choices* (University of New Mexico Press, 1989), p. 80; and personal communication with Richard M. Coughlin, University of New Mexico, August 18, 1992.

39. Some believe that less stigma is associated with SSI because it is administered by the Social Security Administration and therefore gains some of the public acceptance of the social security program. Coughlin communication. Public support for programs targeted at the elderly is also stronger than it is for welfare programs targeted on the nonelderly. When asked whether funding for seven social programs should be increased, maintained, or decreased, public support for programs serving primarily the elderly (such as social security, medicare, and SSI) enjoyed the greatest public support. On a scale from 1 to 3, with 3 indicating support for increases in a program, "mean support scores" ranged from 2.65 for medicare to 2.00 for food stamps. Mean support for SSI was comparable to that for the social security program but significantly lower than the mean support for medicare. Support for SSI was significantly higher than support for medicaid, unemployment compensation, AFDC, and food stamps. Fay Lomax Cook, "Congress and the Public: Convergent and Divergent Opinions on Social Security," in Henry J. Aaron, ed., *Social Security and the Budget* (Lanham, Md.: University Press of America, 1990), pp. 86–87.

40. Hugh Heclo, "The Political Foundations of Antipoverty Policy," in Sheldon H. Danziger and Daniel H. Weinberg, eds., *Fighting Poverty: What Works*

*and What Doesn't* (Harvard University Press, 1986), p. 319; Rainwater, "Stigma in Income-Tested Programs," p. 27; and Michael E. Schiltz, *Public Attitudes toward Social Security: 1935–1965* (Washington: Social Security Administration, 1970), p. 160.

41. Heclo, "The Political Foundations of Antipoverty Policy," pp. 312–40.

42. R. Coughlin, "Welfare Myths and Stereotypes," p. 80.

43. Estimates of the number of elderly nursing home residents with impairment is even higher (58 percent) if those with mental disorders such as schizophrenia and other psychoses but without dementia are included. Tamra J. Lair and Doris Cadigan Lefkowitz, "Mental Health and Functional Status of Residents in Nursing and Personal Care Homes," National Medical Expenditure Survey, Research Findings 7 (Agency for Health Care Policy and Research, Public Health Service, DHHS, Rockville, Md., September 1990), pp. 9–10. See also Judith D. Kasper, "Cognitive Impairment Among Functionally Limited Elderly People in the Community: Future Considerations for Long-Term Care Policy," *Milbank Quarterly*, vol. 68, no. 1 (1990), pp. 81–109.

44. Daniel Yankelovich Group, Inc., *Long Term Care in America: Public Attitudes and Possible Solutions, Executive Summary* (Washington: AARP, January 1990), p. B-6; Research USA, *Membership Survey*, report for the National Committee to Preserve Social Security and Medicare (Washington, December 1988), p. 13; RL Associates, "The American Public Views Long Term Care," survey conducted for the AARP and the Villers Foundation (Princeton, N.J., October 1987), p. 5; and Hugh Heclo, "The Political Foundations of Antipoverty Policy," pp. 312–40.

45. Cook, "Congress and the Public," p. 86. See also R. Coughlin, "Welfare Myths and Stereotypes," pp. 79–80.

46. Robert J. Blendon and Karen Donelan, "The Public and the Emerging Debate over National Health Insurance," *New England Journal of Medicine*, vol. 323 (July 19, 1990), p. 211.

47. William Julius Wilson, *The Truly Disadvantaged: The Inner City, the Underclass, and Public Policy* (University of Chicago Press, 1987) p. 118. Similarly, Lockhart believes that targeting programs on narrow disadvantaged groups also stigmatizes. Charles Lockhart, "The Contradictions of Public Assistance and the Prospect of Social Merging," in R. Coughlin, *Reforming Welfare*, p. 65.

48. Marmor, Mashaw, and Harvey, *America's Misunderstood Welfare State*.

49. Ibid., pp. 35–36; and R. Coughlin, "Welfare Myths and Stereotypes," pp. 79–106. Public opinion about welfare programs has strong racial and ethnic overtones. For example, the popular perception that most medicaid benefits flow to black AFDC families is misleading. Paul Starr, "Health Care for the Poor: The Past Twenty Years," in Danziger and Weinberg, *Fighting Poverty*, pp. 106–32.

50. Expanded coverage falls into two categories: broadened eligibility and increased services. During the last ten years, Congress has required states to extend coverage to certain categories of children and pregnant women. In addition, although the medicare-related portions of the Medicare Catastrophic Coverage Act of 1988 were repealed in December 1989, Congress left in place medicaid requirements protecting a community spouse's income and resources and paying medicare premiums for QMBs. The Family Support Act of 1988, legislation aimed primarily at welfare reform, also expanded medicaid to extend transitional coverage to families moving off welfare and to cover two-parent families where the principle breadwinner is unemployed. Linda Bilheimer, "Fac-

tors Contributing to the Growth of the Medicaid Program," CBO Staff Memorandum, Washington, May 1992, p. 16–22; Joshua M. Wiener and Jeannie Engel, *Improving Access to Health Services for Children and Pregnant Women* (Brookings, 1991), pp. 60–61; Neal R. Peirce, "State of the States," *National Journal*, vol. 23 (September 14, 1991), p. 2229; and *Overview of Entitlement Programs,* Committee Print, pp. 1137–38.

A state's flexibility to change the benefit package is somewhat constrained by four basic federal guidelines that require states to offer comparable services to all eligible enrollees, to ensure that the benefit package is uniform throughout the state, and to give enrollees their choice of providers. Waivers of these requirements can be obtained, although the application process is thought to be cumbersome and the requirement that the state prove that the waiver would not increase costs is difficult to meet.

The Medicaid Voluntary Donations and Provider-Specific Tax Amendments of 1991 restrict the amount of revenue that states can raise by taxing providers to 25 percent of each state's medicaid budget; the amendments also phase out states' reliance on "voluntary donations" from providers. Projections indicate that these recent regulations will result in large losses to many states' overall medicaid budgets. FFIS, "Medicaid 1993 Matching Rates; Projections for 1994; New Medicaid Regulation; Personal Income Data," vol. 91-16 (Washington, September 12, 1991), p. 1; and Teresa A. Coughlin, Leighton Ku, and John Holahan, *Medicaid Since 1980: Costs, Coverage, and the Shifting Alliance Between the Federal Government and the States* (Washington: Urban Institute, 1994), p. 105.

51. Adjusted for general inflation, real medicaid expenditures grew 34 percent between 1981 and 1988, 23 percent between 1988 and 1990, and 22 percent in 1991 alone. Figures are for fiscal years. Bilheimer, "Factors Contributing to the Growth of the Medicaid Program," p. 1.

52. Jerry Gray, "Governors Seek to Shed Burdens of Medicaid," *New York Times,* August 4, 1992, p. A8; Andrew Bates, "Golden Girls," *New Republic,* February 3, 1992, pp. 17–18; Brian Burwell, "Middle Class Welfare: Medicaid Estate Planning for Long-Term Care Coverage," SysteMetrics/McGraw-Hill, Lexington, Mass., September 1991; Stephen A. Moses, "The Fallacy of Impoverishment," *Gerontologist,* vol. 30 (February 1990), pp. 21–25; and Jane Bryant Quinn, "Do Only the Suckers Pay?" *Newsweek,* December 18, 1989, p. 52. This section also draws from Raymond J. Hanley and Joshua M. Wiener, "A Non-Problem: Scheming Oldsters Bilking Medicaid," *Philadelphia Inquirer,* May 11, 1992, p. A11.

53. Omnibus Budget Reconciliation Act of 1993, Public Law 103-66, August 10, 1993.

54. Burwell, "Middle Class Welfare," p. 34.

55. Moses, "The Fallacy of Impoverishment," pp. 21–25.

56. U.S. General Accounting Office, *Medicaid Estate Planning,* GAO/HRD-93-29R (July 20, 1993).

57. Frank A. Sloan and Mary W. Sharpe, "Long-Term Care, Medicaid, and Impoverishment of the Elderly," *Milbank Quarterly,* vol. 71 (1993), pp. 575–600.

58. Hanley, Wiener, and Harris, "The Economic Status of Elderly Nursing Home Users."

59. Authors' unpublished estimates based on HCFA Form 2082 data; and Coughlin, Ku, and Holahan, *Medicaid Since 1980,* table 6-2.

60. Joshua M. Wiener, "A Sociological Analysis of Government Regulation: The Case of Nursing Homes," Ph.D. dissertation, Harvard University, 1981.

61. John A. Nyman, "Excess Demand, the Percentage of Medicaid Patients, and the Quality of Nursing Home Care," *Journal of Human Resources*, vol. 23 (Winter 1988), pp. 76–92; John A. Nyman, "The Effect of Competition on Nursing Home Expenditures under Prospective Reimbursement," *Health Services Research*, vol. 23 (October 1988), pp. 555–74; John A. Nyman, Samuel Levey, and James E. Rohrer, "RUGs and Equity of Access to Nursing Home Care," *Medical Care*, vol. 25 (May 1987), pp. 363–74; Charlene Harrington and James H. Swan, "The Impact of State Medicaid Nursing Home Policies on Utilization and Expenditures," *Inquiry*, vol. 24 (Summer 1987), pp. 157–71; and William J. Scanlon, "A Theory of the Nursing Home Market," *Inquiry*, vol. 17 (Spring 1980), pp. 25–41.

62. Estimates of the difference between medicaid and private payment levels vary from 18 percent, based on data from the 1985 National Nursing Home Survey, to 30 percent in 1987, according to an Institute of Medicine report on the quality of nursing homes. CRS, *Medicaid Source Book*, p. 341; Robert J. Buchanan, R. Peter Madel, and Dan Persons, "Medicaid Payment Policies for Nursing Home Care: A National Survey," *Health Care Financing Review*, vol. 13 (Fall 1991), p. 60; and Institute of Medicine, *Improving the Quality of Care in Nursing Homes* (Washington: National Academy Press, 1986), p. 194. There are exceptions to the rule that medicaid reimbursement is less than that for privately paying clients. For example, Minnesota's Rate Equalization Act prohibits nursing homes from charging private residents more than the medicaid rate.

63. Recently, the industry's concern over medicaid reimbursement rates has focused on how to finance nursing home reforms mandated by Omnibus Budget Reconciliation Act of 1987. "AHCA Faces Struggle to Prove Injury in Reform Suit," *Long Term Care Management*, vol. 20 (May 30, 1991), p. 2.

64. The medicaid clientele is much more important to the nursing home industry than to physicians; still, the administrative hassles and other problems are similar. Stephen M. Davison, "Physician Participation in Medicaid: Background and Issues," *Journal of Health Politics, Policy and Law*, vol. 6 (Winter 1982), p. 711.

65. CRS, *Medicaid Source Book*, pp. 53–54; and Davison, "Physician Participation in Medicaid," p. 711.

66. Spence and Wiener, "Estimating the Extent of Medicaid Spend-Down in Nursing Homes," pp. 607–26.

67. Stephen A. Moses, "How to Resolve Elder Law's Ethical Dilemma," *The Elder Law Report* (October 1990), p. 7.

68. Nyman, "Excess Demand, the Percentage of Medicaid Patients, and the Quality of Nursing Home Care"; Nyman "The Effect of Competition on Nursing Home Expenditures under Prospective Reimbursement"; Nyman, Levey, and Rohrer, "RUGs and Equity of Access to Nursing Home Care"; Harrington and Swan, "The Impact of State Medicaid Nursing Home Policies on Utilization, and Expenditures"; and Scanlon, "A Theory of the Nursing Home Market."

69. Institute of Medicine, *Improving the Quality of Care in Nursing Homes*, p. 195; and Robert E. Schlenker, "Comparison of Medicaid Nursing Home Payment Systems," *Health Care Financing Review*, vol. 13 (Fall 1991), pp. 93–109.

70. Niccie L. McKay, "Quality Choice in Medicaid Markets: The Case of Nursing Homes," *Quarterly Review of Economics and Business*, vol. 29 (Summer 1989), pp. 27–40; and Scanlon, "A Theory of the Nursing Home Market."

71. Medicaid Management Institute, "Medicaid Reimbursement for Nursing Home Reform," American Public Welfare Association, Washington, January 1991, p. 1.

72. The Omnibus Budget Reconciliation Act of 1987 required states to take into account the costs of complying with the nursing home provisions included in this act. The Omnibus Budget Reconciliation Act of 1990 reinforces that requirement. Bilheimer, "Factors Contributing to the Growth of the Medicaid Program," p. 27.

73. See *Wilder v. Virginia Hospital Association*. Linda Greenhouse, "High Court Rules Hospitals Can Sue on Medicaid Rates," *New York Times*, June 15, 1990, pp. A1, A15; and "High Court Affirms Providers' Right to Sue Medicaid in Federal Court," *Long Term Care Management*, vol. 19 (June 21, 1990), p. 1.

74. Joanna K. Weinberg and others, "Nursing Home Litigation under the Boren Amendment: Issues and Analysis," Institute for Health and Aging, University of California, San Francisco, November 1993, table 3.

75. Using the Brookings-ICF Long-Term Care Financing Model, Crown and Burwell showed the effects of increasing medicaid asset levels from the current $2,000 to $12,000, $20,000 and $30,000. Results indicated that levels could be increased to the upper limit of $30,000 at relatively low cost ($1.2 billion in 1994). William H. Crown and Brian Burwell, "An Analysis of Asset Testing for Long-Term Care Benefits," report prepared for the AARP, Washington, September 1993, table 6.

76. Blendon and Donelan, "The Public and Emerging Debate over National Health Insurance," p. 211; Starr, "Health Care for the Poor: The Past Twenty Years," p. 107; and Bruce C. Vladeck, *Unloving Care: The Nursing Home Tragedy* (Basic Books, 1980), p. 75.

## Chapter Seven

1. For the most part, a person is eligible for medicare if he or she receives social security. The percentage of people covered by medicare, however, is larger than the percentage receiving social security because some federal civilians hired before 1983 opted to participate in a separate federal pension program rather than in social security but are still eligible for medicare benefits. *Overview of Entitlement Programs: Background Material and Data on Programs Within the Jurisdiction of the Committee on Ways and Means*, Committee Print, 102 Cong. 2 sess. (Government Printing Office, 1992), p. 115.

2. Susan Van Gelder and Diane Johnson, *Long-Term Care Insurance: A Market Update* (Washington: Health Insurance Association of America [HIAA], January 1991), p. 7.

3. In a public opinion survey conducted in the mid-1980s, the youngest respondents (aged 18 through 34) appeared equally as supportive of social security as those aged 35 through 64; the younger respondents even said that they would be willing to "take action" such as writing letters to legislators and signing petitions to express disapproval of any cutbacks to the program. As expected, elderly respondents (65 years and older) showed greater support, but the difference was not statistically significant. Blacks are somewhat more supportive of social security than whites, and Democrats are more supportive than Republicans. Support for social security consistently declines with income. Interestingly, the only statistically significant difference is between males (who are

significantly less supportive of social security) and females. Fay Lomax Cook, "Congress and the Public: Convergent and Divergent Opinions on Social Security," in Henry J. Aaron, ed., *Social Security and the Budget* (Lanham, Md.: University Press of America, 1990), p. 88.

4. Survey by the American Council of Life Insurance as reported in *American Enterprise*, vol. 1 (March–April 1990), p. 100; and in Robert J. Myers, "Confidence in the Future of Social Security," *Social Security News* (Fall 1991), p. 3.

5. CBS-Times poll cited in National Journal, July 7, 1990, p. 1684; and Robert Y. Shapiro and Tom W. Smith, "The Polls: Social Security," *Public Opinion Quarterly*, vol. 49 (August 1985), pp. 561–72.

6. James Coleman, "Income Testing and Social Cohesion," in Irwin Garfinkel, ed., *Income-Tested Transfer Programs: The Case For and Against* (Academic Press, 1982), pp. 67–88.

7. Paul Light, *Artful Work: The Politics of Social Security Reform* (Random House, 1985), pp. 99–101.

8. ICR Survey Research Group of AUS Consultants, "Long-Term Care Survey," prepared for the American Association of Retired Persons (AARP) (Media, Pa.: 1993). Similarly, in a 1989 poll by the Daniel Yankelovich Group for the AARP, 68 percent of those surveyed stated that they "strongly supported" a "federal government program similar to social security or medicare to help pay for long-term care for the elderly and disabled." Daniel Yankelovich Group, Inc., *Long Term Care in America: Public Attitudes and Possible Solutions, Executive Summary* (Washington: AARP, January 1990).

9. The *Los Angeles Times*, January 21–24, 1990, cited in unpublished information from AARP. Similar results were found in a 1987 survey by RL Associates for AARP; 61 percent of those polled said they wanted a long-term care program "available to everyone regardless of how rich or poor they are." RL Associates, "The American Public Views Long Term Care," survey conducted for the AARP and the Villers Foundation (Princeton, N.J., October 1987). Conjoint analysis on the 1989 poll conducted by Daniel Yankelovich, cited above, showed that most Americans favor universal eligibility for a long-term care program. In contrast, a 1993 survey for the American Health Care Association by the Gallup Organization found that 76 percent of those surveyed want the government to pay for nursing home care only for those who cannot afford it. "Survey Finds Limited Interest in Government-Financed Long-Term Care," *Long-Term Care Management*, vol. 21 (March 10, 1993), pp. 3–4.

10. Daniel Yankelovich Group, Inc., *Long Term Care in America*.

11. The 1993 Gallup Organization survey for the Employee Benefit Research Institute (EBRI) showed that 69 percent of those surveyed supported a "federal program providing long-term care assistance for the elderly (even) if it meant an increase in . . . income taxes." Gallup Organization, *Public Attitudes on Long-Term Care, 1993*, survey prepared for the EBRI (Washington, 1993). See also Gallup Organization for the American Medical Association, January 3–6, 1991, cited in unpublished information from the AARP; Yankelovich, Clancy, and Shulman poll cited in "The Truth About Taxes," *American Enterprise*, vol. 1 (July–August 1990), p. 82; Gallup Organization for Families USA, August 13–19, 1990, cited in unpublished information from the AARP; *Los Angeles Times* poll cited in *National Journal*, vol. 22 (May 26, 1990), p. 1309; Daniel Yankelovich Group, *Long Term Care in America*, p. D-13; *Los Angeles Times* poll, January 21–24, 1990, cited in unpublished information from the AARP; Gallup

poll cited in *National Journal*, vol. 21 (April 29, 1989), p. 1076; *Los Angeles Times* poll, April 1–6, 1989, cited in unpublished information from the AARP; Gallup poll cited in *Public Opinion*, vol. 11 (March–April 1989), p. 21; CBS–*New York Times* poll cited in *National Journal*, vol. 21 (February 4, 1989), p. 306; Gallup poll cited in *National Journal*, vol. 20 (December 10, 1988), p. 3157; Gallup Organization, "Solid Majority Would Accept Tax Hike to Improve Schools," *Gallup Report*, no. 277 (October 1988), p. 33; Gallup Organization for the AARP, June 14–19, 1988, cited in unpublished information from the AARP; and Hamilton, Frederick & Schneiders, "Attitudes of Americans Over 45 Years of Age on Long-Term Care," survey prepared for the AARP, Washington, February 1988, p. 10.

12. In the 1993 ICR Survey Research Group survey, respondents were told that some taxes would be needed to pay for health care reform. When asked whether they would rather pay about $30 a month in additional taxes for a health reform plan that guaranteed everyone hospital and doctor care only, or $50 a month in additional taxes to guarantee hospital, doctor, and long-term care, nearly half opted for the broader coverage; 37 percent preferred the less expensive plan. ICR Survey Research Group, "Long-Term Care Survey." In a 1991 survey by the Gallup Organization for the American Medical Association, almost half of respondents did not know how much they would be willing to pay for a program that provided long-term care to the elderly. Fully 40 percent were not willing to pay more than $100 per year. Cited in unpublished information from AARP. Similarly, another survey found that of the 74 percent who said they would be willing to pay additional taxes for long-term care assistance for the elderly, 42 percent did not know how much they would be willing to pay, and only 29 percent would be willing to pay more than $100 a year. Gallup Organization, *Public Attitudes on Long-Term Care, 1991*, survey prepared for EBRI (Washington, 1993), p. 20.

A 1989 survey by EBRI and the Gallup Organization found that 43 percent of respondents said that they would be willing to pay $100 a month for private or public long-term care insurance. Gallup Organization, *Public Attitudes on Long-Term Care, 1989*, survey prepared for EBRI (Washington, 1989), p. 26. In a 1987 survey by Hamilton, Frederick & Schneiders, from 53 to 65 percent of persons polled said that they would be willing to pay $20 to $58 a month in additional taxes to finance a federal long-term care program for the elderly and disabled. Hamilton, Frederick & Schneiders, "Attitudes of Americans Over 45 Years of Age on Long-Term Care," p. 10.

13. Margaret K. Straw, "Home Care: Attitudes and Knowledge of Middle-Aged and Older Americans," AARP, Washington, September 1991, p. 6; Louis Harris and Associates, "A Telephone Survey of 1,500 Adults Nationwide Conducted Between February 18–23, 1988," cited in Rosita M. Thomas, "Public Opinion on Long-Term Health Care Needs, Costs, and Financing" CRS 90-151-GOV., Congressional Research Service (CRS), Washington, March 19, 1990, p. 44; William J. McAuley and Rosemary Blieszner, "Selection of Long-Term Care Arrangement by Older Community Residents," *Gerontologist*, vol. 25 (April 1985), pp. 188–93; and Marvin Cetron, "The Public Opinion of Home Care: A Survey Report, Executive Summary," *Caring*, vol. 4 (October 1985), pp. 12–15.

14. Around three-quarters of respondents across all age groups and incomes prefer home care to nursing home care. With the exception of those aged 65

and older, with annual incomes greater than $25,000, all groups also prefer care from family and friends rather than paid assistance. Upper-income respondents were more likely to want paid assistance. Straw, "Home Care," pp. 5–6.

15. Only one-quarter of those who would prefer to have care provided at home said that nursing home care was preferable when a disabled family member required twenty-four-hour care. Straw, "Home Care," p. 5.

16. In a 1993 Kaiser-Harris National Health Care Survey, 36 percent of respondents chose prescription drugs, 33 percent chose home care, and 18 percent chose nursing home care. Letter from Dennis F. Beatrice, Vice President, The Henry J. Kaiser Family Foundation, Menlo Park, Calif., May 7, 1993.

17. RL Associates, "The American Public Views Long Term Care."

18. Susan Polniaszek and James P. Firman, "Will Your Insurance Pay If You Need Home Care? An Analysis of Major Long-Term Care Insurance Policies," United Seniors Health Cooperative, Washington, 1990.

19. Medicaid rates for nursing homes are considered an obstacle to public patients' gaining access to needed care. These rates fall 18 to 30 percent below the rate charged private patients. CRS, *Medicaid Source Book: Background Data and Analysis (A 1993 Update)*, prepared for the Subcommittee on Health and the Environment of the House Committee on Energy and Commerce, 103 Cong. 1 sess. (January 1993), p. 341; Robert J. Buchanan, R. Peter Madel, and Dan Persons, "Medicaid Payment Policies for Nursing Home Care: A National Survey," *Health Care Financing Review,* vol. 13 (Fall 1991), p. 60; and Institute of Medicine, *Improving the Quality of Care in Nursing Homes* (Washington: National Academy Press, 1986), p. 194. One might expect a social insurance program for long-term care to have a rate structure comparable to medicare. Medicare rates are more generous than those paid by medicaid but less than private pay rates. Esther Hing, Edward Sekscenski, and Genevieve Strahan, "The National Nursing Home Survey: 1985 Summary for the United States," *Vital and Health Statistics,* series 13, no. 97 (Washington: National Center for Health Statistics, 1989), table 9.

20. John A. Nyman, "The Effect of Competition on Nursing Home Expenditures under Prospective Reimbursement," *Health Services Research,* vol. 23 (October 1988), pp. 555–74.

21. Because of the large market share that medicaid controls, only 29 percent of nursing homes, accounting for 14 percent of the beds, have opted not to participate in the medicaid program. Hing, Sekscenski, and Strahan, "The National Nursing Home Survey," table 1. A social insurance strategy would be expected to have an even greater market share and higher participation rates.

22. William J. Scanlon, "Possible Reforms for Financing Long-Term Care," *Journal of Economic Perspectives,* vol. 6 (Summer 1992), pp. 43–58.

23. U.S. Bipartisan Commission on Comprehensive Health Care (Pepper Commission), *A Call for Action: Final Report* (GPO, 1990), p. 16.

24. In 1990 the United States ranked twenty-third out of twenty-four members of the Organization for Economic Cooperation and Development (OECD) in tax revenues as a percentage of gross domestic product. OECD, *Revenue Statistics of OECD Member Countries: 1965–1991* (Paris, 1992), table 1, p. 74.

25. See, for example, Peter G. Peterson and Neil Howe, *On Borrowed Time: How the Growth in Entitlement Spending Threatens America's Future* (San Francisco: Institute for Contemporary Studies Press, 1988); Daniel Callahan, *Setting Limits: Medical Goals in an Aging Society* (Simon and Schuster, 1987); Phillip Longman, *Born to Pay: The New Politics of Aging in America* (Houghton Mifflin

Company, 1987); Richard D. Lamm, *MegaTraumas: America at the Year 2000* (Houghton Mifflin, 1985); John H. Makin, "Economic Growth and the Health Care Budget," paper presented at a conference on Medicare Reform and the Baby Boom Generation sponsored by Americans for Generational Equity, April 1987; and John Makin, "Social Security: Nothing but a Ponzi Scheme," *New York Times,* October 8, 1988, p. A27.

26. Michael D. Hurd, "Research on the Elderly: Economic Status, Retirement, and Consumption and Saving," *Journal of Economic Literature,* vol. 28 (June 1990), pp. 565–637; Michael D. Hurd, "Issues and Results from Research on Elderly I: Economic Status," Working Paper 3018 (Cambridge, Mass: National Bureau of Economic Research, June 1989); Daniel B. Radner, "Shifts in the Aged-Nonaged Income Relationship, 1979–1985," Working Paper 35 (Office of Research and Statistics, Office of Policy, Social Security Administration, January 1988); and Sheldon Danziger and others, "Implications of the Relative Economic Status of the Elderly for Transfer Policy," in Henry J. Aaron and Gary Burtless, eds., *Retirement and Economic Behavior* (Brookings, 1984), pp. 175–92.

27. Peterson and Howe, *On Borrowed Time*; Callahan, *Setting Limits*; and Longman, *Born to Pay.*

28. Daniel B. Radner, "An Assessment of the Economic Status of the Aged," *Studies in Income Distribution,* no. 16 (Washington: Social Security Administration, Office of Research and Statistics, May 1993), pp. 7–8; and Bureau of the Census, "Poverty in the United States: 1988 and 1989," *Current Population Reports,* series P-60, no. 171 (U.S. Department of Commerce, 1991), pp. 19, 25.

29. Daniel B. Radner, "The Economic Status of the Aged," *Social Security Bulletin,* vol. 55 (Fall 1992), table 5.

30. Raymond J. Hanley and Joshua M. Wiener, "Use of Paid Home Care by the Chronically Disabled Elderly," *Research on Aging,* vol. 13 (September 1991), pp. 310–32.

31. Bureau of Census, "The Need for Personal Assistance with Everyday Activities: Recipients and Caregivers," *Current Population Reports,* series P-70, no. 19 (U.S. Department of Commerce, 1991), p. 1.

32. Raymond J. Hanley, Joshua M. Wiener, and Katherine M. Harris, "Will Paid Home Care Erode Informal Support?" *Journal of Health Politics, Policy and Law,* vol. 16 (Fall 1991), pp. 507–21.

33. Eric R. Kingson, Barbara A. Hirshorn, and John H. Cornman, *The Ties That Bind: The Interdependence of Generations* (Washington: Seven Locks Press, 1986), pp. 129, 131.

34. For example, in a 1992 Gallup Organization survey, 86 percent of people polled "disagreed" or "strongly disagreed" with the statement "In order to slow the rise in health care costs and increase access to health care for all Americans, it would be acceptable to reduce the amount of health care that is available to the elderly." EBRI, "Public Opinion on Health, Retirement, and Other Employee Benefits," *EBRI Issue Brief,* no. 132 (December 1992), p. 16. Data from the 1986 General Social Survey have shown that support for programs for the elderly cuts across all age groups. For example, when asked whether social security spending was "too little," "about right," or "too much," more than half (56 percent) of all respondents said that spending was "too little." Moreover, while 63 percent of respondents under age 35 gave this response, only 42 percent of those 65 years and older did. Michael Ponza and others, "The Guns

of Autumn? Age Differences in Support for Income Transfers to the Young and Old," *Public Opinion Quarterly*, vol. 52 (Winter 1988), p. 463.

35. Hugh Heclo, "Generational Politics," in John L. Palmer, Timothy Smeeding, and Barbara Boyle Torrey, eds., *The Vulnerable* (Washington: Urban Institute Press, 1988) p. 384. Currently, the only federally funded program where the elderly and children directly compete is medicaid.

36. Marc A. Cohen and others, "Long-Term Care Financing Proposals: Their Costs, Benefits and Impact on Private Insurance," *Health Insurance Association of America Research Bulletin*, (Washington, January 1991); and Marc A. Cohen and others, "Financing Long-Term Care: A Practical Mix of Public and Private," *Journal of Health Politics, Policy and Law*, vol. 17 (Fall 1992), pp. 403–23.

37. Joshua M. Wiener, Raymond J. Hanley, and Laurel Hixon Illston, "Commentary on 'Financing Long-Term Care: A Practical Public-Private Mix,'" *Journal of Health Politics, Policy and Law*, vol. 17 (Fall 1992), p. 430.

38. Cohen, Kumar, McGuire, and Wallack, "Financing Long-Term Care: A Practical Mix of Public and Private," p. 414.

39. Bruce Boyd, "LTC Insurance: It's Your Choice," *Generations*, vol. 14 (Spring 1990), pp. 23–27.

40. According to the March 1993 *Current Population Survey*, in 1992, 17.4 percent of the nonelderly population, or 38.5 million people, did not have private or public health insurance. Almost all elderly (96.2 percent) have health insurance coverage through medicare. EBRI, "Sources of Health Insurance and Characteristics of the Uninsured, Analysis of the March 1993 *Current Population Survey*," Washington, January 1994.

41. ICR Survey Research Group for the AARP, October 28–November 7, 1993.

42. Gallup Organization, "Consumers Union–Gallup Survey on Health Care," Princeton, N.J., 1993.

43. ICR Survey Research Group of AUS Consultants, "Long-Term Care Survey."

44. EBRI, "Sources of Health Insurance and Characteristics of the Uninsured," *EBRI Issue Brief*, no. 123 (February 1992).

45. The Clinton administration is hoping to finance a substantial part of expanded long-term care through medicare and medicaid savings.

46. H.R. 2762, "The Medicare Long-Term Home Care Catastrophic Protection Act of 1987," 100 Cong. 1 sess. (1987).

47. Estimates from the Brookings-ICF Long-Term Care Financing Model.

48. Hanley, Wiener, and Harris, "Will Paid Home Care Erode Informal Support?" p. 516.

49. Kenneth G. Manton, "Epidemiological, Demographic, and Social Correlates of Disability among the Elderly," *Milbank Quarterly*, vol. 67, supplement 2, part 1 (1989), pp. 50.

50. Hanley, Wiener, and Harris, "Will Paid Home Care Erode Informal Support?" pp. 507–21.

51. Using the Channeling data set, Coughlin and colleagues observed that prescription drugs and long-term nursing home care were the major sources of catastrophic costs among the frail elderly. Although prescription drugs were a more certain cause of extreme out-of-pocket costs, they were more likely to be burdensome to the poor than to the well-off. On the other hand, long-term nursing home care, when needed, made individuals, regardless of income, ex-

tremely vulnerable to catastrophic costs. Teresa A. Coughlin, Korbin Liu, and Timothy D. McBride, "Severely Disabled Elderly Persons with Financially Catastrophic Health Care Expenses: Sources and Determinants," *Gerontologist*, vol. 32 (June 1992) pp. 391–403.

52. S. 2163, "Life Care, Long-Term Care Protection Act," 101 Cong. 2 sess. (1990); and Robert M. Ball, with Thomas N. Bethell, *Because We're All in This Together: The Case for a Long-Term Care Insurance Policy* (Washington: Families USA, 1989).

53. Pepper Commission, *A Call for Action*.

54. S. 2571, "The Long-Term Care Family Security Act of 1992," introduced by Senators George Mitchell, Jay Rockefeller, Edward M. Kennedy, and others, 102 Cong. 2 sess. (April 9, 1992); and H.R. 4848, introduced by Representatives Henry Waxman and Richard Gephardt, 102 Cong. 2 sess (April 9, 1992).

55. Using aggregated nursing home length of stays, Spence and Wiener report that in 1985, 45 percent of nursing home residents stayed fewer than three months and 10 percent stayed between three and six months. Of those with a stay of less than six months, an estimated 50 percent were discharged alive. Denise A. Spence and Joshua M. Wiener, "Nursing Home Length of Stay Patterns: Results from the 1985 National Nursing Home Survey," *Gerontologist*, vol. 30 (February 1990), p. 18. In estimating the total lifetime use of nursing homes, Kemper and Murtaugh report that about 50 percent of nursing home patients stayed less than one year. Peter Kemper and Christopher M. Murtaugh, "Lifetime Use of Nursing Home Care," *New England Journal of Medicine*, vol. 324 (February 28, 1991), p. 597.

56. The Pepper Commission recommendations, for example, would increase the amount of assets single medicaid patients could keep from $2,000 to $60,000. Pepper Commission, *A Call For Action*.

57. In 1993 medicare paid for up to 100 days (following hospitalization) in a skilled nursing facility for patients needing continued skilled nursing care or skilled rehabilitative services on a daily basis. *Overview of Entitlement Programs*, Committee Print, p. 144.

58. S. 2305, "The Long-Term Care Assistance Act of 1988," introduced by Senator George Mitchell, 100 Cong. 2 sess. (1988).

59. Susan Van Gelder, HIAA, personal communication, October 11, 1990.

60. Joshua M. Wiener, Katherine M. Harris, and Raymond J. Hanley, "Premium Pricing of Prototype Private Long-Term Care Insurance Policies," report for the Office of the Assistant Secretary for Planning and Evaluation/Social Services Policy of the U.S. Department of Health and Human Services, December 1990.

61. Spence and Wiener, "Nursing Home Length of Stay Patterns," p. 18.

62. H.R. 5320, "Elder-Care Long-Term Care Protection Act," introduced by Representative Henry Waxman, 100 Cong. 2 sess (1988); and H.R. 5393, "Chronic-Care Medicare Long-Term Care Coverage Act," introduced by Representative Fortney "Pete" Stark, 100 Cong. 2 sess (1988).

63. Nyman, "The Effect of Competition on Nursing Home Expenditures under Prospective Reimbursement"; John A. Nyman, Samuel Levey, and James E. Rohrer, "RUGs and Equity of Access to Nursing Home Care," *Medical Care*, vol. 25 (May 1987), pp. 361–72; and William J. Scanlon, "A Theory of the Nursing Home Market," *Inquiry*, vol. 17 (Spring 1980), pp. 25–41.

64. Home care use is assumed to be independent of nursing home use.

Consequently, the level of induced demand for home care is the same for each of the options.

65. The Hawaii Long-Term Care Financing Advisory Board has proposed a broad-based program that would cover 80 percent of the costs of nursing home care or a full range of home and community-based care up to a maximum daily rate of $90 for life. This would be available to everyone, regardless of age or income, who needs help with at least two activities of daily living. A 0.4 percent tax on modified adjusted gross income for taxpayers above the poverty line would finance the proposed program. The Long-Term Care Financing Advisory Board, *Report to the Hawaii State Legislature: Long Term Care Financing* (Honolulu: February 1992), p. 22. In 1992 the Vermont legislature passed a bill to begin overhauling the state's health care system. Among other things, the legislation requires recommendations from the Vermont Health Care Authority— a governor-appointed board created to oversee health care reform—for including long-term care in the state's universal access health care system. "Summary of Vermont's Health Care Reform Bill (H. 733)," prepared by the Legislative Council, May 7, 1992.

## Chapter Eight

1. Prospective Payment Advisory Commission, *Medicare and the American Health Care System: Report to the Congress* (Washington, June 1993), table 4-4, p. 112.

2. Notwithstanding the almost universal belief among experts that the impact of public or private insurance on nursing home use would be very modest, the few empirical estimates of price elasticity of nursing home care are quite large. For a review of the literature, see Teresa Fama and David Kennell, "Should We Worry About Induced Demand for Long-Term Care Services?" *Generations*, vol. 14 (Spring 1990), pp. 37–41.

3. Robert L. Kane and Rosalie A. Kane, *A Will and a Way: What the United States Can Learn from Canada about Caring for the Elderly* (Columbia University Press, 1990).

4. Korbin Liu, Timothy D. McBride, and Teresa A. Coughlin, "Costs of Community Care for Disabled Elderly Persons: The Policy Implications," *Inquiry*, vol. 27 (Spring 1990), pp. 61–72.

5. Charlene Harrington and Robert J. Newcomer, "Social Health Maintenance Organizations as Innovative Models to Control Costs," *Generations*, vol. 14 (Spring 1990), pp. 49–54.

6. For a discussion of acute care expenditure caps, see Henry J. Aaron, "Health Care Financing," in Henry J. Aaron and Charles L. Schultze, eds., *Setting Domestic Priorities* (Brookings, 1992), pp. 56–59.

7. Some advocates for the disabled argue that per person costs can be reduced by using a flexible set of services. This contention is based on the presumption that, given a choice, people will choose only the minimum level of the services they actually need rather than a larger amount of a service that does not quite meet their need.

8. Marie-Louise Ansak, "The On Lok Model: Consolidating Care and Financing," *Generations*, vol. 14 (Spring 1990), pp. 73–74.

9. Walter N. Leutz and others, "Adding Long-Term Care to Medicare: The

Social HMO Experience," *Journal of Aging and Social Policy*, vol. 3, no. 4 (1991), pp. 69–87.

10. Robert L. Kane, Laurel Hixon Illston, and Nancy A. Miller, "Qualitative Analysis of the Program of All-Inclusive Care for the Elderly (PACE)," *Gerontologist*, vol. 32 (December 1992), pp. 771–80; and Rivlin and others, *Caring for the Disabled Elderly*, p. 101.

11. Charlene Harrington and Robert J. Newcomer, "Social Health Maintenance Organizations' Service Use and Costs, 1985–89," *Health Care Financing Review*, vol. 12 (Spring 1991), pp. 37–52.

12. Rosalie A. Kane and others, *Quality of Home Care: Concept and Measurement* (University of Minnesota, Division of Health Services Research and Policy, 1991), pp. 57–58.

## Chapter Nine

1. This fiscal constraint was first imposed by law in the 1985 Balanced Budget Act (popularly known as Gramm-Rudman), which established overall deficit targets. The 1990 Budget Enforcement Act required Congress to cover the costs of all new entitlement programs with increased taxes or other spending cuts in other entitlement programs.

2. Kenneth J. Cooper, "Hill Group Backs Broad Health Plan: $66 Billion Tax Cost Is Left Unresolved," *Washington Post*, March 3, 1990, p. A1; and Martin Tolchin, "Panel Says Broad Health Care Would Cost $86 Billion a Year," *New York Times*, March 3, 1990, p. A1. The final report of the Pepper Commission, issued six months later, did assess a variety of different revenue sources against the amount of revenue they would raise, their growth potential, degree of progressivity, and the population affected. U.S. Bipartisan Commission on Comprehensive Health Care (Pepper Commission), *A Call for Action: Final Report* (Government Printing Office, September 1990).

3. Richard A. Musgrave and Peggy B. Musgrave, *Public Finance in Theory and Practice* (McGraw-Hill, 1976), pp. 210–12.

4. Because the payroll taxes used to finance both of these programs are calculated against wages only (that is, they exclude nonwage income such as interest, dividends or capital gains), are subject to income caps, and offer no exemptions, the effect is technically regressive, favoring upper-income individuals. Henry J. Aaron, Barry P. Bosworth, and Gary T. Burtless, *Can America Afford to Grow Old? Paying for Social Security* (Brookings, 1989), p. 27.

5. Sandra Christensen, "The Subsidy Provided under Medicare to Current Enrollees," *Journal of Health Politics, Policy and Law*, vol. 17 (Summer 1992), pp. 255–64.

6. Implicit in this requirement for sound tax structure is the assumption that efficient allocation of resources exists before the imposition of taxes and, therefore, that any tax interferes with the allocation of resources. Musgrave and Musgrave, *Public Finance in Theory and Practice*. In the "real world" there are significant departures from the conditions necessary for this optimum. Joseph A. Pechman, *Federal Tax Policy* (Brookings, 1987), p. 194. Only poll taxes are neutral with regard to all economic choices. Glenn H. Miller, Jr., "Federal Excise Taxes: Approaching Deficit Reduction from the Revenue Side," *Economic Review* (Federal Reserve Bank of Kansas City), vol. 74 (March 1989), pp. 21–35.

7. David Wessel and Rick Wartzman, "Tax Increases Seem Inevitable, Including Some on Middle Class," *Wall Street Journal,* January 22, 1993, p. A-1.

8. *Budget of the United States Government, Fiscal Year 1993,* part 2, table 24-1, pp. 25–28.

9. Richard Kasten and Frank Sammartino, *The Changing Distribution of Federal Taxes: 1975–1990* (Washington: Congressional Budget Office [CBO], October 1987), table B-3, p. 72.

10. According to a 1989 survey by the Gallup Organization, the least fair or worst tax is the local property tax, followed by the federal income tax. Both state income taxes and state sales taxes, however, were viewed as fairer than the "social security [payroll] tax." Gallup Organization, Survey for the Advisory Commission on Intergovernmental Relations, June 10–18, 1989, as cited in *American Enterprise,* vol. 1 (September–October 1990), p. 88. See also National Association of Retired Federal Employees, *Gauging National Healthcare Priorities* (Washington, 1990), graph 5; Hamilton, Frederick & Schneiders, "Attitudes of Americans Over 45 Years of Age on Long-Term Care," survey prepared for the American Association of Retired Persons (AARP), Washington, February 1988, p. 10; and Research USA, Inc., "National Committee to Preserve Social Security and Medicare: Membership Survey," Washington, December 1988, p. 15.

11. "The Budget Reconciliation Bill: The First Round of Cutbacks," *Public Policy and Aging Report,* vol. 5, no. 6 (1993), p. 4.

12. A provision in the Omnibus Budget Reconciliation Act of 1993 removed the cap on taxable earnings, which had previously been set at $135,000 for 1993. Authors' estimates are based on taxable payroll information from the *Annual Report of the Board of Trustees of the Federal Old-Age and Survivors Insurance and Disability Insurance Trust Funds.*

13. To arrive at estimates of payroll needed, annual public long-term care expenditures from the Brookings-ICF Long-Term Care Financing Model were calculated as a percentage of total payroll using estimates from the 1991 social security and medicare board of trustees annual report of effective taxable payroll for each year through 2050. Estimates for selected years represent the financial burden of a pay-as-you-go system. The economic burden of the program would vary, depending on whether the economy grew faster or slower than the assumptions used in the model. *1991 Annual Report of the Board of Trustees of the Federal Old-Age and Survivors Insurance and Disability Insurance Trust Funds,* table 15b.

14. This calculation assumes a fully phased-in program.

15. Jackie Calmes, "With Signature, President Will Erase Reagan's Legacy," *Wall Street Journal,* August 9, 1993, p. A4.

16. In 1990 the United States ranked twenty-third out of twenty-four OECD member countries in tax revenues as a percentage of gross domestic product. OECD, *Revenue Statistics of OECD Member Countries: 1965–1991* (Paris, 1992), table 1, p. 74.

17. *Budget of the United States Government, Fiscal Year 1993,* part 2, table 24-1, pp. 25–28; and U.S. Government Accounting Office (GAO), *Revenue Options,* GAO/OGC-893TR (November 1988), p. 6.

18. GAO, *Revenue Options,* p. 6.

19. *Budget of the United States Government, Fiscal Year 1993,* part 2, table 24-1, pp. 25–28.

20. Revenue loss is calculated against both income and payroll taxes, but this

ignores the fact that money collected in payroll taxes today is paid out in future social security benefits and should probably not be considered a revenue loss. Calculating the revenue loss only against income tax puts the loss at $46 billion in 1993. CBO, *Economic Implications of Rising Health Care Costs* (Washington, October 1992), p. 32; and CBO, *Reducing the Deficit: Spending and Revenue Options* (Washington, February 1992), p. 257.

21. *Budget of the United States Government, Fiscal Year 1993,* appendix 1, p. 57.

22. For the past thirty years or more, income tax as a percentage of federal revenues and federal revenues as a percentage of gross domestic product have remained relatively constant.

23. Musgrave and Musgrave, *Public Finance in Theory and Practice,* pp. 322–41.

24. James M. Poterba, "Lifetime Incidence and the Distributional Burden of Excise Taxes," Working Paper 2833 (Cambridge, Mass.: National Bureau of Economic Research, 1989).

25. Alice M. Rivlin, *Reviving the American Dream: The Economy, the States, and the Federal Government* (Brookings, 1992), p. 144.

26. John L. Mikesell, "State Sales Tax Policy in a Changing Economy: Balancing Political and Economic Logic against Revenue Needs," *Public Budgeting and Finance,* vol. 12 (Spring 1992), p. 83.

27. Robert E. Ebel and Christopher Simmerman, "Sales Tax Trends and Issues," in William F. Fox, ed., *Sales Taxation: Critical Issues in Policy and Administration* (Westport, Conn.: Praeger, 1992), p. 11. Ebel and Zimmerman also reported that in 1988 state and local governments collected $154.9 billion in sales taxes (p. 9). In 1985 retail sales taxes accounted for 21 percent of total state and local revenues (including revenue from the federal government). Pechman, *Federal Tax Policy,* table D-24. General retail sales taxes generated 32 percent of the states' total tax collections in 1984. J. Richard Aronson and John L. Hilley, *Financing State and Local Governments* (Brookings, 1986), p. 94.

28. Ebel and Zimmerman, "Sales Tax Trends and Issues," p. 12; and Pechman, *Federal Tax Policy,* p. 259.

29. Miller, "Federal Excise Taxes: Approaching Deficit Reduction from the Revenue Side."

30. *Budget of the United States Government, Fiscal Year 1992,* part 2, Receipts, p. 11.

31. Executive Office of the President, "Health Security Act," pp. 1075–87.

32. Jon Hakken and Rosemarie Nielsen, *Effects of Adopting a Value-Added Tax* (Washington: CBO, February 1992) p. 1; and Alan A. Tait, "VAT Policy Issues: Structure, Regressivity, Inflation, and Exports," in Alan A. Tait, ed., *Value-Added Tax: Administrative and Policy Issues* (Washington: International Monetary Fund, October 1991), p. 1.

33. VATs account for 12 to 30 percent of revenue. Tait, "VAT Policy Issues," pp. 1-3, and table 1.

34. Figures are authors' calculations of the average of a fully phased-in program based on CBO, *Reducing the Deficit,* p. 395.

35. Rivlin, *Reviving the American Dream,* pp. 139, 145; and Ebel and Zimmerman, "Sales Tax Trends and Issues," p. 3.

36. Hakken and Nielsen, *Effects of Adopting a Value-Added Tax,* p. 49.

37. Ibid.

38. Henry J. Aaron, "The Value-Added Tax: Sorting Through the Practical and Political Problems," *Brookings Review*, vol. 6 (Summer 1988), p. 10.

39. Organisation for Economic Co-operation and Development, *Taxing Consumption* (Paris: OECD, 1988), p. 204.

40. These figures overstate the regressivity of the sales tax because neither low- nor high-income persons reduce or increase their consumption by the entire amount that their income has been altered by the tax. Pechman, *Federal Tax Policy*, pp. 200, 204.

41. Daniel Yankelovich Group, Inc., *Long Term Care in America: Public Attitudes and Possible Solutions, Executive Summary* (Washington: AARP, 1990), appendix D, p. 12; and RL Associates, "The American Public Views Long Term Care," survey conducted for the AARP and the Villers Foundation (Princeton, N.J., October 1987), p. 20.

42. In a 1991 Gallup poll, elderly respondents said they were willing to pay an average of $361 annually in additional income taxes for long-term care. Gallup Organization, *Public Attitudes on Long-Term Care, 1991* (Washington: Employee Benefits Research Institute [EBRI], 1991), p. 21.

43. In 1993, 73.6 percent of the 32.7 million elderly had incomes 150 percent or more above the poverty level. Imposing a $10 a month premium on these 24.1 million people would yield $2.9 billion. Brookings-ICF Long-Term Care Financing Model; and Daniel B. Radner, "An Assessment of the Economic Status of the Aged," Studies in Income Distribution Series (Department of Health and Human Services, Social Security Administration, May 1993), table 5.

44. John R. Gist, *Options for the Public Financing of Long-Term Care* (Washington: AARP, December 1989), p. 14.

45. Jackie Calmes, "With Signature, President Will Erase Reagan's Legacy."

46. For example, if an individual has $8,000 in social security benefits and $30,000 in other retirement benefits, her adjusted gross income equals $36,800 (or 85 percent of the $8,000 plus the $30,000). Two thousand eight hundred dollars ($2,800), or the amount that the adjusted gross income ($36,800) is in excess of the income threshold ($34,000) of the social security benefit, is taxable.

47. The tax change is expected to raise an additional $24.6 billion between 1994 and 1998, which will be channeled into the Hospital Insurance Trust Fund. Paul Leonard and Robert Greenstein, "The New Budget Reconciliation Law: Progressive Deficit Reduction and Critical Social Investments," Center on Budget and Policy Priorities, Washington, August 17, 1993, p. 3; and "Budget Cuts Nearly $63 Billion from Medicare and Medicaid," *Long-Term Care Management*, vol. 22 (August 11, 1993), p. 6.

48. *Overview of the Entitlement Program: Background Material and Data on Programs Within the Jurisdiction of the Committee on Ways and Means*, Committee Print, prepared for the House Committee on Ways and Means, 102 Cong. 2 sess. (GPO, 1992), p. 358.

49. In 1991 the mean income (including social security benefits) for people aged 65 and older was $15,130. Without social security, mean income drops to $8,665. Bureau of Census, *Money Income of Households, Families, and Persons in the United States: 1991*, series P-60, no. 180 (U.S. Department of Commerce, August 1992), p. 178. In that same year, without social security benefits, 48.5 percent of the elderly would have lived in poverty; with these benefits, only 12.2 percent did. Bureau of Census, *Measuring the Effect of Benefits and Taxes on Income and Poverty: 1979–1991*, series P-60, no. 182-RD (U.S. Department of Commerce, August 1992), p. xix.

50. CBO, *Reducing the Deficit*, p. 255.

51. A small amount of revenue could also be raised by recovering money from the estates of medicaid-sponsored nursing home patients. The Omnibus Budget Reconciliation Act of 1993 required states to institute estate recovery programs. That law also lengthened from 30 months to 36 months the period in which people are barred from transferring their assets to others before applying for medicaid. The savings from these two changes is estimated to be only $650 million during the five-year period between 1994 and 1998. "Budget Cuts Nearly $63 Billion from Medicare and Medicaid," *Long-Term Care Management*, vol. 22 (August 11, 1993), p. 6.

52. Pechman notes that income taxes are more likely to affect savings and investment decisions than estate taxes because the timing of income taxes is more proximate to these decisions. Pechman, *Federal Tax Policy*, pp. 234–35.

53. Actual estate and gift taxes were $11.1 billion in 1991. *Budget of the United States Government, Fiscal Year 1993*, p. 2-11.

54. Alicia Munnell, "Wealth Transfer Taxation: The Relative Role for Estate and Income Taxes," *New England Economic Review*, November–December, 1988, p. 4.

55. Barry W. Johnson, "Estate Tax Returns, 1986–1988," *Statistics of Income Bulletin*, vol. 9 (Spring 1990), p. 31.

56. CBO, *Reducing the Deficit*, p. 378.

57. Ibid., p. 375.

58. Paul Glastris, "The Secret Solution to the Deficit," *Washington Monthly*, February 1991, p. 27.

59. George J. Schieber, Jean-Pierre Poullier, and Leslie M. Greenwald, "Health Spending, Delivery, and Outcomes in OECD Countries," *Health Affairs*, vol. 12 (Summer 1993), exhibit 2, p. 122.

60. Ibid., exhibit 1, p. 121.

61. Medicare expenditures increased by 14 percent a year between 1980 and 1985, and by 9.4 percent a year between 1985 and 1991. Authors' calculations based on Suzanne W. Letsch and others, "National Health Expenditures, 1991," *Health Care Financing Review*, vol. 14 (Winter 1992), table 4, p. 9; and Prospective Payment Assessment Commission, *Medicare and the American Health Care System: Report to the Congress* (Washington, June 1993), figure 1-4, p. 20.

62. Randall S. Brown and others, "The Medicare Risk Program for HMOs—Final Summary Report on Findings from the Evaluation," Mathematica Policy Research, Inc., Princeton, N.J., February 18, 1993, pp. xx–xxi.

63. Yung-Ping Chen, "A 'Three-Legged Stool': New Way to Fund Long-Term Care?" in *Care in the Long-Term: In Search of Community and Security*, the Herman M. Somers Memorial Symposium (Washington: National Academy Press, 1993), pp. 54–70.

64. Gallup survey cited in *Employee Benefit Notes*, vol. 13 (Washington: EBRI, October 1992), p. 9; and Gallup survey cited in *Employee Benefit Notes*, vol. 12 (December 1991), p. 5.

65. Social security expenditures were $266.8 billion in 1991. *Budget of the United States Government, Fiscal Year 1993*, appendix 1, p. 146.

66. With a balanced budget and a surplus in the social insurance trust fund, the surplus could be used to buy public bonds back from the private sector (which offers less favorable interest rates) and each year a portion of the national debt could be retired. Those sums no longer needed to finance the debt would

then be available to supplement national savings, and the future level of productivity and output would be raised. Aaron, Bosworth, and Burtless, *Can America Afford to Grow Old?*, pp. 79–82.

67. Alice M. Rivlin, "What Kind of Social Security System?" and Charles L. Schultze, "Effects on National Saving," in "Four Reasons Not to Cut Social Security Taxes," *Brookings Review*, vol. 8 (Spring 1990), pp. 3–4.

68. Robert D. Hershey, Jr., "Michigan's Singular Tax Is Studied as U.S. Model," *New York Times*, July 13, 1992, p. D1.

69. Joseph P. Newhouse, "An Iconoclastic View of Health Cost Containment," *Health Affairs* (Supplement 1993), exhibit 4, p. 163.

## Chapter Ten

1. U.S. Bipartisan Commission on Health Care Reform (Pepper Commission), *A Call for Action, Final Report* (Government Printing Office, 1990).

2. Executive Office of the President, *Health Security Act* (Government Printing Office, 1993).

3. John R. Gist, "Did Tax Reform Hurt the Elderly?" *Gerontologist*, vol. 32 (August 1992), p. 474.

4. "Budget Cuts Nearly $63 Billion from Medicare and Medicaid," *Long-Term Care Management*, vol. 22 (August 11, 1993), p. 6.

5. Estimates for continued federal, state, and local spending at current levels and population estimates for elderly with incomes greater than 150 percent of poverty are from the Brookings-ICF Long-Term Care Financing Model. Authors' payroll estimates are based on Social Security Administration and Office of the Actuary estimates of total future payroll. It is assumed that premiums increase at 1.5 percent above real inflation, or 5.5 percent. The estimates also assume that medicare savings will grow at 5.5 percent each year.

## Appendix A

1. *1988 Annual Report of the Board of Trustees of the Federal Old-Age and Survivors Insurance and Disability Insurance Trust Funds.*

2. Howard N. Fullerton, Jr., "Labor Force Projections 1986–2000," *Monthly Labor Review*, vol. 110 (September 1987), pp. 19–29; and George T. Silverstri and John L. Lukasiewicz, "A Look at Occupational Employment Trends to the Year 2000," *Monthly Labor Review*, vol. 110 (September 1987), pp. 46–63.

3. Raymond J. Hanley and others, "Predicting Elderly Nursing Home Admissions: Results from the 1982–1984 National Long-Term Care Survey," *Research on Aging*, vol. 12 (June 1990), pp. 199–228.

4. Denise A. Spence and Joshua M. Wiener, "Nursing Home Length of Stay Patterns: Results from the 1985 National Nursing Home Survey," *Gerontologist*, vol. 30 (February 1990), pp. 16–20.

5. *Duggan v. Bowen*, 691 F. Supp. 148 (D.D.C. 1988).

6. *1989 Annual Report of the Board of Trustees of the Federal Old-Age and Survivors Insurance and Disability Insurance Trust Funds.*

7. Denise A. Spence and Joshua Wiener, "Estimating the Extent of Spend-Down in Nursing Homes," *Journal of Health, Politics, Policy and Law*, vol. 15 (Fall

1990), pp. 607–26; Korbin Liu, Pamela Doty, and Kenneth Manton, "Medicaid Spend-Down in Nursing Homes," *Gerontologist,* vol. 30 (February 1990), pp. 7–15; Brian O. Burwell, E. Kathleen Adams, and Mark Meiners, "Spend-Down to Medicaid Eligibility among Nursing Home Recipients in Michigan," *Medical Care,* vol. 28 (April 1990), pp. 349–62; and Leonard Gruenberg and others, "An Analysis of the Spend-Down Patterns of Individuals Admitted to Nursing Homes in the State of Connecticut," Research Institute Discussion Papers 1-89 (State of Connecticut, Office of Policy and Management, September 1989).

8. *1992 Annual Report of the Board of Trustees of the Federal Old-Age and Survivors Insurance and Disability Insurance Trust Funds.*

## Appendix B

1. See, for example, National Association of Insurance Commissioners Long-Term Care Actuarial Task Force, "Inflation Protection and Nonforfeiture Benefits in Long-Term Care Insurance Policies: Final Report," Kansas City, Mo., 1991, p. 6; and William M. Mercer, Inc., *Inflation Protection and Nonforfeiture Benefits in Long-Term Care Insurance Policies: New Data for Decision Making* (Washington: American Association of Retired Persons, 1992), p. 7.

2. Teresa Fama and David L. Kennell, "Should We Worry About Induced Demand?" *Generations,* vol. 14 (Spring 1990), pp. 37–41.

3. Social Security Technical Panel, *Report to the 1991 Advisory Panel on Social Security* (Baltimore, Md.: Social Security Administration, 1990), p. 24.

4. This life table was provided by Alice Wade, Office of the Actuary, Social Security Administration, Baltimore, Md.

5. Daniel R. Disseizor and others, "Health Expenditures by Age Group, 1977 and 1987," *Health Care Financing Review,* vol. 10 (Summer 1989), pp. 111–20, tables 3, 4.

6. This life table was provided by Alice Wade, Office of the Actuary, Social Security Administration, Baltimore, Md.

7. National Association of Insurance Commissioners, *Long-Term Care-Insurance Model Regulation* (Kansas City, Mo., December 7, 1990), p. 16.

# Index